AQA History

A2
Unit 3

Emergence of a Great Power? Spain, 1492–1556

Exclusively endorsed by AQA

Paula McClive
Series editor
Sally Waller

Nelson Thornes

Published in 2009 by:
Nelson Thornes Ltd
Delta Place
27 Bath Road
CHELTENHAM
GL53 7TH
United Kingdom

09 10 11 12 13 / 10 9 8 7 6 5 4 3 2 1

A catalogue record for this book is available from the British Library

ISBN 978 1 4085 0318 8

Cover image by: Alamy/Stephen Bisgrove

Illustrations by: Karen Donnelly Illustration, David Russell Illustration,
Thomson Digital

Page make-up by Thomson Digital

Printed in Croatia by Zrinski

Contents

Introduction

Nelson Thornes and AQA

Nelson Thornes has worked in collaboration with AQA to ensure that this book offers you the best support for your AS or A Level course and helps you to prepare for your exams. The partnership means that you can be confident that the range of learning, teaching and assessment practice materials has been checked by the senior examining team at AQA before formal approval, and is closely matched to the requirements of your specification.

How to use this book

This book covers the specification for your course and is arranged in a sequence approved by AQA.

The features in this book include:

Timeline

Key events are outlined at the beginning of the book. The events are colour-coded so you can clearly see the categories of change.

Learning objectives

At the beginning of each section you will find a list of learning objectives that contain targets linked to the requirements of the specification.

Key chronology

A short list of dates usually with a focus on a specific event or legislation.

Key profile

The profile of a key person you should be aware of to fully understand the period in question.

Key terms

A term that you will need to be able to define and understand.

Did you know?

Interesting information to bring the subject under discussion to life.

Exploring the detail

Information to put further context around the subject under discussion.

A closer look

An in-depth look at a theme, person or event to deepen your understanding. Activities around the extra information may be included.

Sources

Sources to reinforce topics or themes and may provide fact or opinion. They may be quotations from historical works, contemporaries of the period or photographs.

Cross-reference

Links to related content within the book which may offer more detail on the subject in question.

Activity

Various activity types to provide you with different challenges and opportunities to demonstrate both the content and skills you are learning. Some can be worked on individually, some as part of group work and some are designed to specifically 'stretch and challenge'.

■ Question

Questions to prompt further discussion on the topic under consideration and are an aid to revision.

■ Summary questions

Summary questions at the end of each chapter to test your knowledge and allow you to demonstrate your understanding.

AQA Examiner's tip

Hints from AQA examiners to help you with your study and to prepare for your exam.

AQA Examination-style questions

Questions at the end of each section in the style that you can expect in your exam.

Learning outcomes

Learning outcomes at the end of each section remind you what you should know having completed the chapters in that section.

■ Web links in the book

Because Nelson Thornes is not responsible for third party content online, there may be some changes to this material that are beyond our control. In order for us to ensure that the links referred to in the book are as up-to-date and stable as possible, the websites provided are usually homepages with supporting instructions on how to reach the relevant pages if necessary.

Please let us know at **kerboodle@nelsonthornes. com** if you find a link that doesn't work and we will do our best to correct this at reprint, or to list an alternative site.

Introduction to the History series

When Bruce Bogtrotter in Roald Dahl's *Matilda* was challenged to eat a huge chocolate cake, he just opened his mouth and ploughed in, taking bite after bite and lump after lump until the cake was gone and he was feeling decidedly sick. The picture is not dissimilar to that of some A Level History students. They are attracted to history because of its inherent appeal but, when faced with a bulging file and a forthcoming examination, their enjoyment evaporates. They try desperately to cram their brains with an assortment of random facts and subsequently prove unable to control the outpouring of their ill-digested material in the examination.

The books in this series are designed to help students and teachers avoid this feeling of overload and examination panic by breaking down the AQA History specification in such a way that it is easily absorbed. Above all, they are designed to retain and promote students' enthusiasm for history by avoiding a dreary rehash of dates and events. Each book is divided into sections, closely matched to those given in the specification, and the content is further broken down into chapters that present the historical material in a lively and attractive form, offering guidance on the key terms, events and issues, and blending thought-provoking activities and questions in a way designed to advance students' understanding. By encouraging students to think for themselves and to share their ideas with others, as well as helping them to develop the knowledge and skills they will need to pass their examination, this book should ensure that students' learning remains a pleasure rather than an endurance test.

To make the most of what this book provides, students will need to develop efficient study skills from the start and it is worth spending some time considering what these involve:

- Good organisation of material in a subject-specific file. Organised notes help develop an organised brain and sensible filing ensures time is not wasted hunting for misplaced material. This book uses cross-references to indicate where material in one chapter has relevance to material in another. Students are advised to adopt the same technique.

- A sensible approach to note-making. Students are often too ready to copy large chunks of material from printed books or to download sheaves of printouts from the internet. This series is designed to encourage students to think about the notes they collect and to undertake research with a particular purpose in mind. The activities encourage students to pick out information that is relevant to the issue being addressed and to avoid making notes on material that is not properly understood.

- Taking time to think, which is by far the most important component of study. By encouraging students to think before they write or speak, be it for a written answer, presentation or class debate, students should learn to form opinions and make judgements based on the accumulation of evidence. These are the skills that the examiner will be looking for in the final examination. The beauty of history is that there is rarely a right or wrong answer so, with sufficient evidence, one student's view will count for as much as the next.

Unit 3

The topics chosen for study in Unit 3 are all concerned with the changing relationship between state and people over a period of around 50 years. These topics enable students to build on the skills acquired at AS Level, combining breadth, by looking at change and continuity over a period of time, with depth, in analysing specific events and developments. The chosen topics offer plentiful opportunities for an understanding of historical processes enabling students to realise that history moves forward through the interaction of many different factors, some of which may change in importance over a period of time. Significant individuals, societies, events, developments and issues are explored in a historical context and developments affecting different groups within the societies studied from a range of historical perspectives. Study at Unit 3 will therefore develop full synoptic awareness and enable students to understand the way a professional historian goes about the task of developing a full historical understanding.

Unit 3 is assessed by a 1 hour 30 minute paper containing three essay questions from which students need to select two. Details relating to the style of questions, with additional hints, are given in the accompanying table and helpful tips to enable students to meet the examination demands are given throughout this book. Students should familiarise themselves with both the question demands and the marking criteria which follow before attempting any of the practice examination questions at the end of each section of this book.

Answers will be marked according to a scheme based on 'levels of response'. This means that an essay will be assessed according to which level best matches the

Unit 3 (Three essay questions in total)	Question Types	Marks	Question stems	Hints for students
Two essay questions	Standard essay questions addressing a part of the specification content and seeking a judgement based on debate and evaluation	45	These are not prescriptive but likely stems include: To what extent … How far … A quotation followed by, 'How valid is this assessment/view?'	All answers should convey an argument. Plan before beginning to write and make the argument clear at the outset. The essay should show an awareness of how factors interlink and students should make some judgement between them (synoptic links). All comments should be supported by secure and precise evidence
One essay question	Standard essay question covering the whole period of the unit or a large part of that period and seeking a judgement based on debate and evaluation	45	As above	Evidence will need to be carefully selected from across the full period to support the argument. It might prove useful to emphasise the situation at the beginning and end of the period, identify key turning points and assess factors promoting change and continuity

historical skills it displays, taking both knowledge and understanding into account. All students should keep a copy of the marking criteria in their files and need to use them wisely.

Marking criteria

Level 1 Answers will display a limited understanding of the demands of the question. They may either contain some descriptive material which is only loosely linked to the focus of the question or they may address only a part of the question. Alternatively, they may contain some explicit comment but will make few, if any, synoptic links and will have limited accurate and relevant historical support. There will be little, if any, awareness of differing historical interpretations. The response will be limited in development and skills of written communication will be weak. *(0–6 marks)*

Level 2 Answers will show some understanding of the demands of the question. They will either be primarily descriptive with few explicit links to the question or they may contain explicit comment but show limited relevant factual support. They will display limited understanding of differing historical interpretations. Historical debate may be described rather than used to illustrate an argument and any synoptic links will be undeveloped. Answers will be coherent but weakly expressed and/or poorly structured. *(7–15 marks)*

Level 3 Answers will show a good understanding of the demands of the question. They will provide some

assessment, backed by relevant and appropriately selected evidence, which may, however, lack depth. There will be some synoptic links made between the ideas, arguments and information included although these may not be highly developed. There will be some understanding of varying historical interpretations. Answers will be clearly expressed and show reasonable organisation in the presentation of material. *(16–25 marks)*

Level 4 Answers will show a very good understanding of the demands of the question. There will be synoptic links made between the ideas, arguments and information included showing an overall historical understanding. There will be good understanding and use of differing historical interpretations and debate and the answer will show judgement through sustained argument backed by a carefully selected range of precise evidence. Answers will be well-organised and display good skills of written communication. *(26–37 marks)*

Level 5 Answers will show a full understanding of the demands of the question. The ideas, arguments and information included will be wide-ranging, carefully chosen and closely interwoven to produce a sustained and convincing answer with a high level of synopticity. Conceptual depth, independent judgement and a mature historical understanding, informed by a well-developed understanding of historical interpretations and debate, will be displayed. Answers will be well-structured and fluently written. *(38–45 marks)*

Introduction to this book

Merely 'a geographical expression'; this is a description that can appropriately be applied to Spain in the late 15th century, although it was originally used with reference to Italy in the 19th century. In 1492, when this study starts, Ferdinand had been King of Aragon for 13 years and Isabella had been Queen of Castile for 18 years. The Spanish peninsula they ruled was divided into five kingdoms: Aragon; Castile; Granada; Navarre; and Portugal, although Navarre was soon absorbed by Castile. Even the largest of these kingdoms was a collection of different provinces. For example, Castile was made up of Anadalucia, New Castile, Old Castile, Leon, Galicia, Asturias, Cantabria and the Basque provinces.

In Aragon there were also the provinces of Catalonia and Valencia. Granada was in the hands of the Moors and was the last remaining territory claimed by the descendants of those who had originally invaded from North Africa. Portugal remained independent, but two states, Granada in 1492 and Navarre in 1512, subsequently became part of the lands of Ferdinand and Isabella, usually known after their marriage as the 'Catholic Monarchs'.

Not everyone greeted the new monarchs with enthusiasm. The contemporary historian, Palencia, complained about 'the arrogance and massive power of Lady Isabella, in no way disposed to accept the rules of government, which, since the most remote centuries, have favoured the male'. There is also criticism of Ferdinand, this time from a modern historian, Ryder, who stated, 'No counsellor, however exalted, however intimate, and no private secretary, however close, entered unreservedly into his confidence.' Together, however, Ferdinand and Isabella began the work that was to create a strong and powerful Spain. The following brief picture of the country as it was in the period leading up to 1492 will help to explain why this great change occurred.

Did you know?

Navarre was a small independent state on the border between Spain and France. It had been ruled previously by John II of Aragon. In 1494, the Queen of Navarre had accepted that the state was under Castilian rule but no further action was taken until 1512 when Ferdinand requested that Spanish troops be allowed to go through Navarre to attack Bayonne in France. Catherine of Navarre refused; Ferdinand promptly sent a force to occupy Navarre, indicating that his second wife, Germaine de Foix, had a claim to the throne. The Pope deposed Catherine and the state became a part of Castile. This was perceived as a great triumph.

Religious issues

Spain was, and still is, geographically a relatively isolated state; the large peninsula is tagged on to southern Europe, its main border with France in the north, clearly separated by the Pyrénées. The only other approach in the late 15th and early 16th centuries was by sea; the Atlantic to the west and the Mediterranean to the south and east. A narrow passage, the Strait of Gibraltar, between south-west Spain and North Africa, had been crossed on various occasions before this by raiding parties from Africa. In the 8th century, these largely Muslim raiders worked their way northwards through Spain, claiming control. This did not always result in conflict; there are examples of *convivencia* (differing religious groups living together peacefully), for example Christians reading Arabic literature and Jewish communities based largely in Castile who were tolerated and made a living through trade.

Key terms

Reconquista: Christian reconquest or regaining of land lost to Muslims. The last extensive reconquest was in the 13th and 14th centuries, but the process in Spain went back to the 7th century. Reconquest tended to be a divisive activity as the land regained was then often divided and given to the military orders, the Church and the nobles. By the 13th century, the process slowed down and the concept of *convivencia* also began to break down. Reconquest began again in 1482; the last campaign was against Granada.

Nevertheless, in the 10th century, the native Christian population responded in what was known as the ***reconquista*** or 'reconquest'. This process was largely complete by the mid-14th century. One of the earliest manifestations of the *reconquista* was the work of El Cid, a Christian who, in 1094, conquered and ruled the Muslim kingdom of Valencia.

However, El Cid did not impose religious unity on his conquests. Another reconquest saw the emergence of Portugal in 1249. Relations between the different groups remained fluid. For example, Christian rulers sometimes made agreements with Muslim leaders to defend themselves against another Christian leader. A historian, Kamen, states that Ferdinand III of Castile, who ruled in the 13th century, gave himself the title of 'King of the Three Religions'. However, by the mid-14th century, after a period of about 500 years, the process of *reconquista* was largely complete. Spain did not lose all of its Muslims; some Moorish communities remained; the size of Spain and the distances between different communities acted as a buffer against conflict. *Conversos* or New Christians/converted Jews also gained significant roles in commerce and government. Nevertheless, this mix of cultures and religions was to become a more difficult issue in the reign of Ferdinand and Isabella, known for their piety and devotion to Catholicism as the Catholic Monarchs. By 1492, Jews had been expelled and the Moors defeated.

From the beginning, both monarchs saw the Catholic Church as a rich and powerful institution. There were seven archbishoprics and 40 bishoprics in Castile alone. The total income of the Church was in the region of 6 million ducats (£198,000) per annum. Not only was the Church wealthy, it had a number of significant privileges; for example in Castile, it was exempt from taxation, owned a substantial amount of land and some rights to clerical appointments. Cathedral chapters chose their own members. In contrast, the crown even had difficulty in getting the clergy together for discussion. The monarchs attempted to summon an ecclesiastical council to Seville in 1478 to consider the issue of appointments. The council sent a delegation to Rome, but no agreement was reached. A vacancy in Cuenca in 1479 gave Ferdinand the chance to act; he made the appointment and the Pope had to agree. However, there was no guarantee that further appointments could be made by the crown. Only when the monarchs fought the war in Granada against the 'infidel', and the conquest was in sight, did Ferdinand manage to get the agreement of the Pope, who needed help in Italy, that all benefices in Granada would be crown appointments. The precedent had been set, and when the time came to appoint to high clerical office in the new lands in America, the monarchs did exercise all the rights.

■ Political issues

In terms of government, Spain was not yet a coherent state. Even the word 'Spain' was rarely used. Its inhabitants were Aragonese, Catalan, Castilian, etc. Systems needed to be developed. The nobility had tended to dominate; they had land and wealth and were not eager to give up their power. However, Elliott suggests that the initial union came at a time when Aragon was 'a society in retreat'; in comparison, Castile was more outward and forward looking and thus became the superior power.

Elliott also suggests that 'in the union of crowns, youth (Isabella?) and experience (Ferdinand?) walked hand in hand', Castile supplying the 'dynamism' and Aragon the 'administrative experience, techniques of diplomacy and government', thus giving benefits to both kingdoms. The different nature of the two crowns was emphasised by the fact that the monarchs were 'absolute monarchs in Castile' but 'constitutional monarchs in the states of the Crown of Aragon' so that '... the dualism of the two crowns was intensified and perpetuated.' In its initial form, there was no obligation on the King to summon the Castilian Cortes; no-one had the specific right to attend and it could not pass laws, although it could draw up petitions. From 1480 to 1498, no Cortes was summoned in Castile at all. Catalonia remained a medieval-style state with a contractual understanding between monarch and subjects to retain their 'customary laws and liberties'.

The most important change Ferdinand made here was to allow the peasants to leave their land, sell or grant it away without the consent of the lord. This agreement was called the *Sentencia de Guadalupe* and usefully allowed greater mobility. Ferdinand was the monarch who had more freedom of action; he governed the smaller state. Viceroys and the Council of Aragon supported his rule. However, he was very much an absentee monarch as the Castilian constitution allowed him more freedom of action. Ferdinand spent most of his time in Castile and during the Granadan campaign did not visit his own territories for 11 years.

The imposition of greater royal authority began with an increase in the monarchs' involvement with day-to-day government. It was undoubtedly the consequence of the upheaval of earlier years and the determination of two young monarchs to make a difference and establish their authority, aware that if law and order was not maintained, the nobility would look for loopholes. This was also a reason for the royal progress through Castile and the opportunity to meet significant individuals, noble or otherwise. Such constant movement hampered the growth of bureaucracy, but kept the monarchs and their subjects in touch. In some ways this was beneficial; an extensive and static bureaucracy would inevitably have grown and been expensive to maintain.

These measures to impose royal authority on Castile have been called by some historians the 'new monarchy'. There certainly was an increase in royal activity, as seen in the royal progress through Castile.

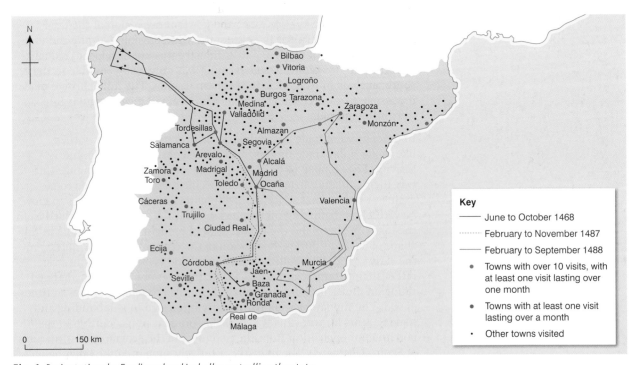

Fig. 1 *Peripatetic rule: Ferdinand and Isabella controlling the state*

Social and economic issues

Socially, the great aristocratic dynasties dominated; Elliott speaks of their 'unrestrained power' and quotes the heiress to the Alburquerque fortune who could travel from Castile to Aragon and Portugal without leaving her own estates. Kamen comments that the monarchs were unlikely to challenge the nobles; combined, they could have destroyed the crown. Alliances were the order of the day; these were made with families such as the Mendozas and the Velascos. One noble had 150,000 vassals (workers tied to the land). Force was often needed to keep these people in control. Another issue was the fact that many nobles had seized lands belonging to the crown; in the early days of their reign, Ferdinand and Isabella tried to regain these lands and were successful to a degree, often by compromise and an agreed settlement. Kamen comments that these early attempts to control the nobility were often successful and many of them 'now used their energies in the service of the crown rather than against it and each other'.

The presence of large Muslim and Jewish populations made Spain very different from the rest of Europe. This was a social and not just a religious issue. Many Muslims and Jews converted and were hard-working, but their contribution was not always appreciated. They often became the scapegoats when times were hard. The establishment of the Inquisition further added to their difficulties.

In economic terms, this period was initially one of development. Castile, where 97 per cent of the land was owned by only 3 per cent of the people, was being regenerated by the wool trade, although much of its development was in the hands of Genoese merchants rather than the Castilians. Seville had become an important port, fairs were set up at Medina del Campo and the fleet was rapidly expanded. A guild was established at Burgos. Sheep farming was particularly popular with the aristocracy who liked the fact that they did not need to employ large numbers of workers and pastures needed limited maintenance. However, there were drawbacks – for example, constant expansion of the land devoted to sheep resulted in deforestation and erosion. Despite the ready availability of wool, a textile industry was not developed, reducing opportunities for profit. Arable farming was only really possible in the south, such as in Andalusia in southern Castile. The mild climate made it possible to grow cereal crops, but high demand meant regular imports were also required.

In other areas of trade and industry the operation of guilds, rather like modern-day trade unions, also created obstacles to economic activity. They tended to be old-fashioned and unwilling to change the way their workers carried out their specific roles. They wanted to be exclusive bodies, and so were unwilling to allow their industries to grow. Nevertheless, Lotherington emphasises that the government gained from the taxes on sheep and the export of wool brought further income in the shape of customs duties. Regulation of the economy could be quirky; in the early years, it depended on Ferdinand and Isabella's own interests rather than commercial needs – for example, at one point they banned riding on mules because they might be needed to replace horses in times of war. The monarchs were particularly interested in shipbuilding and making arms for war; this was probably prudent in recognition of the potential for opposition from the nobility and the geographical situation of Spain. Ultimately, the industry effectively supported the opening up of the New World and colonial development.

In truth, in the late 15th century, on the accession of these two young people, Spain was not a 'joined-up' state despite the royal marriage. Castile and Aragon were only just coming together in the 'Union of Crowns' where 'youth and experience walk hand in hand'. Nevertheless, Elliott stresses that, 'They worked in double harness, each complementing the other; united in their determination to bring greatness to their kingdoms.'

The gradual merging of the disparate kingdoms and states into what we would now call Spain began in earnest in this period. By the end of 1556, Spain was acknowledged as a strong state internally, although there were still inequalities between the states. Castile was clearly the dominant Spanish state, and also an important European state. Did this also mean that Spain was a 'Great Power'? Coming to a judgement about this issue is a central theme of this book. As you read, you will learn about the development of the differing elements of government, including religion, finance, law and order, the challenge of economic and social change, the growth of the state and the development of empire. An important activity will be for you to analyse the strengths and weaknesses of the individuals who ruled, and also of the monarchy as an institution. You will also need to assess the contribution of other specific individuals, and of groups such as the nobles, to the emerging state. An understanding of religious diversity, its causes and effects, will be significant in enabling you to assess the strengths and weaknesses of the Catholic Church and other religious groups. Overall, your study will enable you to understand and assess the political, religious, economic and social challenges the monarchy faced in this period, and thus to judge the extent to which Spain was a 'Great Power' by 1556.

■ Timeline

The colours represent different types of events as follows: Social, Political, Economic, Religious, International.

1469	1474	1476	1478	1479	1480	1482
Isabella of Castile and Ferdinand of Aragon marry	Isabella becomes Queen of Castile	The *Hermandad* set up as a peacekeeping force	Isabella has a son, strengthening her position as Queen of Castile Isabella's request to the Pope to set up an Inquisition is accepted	Ferdinand becomes King of Aragon	Jews are confined to ghettos	An Inquisition is set up in Seville

1493	1494	1495	1497	1499	1500
All members of the Royal Council are *letrados* (law graduates)	The Council of Aragon is formed Burgos becomes the acknowledged centre of the wool trade	The Canary Islands are captured	Meeting of the Cortes, the first since 1483 The three main coins in both kingdoms are given the same value	Muslims living under Christian rule have to be baptised	Ferdinand becomes president of the three Orders of Chivalry Freer trade allowed in grain and trade guilds have to maintain the roads in their area Revolt of Moors; many convert and become known as *Moriscos* *Corregidores* appointed to supervise some Castilian towns Settlement in the New World grows

1507	1508	1511	1512	1516	1518
Cardinal Cisneros is appointed Inquisitor-General Rising prices begin to cause industrial decline and unemployment	Cardinal Cisneros becomes Regent briefly and sets up a new university at Alcalá Ferdinand rules all Spain until 1516	Cuba is acquired for Spain	Ferdinand conquers Navarre The Laws of Burgos (the New Laws) are introduced to regulate relations between Spaniards and the native inhabitants of the 'new' lands	Death of Ferdinand; Charles becomes King of Spain 64 towns now have *corregidores*	The Cortes begin to make demands on the new King and are less pliable from this time onwards

1527	1528	1529	1530	1532	1534	1536	1539
Inflation is a significant problem; wages rise less than prices	First arrest of a Protestant	Some Castilian ports given concessions to trade with the New World Charles leaves Spain to take up his new role as Holy Roman Emperor	Charles is crowned as Holy Roman Emperor	Charles defends Vienna against the Turks	The *alcabala* tax becomes a fixed sum	Spain is defeated by the Turks in the naval battle of Prevesa; Turks control the Mediterranean	Prince Philip, Charles' son, becomes the Regent of Spain, initially under his mother's guidance

1483

The Council of the Supreme Inquisition is created

Boabdil becomes the Emir of Granada

1488

Tomas de Torquemada becomes the first Spanish Inquisitor-General

The Council of the Inquisition is created

1491

The Treaty of Granada is drawn up

1492

Isabella becomes Co-Regent, Governor and Administrator-General in Aragon

The Royal Council is reorganised with Ferdinand and Isabella in command

The conquest of Granada is completed

Ferdinand and Isabella are given the new title of 'Catholic Monarchs'

A total of 26 Inquisitorial tribunals operated

All Jews are ordered out of Spain – the end of *convivencia*

Columbus embarks on his first voyage to the New World

1501

Sheep farmers' rights to graze their sheep are extended

All copies of the Qu'ran are to be burned

Prices begin to rise

1502

Mudéjars (Muslims) are forced to convert or be exiled

Harsher treatment of converted Muslims (*Moriscos*) – for example, they cannot travel to Granada. No Castilian is to shelter a Muslim

1503

The *Casa de la Contratción* is set up to control trade with the New World

1504

Death of Isabella; Joanna of Castile (Isabella's eldest daughter) and her husband, Philip, succeed

134 *conversos* are burned in Córdoba

1505

New laws of 'entail' mean nobles can pass their entire estate to one heir

A permanent law court is established in Granada

Ferdinand remarries. His bride is Germaine de Foix, niece of the French king

Freer trade in grain is permitted throughout Spain

1519

Charles I is elected Holy Roman Emperor. From 1519, most of his time is spent in the empire

The Germania Revolt

1520

The Comuneros Revolt

1521

The Battle of Villalar

Lutheran books are banned

1522

Cisneros promotes the production of the Complutensian (Polyglot) Bible

Council of War is created

1523

Council of Finance is set up

1524

Trade opens up for foreigners in the Americas

1525

All Muslims are ordered to leave Spain

1526

Many Muslim practices are forbidden, such as the ritual slaughter of animals

Council of State and Council of the Indies are set up

1540

Foundation of the Jesuits

1542

Las Casas attacks the treatment of Indians in the colonies

1543

Repayment of loans rise to 65 per cent of revenue

Philip becomes Regent in his own right

1547

First list of books banned in Spain

1548

Interim of Augsburg; an attempt to settle religious differences in the empire

1555

Charles negotiates peace with the German princes (Peace of Augsburg)

1556

Charles abdicates from the Holy Roman Empire

Spain is technically bankrupt

In this chapter you will learn about:

- the union of the crowns of Aragon and Castile and its significance

- the structure of Ferdinand and Isabella's government as exemplified in the personal authority of the monarchs

- the role of the Royal Council, the Cortes, the *letrados* and *corregidores*; the aristocracy and the extent of the threat they posed.

Fig. 1 *Painting entitled 'The Virgin and the Catholic Monarchs' celebrating Ferdinand and Isabella's accession*

Key chronology

1469 Ferdinand and Isabella marry.

1471 The Pope gives his blessing.

1474 Isabella becomes Queen of Castile.

1478 The Inqusition is established.

1479 Ferdinand becomes King of Aragon.

1492 Ferdinand and Isabella become joint rulers in Aragon. Columbus discovers the New World. Jews are expelled from Castile. War with Granada.

The union of the crowns of Aragon and Castile

October 1469 was a special time for Isabella of Castile, for this was when she first met, and then secretly married, Ferdinand of Aragon. He was 17, Isabella was 18, but, despite their apparent youth, both were aware of the immense responsibilities they would eventually have as monarchs in their own states. Isabella was not regarded as a beauty; she is described by one observer as having 'a plain face, endearing only because of its youthful freshness. Pale eyebrows were set high in it; the nose was irregular, the mouth slightly pouting'. Ferdinand, according to one historian, was 'by nature a philanderer, of a disposition little given to love'. However, in his marriage concessions of 1469, Ferdinand solemnly declared, 'I will personally go to these kingdoms (Castile and

Leon) to reside and be in them with Her Highness the princess, and I will not leave them without her will and counsel, and I will not remove her from them without her consent and will.' If Ferdinand was not going to be faithful, he would at least honour the political demands of the union.

Fig. 2 *Ferdinand of Aragon, husband of Isabella of Castile*

■ A closer look

Ferdinand's marriage concessions, 1469

Both Ferdinand and Isabella wanted their marriage to advantage their states; for Isabella of Castile, this was particularly important. She wanted Castile to become an internationally well-known state and to ensure that her claim to Castile was strong. Ferdinand of Aragon considered that the alliance with Castile would protect Aragon from the French. Ferdinand had to make a wide range of concessions, 24 in total, to reassure the inhabitants of both states, particularly the politicians, that he had no intention of trying to seize the throne from Isabella. Source 1 shows a few of these concessions.

No 4: I will observe and have proper justice observed and administered in all the kingdoms ... and I will listen to all of those who come to me seeking justice, as a good and proper Catholic king should, and I will see to the assistance of the poor and needy persons.

No 6: I will observe and maintain established ways and the laudable customs, laws, *fueros* and privileges of these kingdoms, in all their cities, towns and places, as it is customary for kings to do when they come to power.

No 11: If God should grant us offspring, either sons or daughters, as we may hope, I will never remove them from her, nor will I remove them from those kingdoms.

No 13: All the privileges, letters and other documents that shall be written, drawn up, or sent, by her or by me, must be signed jointly by both of us.

No 22: I will not go anywhere in these kingdoms, under any pretext or reason, without her consent or due counsel.

No 24: I will undertake no war or peace treaty, with any neighbouring king or lord of any kind, not with any knight or lord of said kingdoms, whether ecclesiastical or secular, without the will and knowledge of Her Highness, the princess and her counsellors.

1   *Quoted in J. Cowans (ed.),* **Early Modern Spain: A Documentary History***, 2003*

■ Key terms

Fueros: a word for laws or rights. In Aragon, the King took an oath to maintain existing *fueros*. Even into the next century, the Aragonese were saying that 'the prince can no more be exempt himself from them than he can exempt himself from a contract.' He was subject to the law just as any other person.

However, initially, the marriage was not without its problems; Isabella had not consulted either Henry IV, her brother and King, or the Royal Council. Admittedly, Isabella and Ferdinand's personal union did not, and could not, immediately bring political union; even had it done so, they would not have ruled all of Spain. Portugal and Granada lay outside their authority. A further complication was that Ferdinand

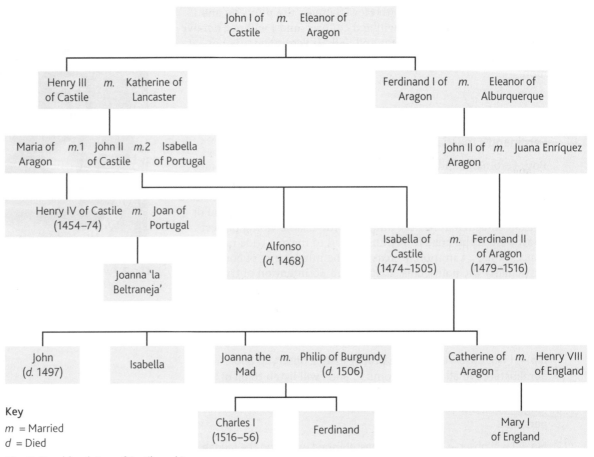

Fig. 3 *Royal family tree of Castile and Aragon*

and Isabella were cousins and had to wait until 1471 before the Pope eventually gave his blessing.

Isabella became Queen of Castile, the largest kingdom in the Spanish peninsula, in 1474 on the death of her half-brother Henry. She was crowned quickly to avoid challenges from other claimants, particularly from Joanna of Castile, Henry's daughter. In view of this situation, Isabella's support was limited; the coronation ceremony was not attended by high-ranking individuals. In that ceremony, held in the main square in Segovia, Isabella made a series of promises to support her country and her people.

Although the assembly (parliament) of Castile was willing to accept Isabella as queen, others were less so. Isabella's struggle for acceptance as queen lasted for the next five years. An inconclusive battle was fought at Toro in 1476. This had the positive effect, however, of allowing Isabella to summon the Cortes, an act which clearly did define her as the ruling monarch. Nevertheless, the Archbishop of Toledo remained one of her fiercest opponents and controlled a large numbers of troops, castles and supporters; he did not surrender until 1478. Many towns also resisted, particularly in the north and south of Castile. Isabella was, however, steadfast; she has been described as 'a determined and resourceful woman, with a street fighter's instinct for survival'. Her position was eventually further consolidated by the birth of a son in 1478. Even so, she may not have been victorious without the failure of King Alfonso of Portugal to support the claim of Joanna of Castile to the throne and the strong support of her husband, Ferdinand. It was only in 1479 that Isabella could feel reasonably secure on her throne. Joanna eventually became a nun, thus ensuring she would not mount another challenge. In the same year, Ferdinand became the King of Aragon, which further consolidated Isabella's authority and also opened up the possibility of a more united future for Spain through the two monarchs.

When Ferdinand became King of Aragon in 1479, he also inherited a number of other states – Granada, Valencia and Catalonia – each with their own rulers, customs and laws. Catalonia made unsuccessful attempts to become independent. Despite the ties of marriage and inheritance however, Portugal remained a distinct and separate kingdom until 1580. As in Castile, the nobility in Aragon were powerful and a considerable threat; they had large amounts of land and controlled large numbers of peasants, very much in the feudal tradition. Nevertheless, Aragon's extensive Mediterranean coastline had allowed it to extend its authority to islands such as Sicily and Sardinia, and it had even established a foothold in southern Italy. In contrast, relations with France were poor throughout the period. However, Ferdinand's marriage to Isabella of Castile was useful in strengthening Aragon's position; by combining Aragon and Castile through marriage there was the prospect of developing some level of cooperation which could be beneficial for the Spanish peninsula as a whole, and for Aragon and Castile in particular.

■ Activity

Thinking point

Study the map of Spain in 1474 (Fig. 4).

Work in pairs.

1 Discuss how big an issue the multiplicity of states could be to the new monarchs in this very early stage of their rule.

2 Discuss what you think was the most significant benefit of the 'union' of the two crowns? Would a contemporary have a different view? Why might that be?

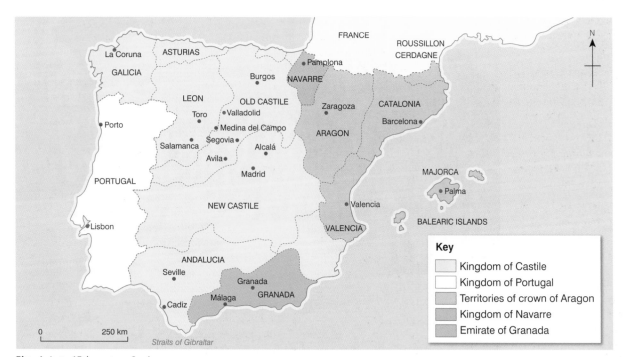

Fig. 4 *Late 15th century Spain*

Similarities and differences: Castile and Aragon

It was not only size that differentiated Aragon and Castile, although that was important. Castile was the larger state geographically and had the larger total population, possibly five times that of Aragon – approximately 5 million in Castile and 1 million people in Aragon. Castile also had several cities of 50,000 people. Although not large by modern-day standards, these cities dwarfed those of Aragon by 20,000 or more. Aragon also had fewer cities in total.

Castile was the more unified state; its government was acknowledged throughout – there was a single representative body, the Cortes, whereas Aragon had three Cortes as a result of the division into three separate kingdoms. The powers of the monarchy were therefore more limited in Aragon, as all laws had to be agreed by each of the Cortes. There could be difficulties with this as the *fueros*, which were specific privileges of each of the three kingdoms, might be implemented to prevent change. However, a legal official, called the justicia, could challenge any attempted change to these privileges. Castile, unlike Aragon, had a single coinage and language. The Basque area in the north had the potential to cause problems, but this was limited enough not to create an insurmountable obstacle to some form of unification. Castile was also developing commercially, courtesy of the wool trade controlled by the Mesta (a consortium of all wool traders in the region). Burgos became a trading city, sending goods as far as the Netherlands and England. In contrast, Aragonese towns competed against each other rather than cooperating with each other.

Fig. 5 *The pacification of Castile, 1485*

Table 1 *Key comparisons between Castile and Aragon*

Size	Castile was larger than Aragon and its population matched the geographical difference; Castile had 5 million inhabitants to Aragon's 1 million.
Parliaments	The Castilian Cortes had three houses, whereas the Aragonese state had four houses – two of these were for the nobility. Each state in Aragon had a committee to act when the Cortes were not in session, thus limiting the power of the monarch.
Population	Both states were mixed: Christians, Jews, Moriscos (Castile) and Moors (Aragon).
Economy	Farming and trade were the biggest industries in Aragon; sheep (wool) were the predominant business in Castile.
Authority	Castilian monarchs had more authority generally, but needed the Cortes to validate decisions; Aragonese monarchs could not make new laws without consent from the Cortes.
Royal presence	The monarchs of Castile were more peripatetic, allowing the population in more remote areas to see them; the Aragonese rarely saw their monarchs (Ferdinand spent considerable time in Castile).
Professional classes	Jews and Muslims were more likely to have prominent positions in Aragon than in Castile.

■ Activity

Talking point

Divide into groups of no more than four. What was the single most important difference between Aragon and Castile? Be prepared to defend your view.

■ The personal authority of the monarch

The reign of Ferdinand and Isabella has been seen by some historians as a 'fresh start' for Spain. Elliott comments that, 'Castilian society was being transformed and invigorated by the economic changes which the wool trade was bringing in its train' and 'the monarchs established strong personal rule, combining this with an effective administration and a degree of centralisation which had not occurred before'. Hunt perceives that, 'in Aragon, the aim was to restore royal authority. Ferdinand's main target was the nobility, but he was also anxious to bring under control the great city of Barcelona.' Kamen's view is 'old habits had to be altered and far reaching changes were required in political, economic and social life.' W. H. Prescott, writing much earlier in 1837, declared their reign to be 'the most glorious epoch in the annals of Spain.' The fact that so many historians agreed that significant progress was made, suggests that there was a definable change: a '**new monarchy**'.

Ferdinand and Isabella had brought together the states of Aragon and Castile. To contemporaries also, this seemed to generate new strengths and possibilities for their reign, for example, to rid Spain and the Mediterranean of the Turkish threat and to subjugate the Moors in Spain. One chronicler wrote, 'With this conjunction of two royal sceptres, our Lord Jesus Christ took vengeance on his enemies and destroyed him who slays and curses.' Fernandez-Armesto talks about a 'millenial fever' (as the next century grew closer) in which Ferdinand, in particular, was perceived as the man who could defeat Islam.

The concept of 'new monarchy' is now much less used by historians; the continuities with the past, as much as the differences, are also seen

■ Key terms

New monarchy: some characteristics were: concentrating more authority in the hands of the monarchy; finding new ways of raising money; controlling ambitious nobles and developing more efficient administrative systems. The historian Lynch considers the changes were simply refining existing methods rather than a real departure from the past. Woodward suggests their achievements were exaggerated, for example revolts after 1506 suggest that the aristocracy was not 'tamed'.

as significant. Nevertheless, most historians do concede that Ferdinand and Isabella left Spain a much stronger country than they found it. They often use the term 'absolute' rulers, suggesting a step beyond 'new monarchy'. This is a concept more often associated with 17th-century monarchs, such as the Stuarts in England and Louis XIV in France, indicating that they wielded extensive power. Absolutism implied that there were no restraints on the monarchs' personal authority. Councillors and ministers, for example, could be ignored, parliaments never summoned and all aspects of government, including questions of succession, war and peace, were at the sole command of the monarchs. Historians such as Kamen doubt this and suggest that Ferdinand and Isabella were supporters of strong authority, but were not impelled, or even able, in the first instance, to exercise it. They had 'no capital, no standing army, no bureaucracy, no reliable income and certainly no theory of **absolutism**.'

Nevertheless, there is some evidence supporting this view of a strong centralised government in Castile; Isabella used the phrase 'absolute power' seven times in her testament. Stronger evidence is apparent in the use of decrees (*pragmaticas*) rather than statute law, especially in Castile. After 1480, there was a 20-year gap before the Cortes was summoned again. Even when it was summoned it was not always representative; on one occasion only 18 towns were represented by 36 men in the Castilian Cortes. There was also certainly an increase in the number of officials appointed by the crown to keep the peace such as the *corregidores*.

However, the relationship between the rulers and the governed in Aragon differed. For example, Ferdinand had to swear to uphold the laws of the kingdom three times, once in each of the different Cortes of Aragon, that is, in Catalonia, Aragon and Valencia, rather than the single occasion on which Isabella did this. Despite that was agreeing to uphold the laws of the Kingdom; these were often different laws in each of the Aragonese territories. Governor-generals or lieutenant-generals were appointed to each territory and, at one point, Isabella held some of these positions. Ferdinand also used his illegitimate son, Alfonso, to stand in for him in Aragon for most of his reign.

Despite their marriage, Ferdinand and Isabella are usually perceived as ruling their territories independently through different institutions, although often following the same policies. Customs barriers remained, they never called themselves the monarchs of Spain, but referred only to their own territory. Any authority they had in each other's kingdom was exercised with the agreement of their partner. Ferdinand was the more experienced ruler, but had to respect his wife's authority and the traditions of Castile; Isabella, similarly, initially had limited influence in Aragon.

By 1492, Ferdinand seemed to have agreed to what amounted to joint rule in Aragon by making Isabella 'Co-Regent, Governor and Administrator General in the kingdoms of the Crown of Aragon in our presence and absence alike'. This suggests some kind of implicit political unification or centralisation, although there is little direct evidence of any actions taken, without consultation, by Isabella alone, in Aragon. Armesto also argues that government in Castile was similarly joint and that each of them took differing roles. However, when Isabella died in 1504, a Regency Council was created and Ferdinand did not become King.

Whatever the reality of joint rule, it is clear that Ferdinand and Isabella had no fixed place from which to direct operations, but moved around their territories, and their ministers and officials moved with them.

Key terms

Absolutism: a form of government where **all** power is vested in the monarchy and its appointed officers; its concepts are built upon those of 'new monarchy'. Absolutism became particularly strong in 17th century Europe, although earlier kings, for example in Spain, as early as the 15th century, had claimed they were absolutist. Juan II claimed that 'his authority is not from men but from God, whose place he occupies in temporal matters'.

Activity

Group activity

In groups, carry out one of the following:

1 Write and display a definition of 'New Monarchy'; start with one student suggesting a definition; others can challenge or add until the group view is agreed.

2 Using pages 13–15, create a table to illustrate the similarities and differences between the governments of Castile and Aragon.

This was known as the royal progress. In this way, they each exercised a very personal, authoritative and traditional style of monarchy, clearly demonstrating their authority to their subjects and also showing some support for and solidarity with nobles, landowners and churchmen. This system of personal monarchy was becoming more unusual in much of early modern Europe, but was considered necessary in Spain; the country was large, nobles were ambitious, fought almost continuous wars and needed to be held in check. Taxes had to be collected, religious deviation had to be suppressed and the laws of the land had to be enforced. Direct intervention by the monarchs was important.

In positive terms, this system worked well; seeing their king or queen in the flesh was a clear reminder to their subjects where the power lay and of the obedience that was owed to their rulers. However, there was also a negative side to such an itinerant monarchy. It was very demanding as the monarchs were constantly travelling and despatching business as they did so. Ferdinand and Isabella did not manage to visit all parts of their realm; when they did visit, they did not linger. Nevertheless, what was important for Spain and their monarchy, was that they were seen to be alive and well, enforcing order and exercising their personal authority.

Such close personal attention to their subjects by the monarchs did not necessarily mean that Spain was an orderly place; towns were often places of unrest and could easily 'boil over' such as in Salamanca in 1493 when noble factions threatened to take control. On another occasion, the gates of Vitoria were closed until Isabella agreed to confirm its privileges. Enforcing order was a slow process, complicated by politics, finance and religion among other factors; it was also a continuous process and even by the end of the reign, although Spain had changed considerably, it could not necessarily be thought of as a united and stable country.

Certainly, Ferdinand and Isabella were 'hands-on rulers'; Isabella spoke of her 'royal absolute power'. This might be supported by the comment of a foreign visitor that 'everyone trembles at the name of the Queen'. However, the Queen was not given the title of 'Majesty' but of 'Highness'. The itinerant nature of their rule mitigated against absolute authority which requires a degree of centralisation; the differing nature of their systems supports this view.

Fig. 6 *Procession on Good Friday in remembrance of the crucifixion*

■ Activity

Source analysis

Study Sources 2 and 3.

1 In what ways do these two sources suggest that the full union of the two kingdoms under Ferdinand and Isabella was unlikely to be acceptable to either kingdom?

2 How far do these two sources differ in their views about the extent of unity between Castile and Aragon in the reign of Ferdinand and Isabella?

3 To what extent do these sources confirm or challenge the description given of Ferdinand and Isabella as 'hands-on' rulers?

■ Cross-reference

For more information on the establishment of the Inquisition in Spain, see page 30.

■ Did you know?

The Inquisition was originally part of the Roman legal system set up to deal with criminals, but by the 4th century it was used to identify those who did not accept Christianity. The Inquisition as a religious body was first established in France in 1233 in response to a growth of heresy. A papal edict of 1234 allowed suspected heretics to be convicted without appeal. Death by burning became the standard punishment. The Inquisition first arrived in Spain in 1238, but only in Aragon. It was not established in Castile until 1376 and was under the control of the Pope. Ferdinand and Isabella set up the Spanish Inquisition, i.e. having authority throughout the kingdoms of the Catholic Monarchs, in 1478. Its main task was to deal with New Christians, i.e. Jews who had converted to Christianity.

Both Ferdinand and Isabella took great care to perfect their political partnership. All their recorded decisions were made in full agreement even when one happened to be absent, for 'though necessity separated their persons, love held their wills together'. Beyond the personal union no attempt was ever made to disturb the complete autonomy of Castile and Aragon.

2 *H. Kamen,* **Spain, 1469–1714: A Society of Conflict**, *1991*

The Inquisition was introduced into both Castile and Aragon and the Council of the Inquisition was responsible for its activities in the two realms. There is more evidence to be found if signs of informal unity are sought. Ferdinand and Isabella worked closely together on a personal level; there was usually a common attitude on religious matters. Castilian gradually became the dominant language. Many resented the Castilians who received the majority of the awards and offices that the union of the two realms brought. Finally, it must be remembered that, after the death of Isabella, the two kingdoms would go again their separate ways.

3 *J. Kilsby,* **Spain: Rise and Decline, 1474–1643**, *1987*

■ The role of the Royal Council, the Cortes, the *letrados* and the *corregidores*

The Royal Council

By 1492, the Catholic Monarchs, as Ferdinand and Isabella were now known, had a reasonably defined structure for their governments. Some of these structures were inherited and continued to develop over their reign. The aim of establishing a clear system that gave the monarchs effective control over the country was always the driving force. The ways in which the Spanish monarchs set up and used their councils and those who manned them, moved the monarchy into a more 'modern' form of government. Most of the development work was channelled through this

Fig. 7 *Nobles at court*

typical organ of early modern governments, the most important of which was the Royal Council.

The Royal Council (*Consejo Real*) was not a new body, but was reorganised by the monarchs. It was the hub of government; it met daily and its main duty was to advise the monarchs and deal with matters that affected Spain as a whole. It also considered individual issues relating to specific localities. Its decisions, or rulings, were then written up as 'royal provisions'. In its earlier form, all bishops, **grandees** and the heads of **military orders** had the right to attend council. This was no longer allowed by the Catholic Monarchs.

The Royal Council had four main officers: the Grand Chancellor; Chancellor of the Privy Seal; Constable; and Admiral. They were aided by lawyers or *letrados*; graduates in law who had spent at least 10 years in practice and were therefore considered experienced and able to make appropriate judgements. Although other councillors initially came from different backgrounds, it soon became clear that those with legal experience were the most useful. Eventually, all councillors were *letrados*. After 1489, the council was sometimes headed by a president who stood in for Ferdinand and Isabella when they were absent on their travels around their kingdoms. Woodward suggests that the council was a centralised structure, i.e. a series of interlinked departments working together for an agreed purpose. In reality, their only connection was to the monarchs and not to each other. Woodward concluded it was 'only in the early stages of developing a professional bureaucracy'.

The Royal Council also had a role as the highest court of justice. It sat twice each a week to hear cases. Ferdinand and Isabella were personally present and made judicial decisions but, as their responsibilities increased, trained judges took over and professional courts of appeal (*audiencias*) were established. Its aim was to develop impartial judicial processes, but sometimes harsh decisions were made.

Key terms

Grandees: the noblemen of the highest rank. In Castile, they accounted for 2–3 per cent of the population whilst owning 97 per cent of the land. The most significant of them were the Enriquez, Mendoza and Guzman families. Beneath them were the *titulos* or lesser nobles and the *segundones*, the younger sons of the three main families.

Military orders: three military orders were created in the 12th century. They were the Orders of Calatrava, Alcantara and Santiago in Castile and of Montesa and St John in Aragon and were dominated by the nobility. They were set up to defend the frontiers against Muslims in the kingdom of Granada. As the mastership of these orders became vacant, Isabella appointed Ferdinand to them. They owned large estates; the Order of Santiago had the most territory. By 1489, they were administered by a Council of Orders.

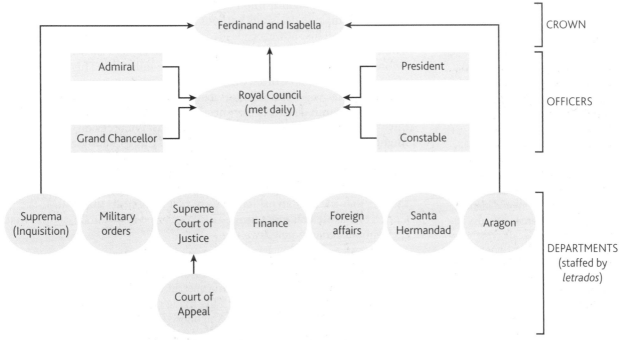

Fig. 8 *The structure of the Royal Council in the reign of Ferdinand and Isabella*

Activity

Revision exercise

Copy Figure 8. Use the text in this chapter and your own research to add information to the diagram about the work of the different bodies and officials. Write one or two paragraphs to explain what this tells you about Ferdinand and Isabella's authority.

Key terms

Hermandad: often called the *Santa Hermandad*. This was set up in 1476 initially in towns of more than 50 inhabitants, then developed as a peacekeeping institution from 1481, acting as both police and judges. It operated first in Castile and was then instituted in Aragon by Ferdinand. By the late 1480s, the organisation was building ships and collecting taxes. More information can be found in Chapter 2.

Cross-reference

For more information on the *Hermandad*, see page 29.

Activity

Group activity

What do you think were the strengths and weaknesses of the partnership between Ferdinand and Isabella?

Work in pairs or threes. Using a large piece of paper make a two-column chart – one column headed strengths and the other weaknesses. Fill in the chart as far as you can. Put your charts up around the room and identify the common themes. Discuss any differences and decide whether they are valid suggestions or not; ask the writer to justify the claim if you have any doubts.

The monarchy continued working to establish effective judicial processes across Spain that would deploy professional judges. For example, a court of appeal was set up in 1489 in Valladolid, as also were provincial courts in Santiago and Seville.

The Royal Council also supervised the main departments of state, i.e. justice, finance, foreign affairs, the **Hermandad** (although this was not functional after 1498) and the Inquisition. The Council of the Supreme Inquisition was added in 1483 and the Council of Aragon in 1494. All the constituent parts of the council were seen as important. Kamen sees the council, not as a centralising body, but an organisation that simply grew according to the needs of the state. Power was devolved by the crown as a practical measure, as the monarchs could not be everywhere at once.

The Cortes

Parliaments are often seen as modern developments, but they were certainly being held in some countries in medieval times and the Spanish kingdoms were some of the first to hold such assemblies. They usually included a mixture of the aristocracy, the clergy and some representatives of the towns. Representation of the towns in the Spanish Cortes is particularly noteworthy when many early modern parliaments in other states generally ignored the lower classes. The Cortes were not summoned regularly. Nevertheless, they were summoned more times in the reign of Ferdinand and Isabella than any later rulers of Spain.

Castile and Aragon each had their own separate Cortes. Their specific functions were to:

■ vote money for the monarch's use

■ agree royal legislation

■ give advice when requested to do so

■ express the grievances of their constituents.

The monarchs thought it important to show that they were consulting rather than making decisions without reference to the representatives of the people. This, however, clashed with their need to raise money. The Cortes, for their part, wanted to be able to express their grievances before granting money and thereby gain some influence. This conflict of interests meant no Cortes was summoned between 1483 and 1497. When a Cortes was summoned, Isabella selected the individuals to be summoned. Hunt describes one meeting when Isabella called only the town representatives of a select group of towns. On occasion, the Cortes might consist of less than 40 representatives. Consequently, relations between the monarchs and the Cortes were often poor; both sides found the situation frustrating. This was particularly true of the Aragonese Cortes. Meetings of the Aragonese Cortes were therefore irregular, despite the fact that the monarchs' hands were tied without it. In contrast, the Cortes of Castile had more limited authority and it was not essential that they should agree to new laws.

Consequently, much of the money needed to run their governments had to come from the Castilian Cortes rather than the Aragonese Cortes. This was achieved by voting special taxes and, from 1474, tax revenue increased exponentially. This made the Castilian Cortes seem quite weak in comparison to the Aragonese Cortes. However, despite this, Isabella continued to ensure that laws were always legitimised by the Cortes whilst also maintaining that her power was absolute. Other sources of money were the Military orders, the *Hermandad* and grants from the papacy. The monarchs also took out loans (*juros*) and used the proceeds of customs duties, which were growing as a result of increased trading.

A further significant restriction on Ferdinand in Aragon was that he was unable legally to remove the justicia who headed the legal system. He could not pass laws, raise taxes or create an army – all vital functions for any head of state. Taxation was a particular concern for obvious reasons; the Cortes set up committees to collect customs duties and taxes on goods. Ferdinand was not able to reduce their power. He had to look elsewhere for other sources of revenue.

The *letrados* and *corregidores*

Bureaucracy grew rapidly in Spain. By 1493, it was expected that all members of the Royal Council were *letrados*, i.e. officers who had studied law and would be able to offer appropriate advice. Their role was not new in its purpose, but there were many more of them at work under Ferdinand and Isabella.

Corregidores were civilian officials whose role was to work 'in the field', usually in towns and mostly in Castile. Their role was originally created by Henry IV in the 1460s, but they seemed to disappear when civil war broke out in 1464. However, by 1500, they had re-emerged with wide-ranging responsibilities. *Corregidores* usually came from different localities to the one in which they worked, so that they could not be pressurised.

Their main responsibilities were to:

- ensure public order
- maintain the authority of the local government
- administer justice based on the laws of Castile
- ensure all citizens maintained loyalty to the crown
- ensure there was sufficient food for the community
- ensure that town halls were built
- maintain detailed public records.

Corregidores acted as tax collectors and were expected to ensure that the wishes of the monarchs were put into effect. This also often involved settling disputes. They presented regular reports about issues arising in their area, and often had to make sure that the nobles or members of the Church were not obstructing the government in any way. They also had a military role. Not surprisingly, they were not always greeted with enthusiasm by the town authorities, despite the need for their presence in view of the lawless state of some towns. Toledo was one of the towns that openly and successfully refused to accept a *corregidor*. Much opposition centred around the fact that the towns had to pay their salaries.

Ferdinand and Isabella made a point of visiting every town in their territory, sometimes staying for several weeks. The monarchs occasionally intervened themselves to ensure peace; this was not always welcome, but Isabella persisted and, over time, there was greater acceptance of such central control. The *Hermandad* was also employed to enforce order. This was a kind of 'brotherhood' or association of individuals who had come together freely to work for law and order, and continued to do so until the turn of the century.

Did you know?

Not only were relations with the Cortes difficult, but the Coronation Oath also imposed limitations on the monarchs of Aragon. It stated: 'We, who are as good as you, swear to you, who are no better than we, to accept you as our sovereign king and lord, provided that you observe our liberties and laws, but if not, not.' Taking on the kingship on these terms was therefore rather like contemplating a poisoned chalice.

Cross-reference

For more on the financial situation of the period, see Chapter 3 (pages 42–5) and Chapter 6 (pages 84–6).

Cross-reference

There is more detail on the Cortes in Chapters 3 (page 43), 5 (pages 73–5), 7 (pages 101–3) and 8 (pages 120–1).

Cross-reference

The development and role of the *Hermandad* are considered in greater detail on pages 29–30.

Activity

Thinking point

What have Ferdinand and Isabella achieved so far in their reign? How would their subjects grade those achievements on a scale of A – excellent, B – fair or C – poor?

The threat from the aristocracy

Spanish society was generally hierarchical and the nobility were usually not expected to do manual work of any kind. Their power had grown strongly during the 14th century and, across both Castile and Aragon, the clergy and nobility owned 90 per cent of the land, suggesting that feudal ties between monarch and subjects were already weakened; this made it difficult for the crown to control them. There were 15 very powerful families; one such was the influential Mendoza family in Castile. Lesser nobles brought the figure up to over 60.

Fig. 9 *Nobles pledging obedience to the monarch*

Key terms

Entail: this was a legal measure indicating to whom a landed estate could be bequeathed, usually the eldest son. This was confirmed by law in 1505. The measure was introduced by Ferdinand and Isabella, possibly to gain support from the nobles, but also to ensure that there was limited conflict between siblings and other claimants on the death of the owner. This did not always have the anticipated outcome as it created power blocs that could threaten the crown. For example, the Duke of Infantado could draw upon a population of 93,000 in support of him.

Key profile

The Mendoza family

The Mendoza family had large amounts of land in the north of Castile. They were related to Ferdinand and were prepared to help him gain support for Isabella's claim to the throne of Castile in 1474. Power came from their wealth, mostly drawn from the proceeds of sheep farming. They benefited from laws passed in 1505 that allowed them to pass on their estates intact to one heir only, i.e. no sub-divisions. This was called '**entail**' and often caused feuding between siblings. These powerful men were, however, excluded from holding any important position in the government.

In Aragon, the relationship between the crown and the nobles was less stable than that in Castile, even though there were fewer nobles – possibly 20 in Aragon, which was a much smaller state than Castile. By virtue of the extent of their wealth, property and influence, nobles could be a major source of opposition to the crown. They had built up their landholdings.

For example, in Salamanca, 63 per cent of the land and more than 60 per cent of the population was controlled by the nobility. Other threats which they posed were tax exemptions and rights to and control of the sheep walks used by the Mesta. The latter also enabled them to collect tolls which rightfully belonged to the crown. They also had vassals who could only be employed to work on the land or be drafted into the armies if required. The Velasco family held the post of Constable of Castile and controlled more than 250 towns and villages; another family nominated more than 500 public officers across Spain. Power had also, in the past, been gained by the masterships of the military orders, although by *c.*1501 these posts were held by Ferdinand. Kamen therefore sees the nobles as a potentially very serious threat to the monarchy, saved only by the rivalry between the nobles themselves.

Ferdinand and Isabella were quick to see the need to limit noble activities as much as possible. Despite this, Ferdinand never fully succeeded in suppressing the nobles, nor did he achieve any significant level of cooperation from them. They continued to be dominant in the Cortes, they were high profile in town councils and had a firm grip on the countryside where high rents and feudal services were imposed. Central government had some limited success in attempting to break their dominance, particularly because of the grant of entail, which did avoid significant disputes and local disputes that could develop into wider conflict. The power of the nobility was one area of affairs where the government appeared to have had some sympathy with the lower classes.

Summary questions

1. How strong was Ferdinand and Isabella's government in this period?

2. What evidence is there that the monarchs had increased their authority by 1500?

2 Race and religion

Fig. 1 *The Courtyard of Lions of the Alhambra in Granada*

In this chapter you will learn about:

- war against Granada and its outcome in religious and political terms

- the role of the Holy Brotherhood (*Santa Hermandad*) and the concept of a 'crusade'

- the establishment of the Inquisition in 1478

- the expulsion of the Jews in 1492 and its religious and social implications

- the extent and end of *convivencia*; forced conversions and the consequences

- the beginnings of Church reform.

In 1483, a 19-year-old man named Boabdil, son of the Emir (ruler) of Granada, and a Moor, became the centre of a palace revolution in Granada. He was supported by the Spaniards, and was made king in place of his father, Mulay Hassan. He was tiny in stature and often called 'Boabdil the Small'; more importantly he had little political experience. However, he was used as the '**Trojan horse**' enabling Ferdinand and Isabella to win their war against Granada, and the Muslim faith, having divided the loyalties of the Granadans. Boabdil eventually became a victim of the Catholic Monarchs himself.

Key profile

Boabdil

Boabdil (*c*.1459–1528) was the son of the Emir of Granada. At the age of 19, he was captured by Spanish troops, following an ambush by the Spaniards. He then agreed to a treaty with Ferdinand and Isabella to help them fight against his father. However, by 1486, he had made an alternative agreement with his uncle in defence of Granada. Twice he played a double game and it was not until 1490 that he began to work for peace, concluding the treaty in 1492, with 500 hostages held to ensure his loyalty. Boabdil was duly rewarded with land.

Religious conflict in Spain was not new; as early as 792 conflict between Jews, Christians and Muslims was common and reflected in political and military affairs. Over time, the mindset of 'crusade' and the desire of the monarchs to establish Catholicism as the sole religion throughout Spain developed, and was supported by the Inquisition. In the reign of Ferdinand and Isabella, fear of Islam was strong. Potential links between Muslims in their state of Granada and the Ottoman Empire in the eastern Mediterranean were a threat in religious and political terms. The economic threat was also strong; the kingdom of Granada bordered on the Mediterranean and had easy access to trade; in addition, it produced commodities such as silk which was a highly prized luxury.

War against Granada and its outcome in religious and political terms

Background

There are many reasons why the Catholic Monarchs decided to conquer Granada. In some respects it was a purely political decision made for the sake of unity, having already brought together Castile and Aragon in a form of political union. There was also a strong wish, not unusual at the time, to ensure the dominance of Catholicism in the Spanish peninsula. For monarchs of the 15th and 16th centuries, religious issues were always a top priority; conflict with those of a different faith was seen as a **crusade**.

This view is confirmed by the inscription on the Catholic Monarchs' tomb recording their success in 'the destruction of the Islamic sect'. Not only this, but the marriage concessions made by Ferdinand in 1469 said:

> We will be obliged to wage war on the Moors, enemies of the holy Catholic faith, as other preceding Catholic Monarchs have done …

Quoted in J. Cowans (ed.), **Early Modern Spain: A Documentary History**, 2003

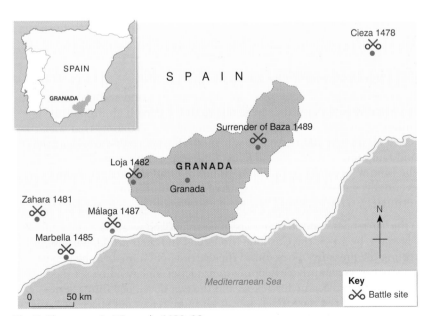

Fig. 2 The war against Granada, 1482–92

Exploring the detail

Trojan horse

This is a reference to the way in which the city of Troy, in ancient times, was captured by the Greeks. The Greeks built a huge wooden horse, put soldiers inside it and took it to the gates of the city of Troy. When the inhabitants opened the gates of the city, the soldiers emerged and the rest of the army was able to force its way in. Troy was taken and the Greeks were triumphant.

Key terms

Crusade: in general terms, this describes a campaign against a person, or an action or decision made by a public body, in an attempt to stop their activity. Historically, it is the word used to describe Christian expeditions in the Middle Ages to regain the Holy Land.

Did you know?

A certain Ibrahim al-Jarbi decided to raise the siege of Málaga, declaring that he would kill Ferdinand and Isabella. He asked to see them, claiming that he had an important message for them. He was kept waiting, taken to another tent and eventually killed and his body was cut up. It was later sewn together and given a Muslim burial. The Muslims, in retaliation, captured a Christian, killed him and put him on an ass facing the Castilian lines of encampment. The Málagans surrendered shortly afterwards, although the war continued to the eventual surrender in 1492.

■ Key terms

Conversos: Jews who had converted to Christianity; also sometimes called New Christians. They were the main target of the Inquisition. They were not trusted as true believers and were thought to continue their Jewish beliefs and traditions privately. The Church failed to instruct these converts fully; eating unleavened bread or refusing to eat bacon or pork were seen as evidence of nonconformity. *Conversos* were not always persecuted, but many were discriminated against.

Convivencia: used to describe the relationship between the different faith communities in the period up to the reign of Ferdinand and Isabella. It means co-existence or a mutual tolerance between the differing faiths of Islam, Judaism and Christianity. The extent to which it was practised could vary. A Castilian king in the 13th century called himself 'king of the three religions' and an orphan, who was Christian, was given alms by both Jews and Muslims in the 1470s.

■ Exploring the detail

Cruzada tax

Although first raised to help pay for the Granadan War, this tax eventually became a tax on papal indulgences. Indulgences were written documents originally given to popes who risked their lives campaigning against non-believers. By the early 16th century, they could also be given by the Pope to others, for example, to those who confessed their sins and wanted forgiveness. Indulgences could also be granted to individuals who had supported the Church, for example by giving money or perhaps building a cathedral or a hospital. The benefit gained from this for the individual was a lighter penance or punishment for failing to keep religious laws/observe practices, etc.

Both Isabella and Ferdinand were personally very pious Christians. However, although there were more Christians in total in the Spanish peninsula, their lands were also home to both Jews and Muslims. Jews who had converted to Christianity were known as ***conversos***. Practitioners of the Islamic faith were well represented in Castile and Aragon. They were known as *Moriscos* in Castile and *Mudéjars* in Aragon. These three different groups – Jews, Muslims and Christians – had generally tolerated each other in the past, i.e. they lived in a state of ***convivencia***. Muslim styles of architecture were common and even the royal palace in Seville displayed excerpts from the Qu'ran. On ceremonial occasions the Catholic Monarchs often wore Moorish dress.

Tensions and war

The situation was about to become more complicated. There had been conflict on the border between Castile and Granada for a long time. The conquest of Granada, known as the *reconquista* and perceived as a crusade, lasted 10 years, ending in 1492, making the territory of the Catholic Monarchs by far the largest proportion of the Spanish peninsula and leaving Portugal as the only other kingdom. Granada was, however, very different to both Aragon and Castile; its population was largely Moorish by race and Muslim by religion.

The Pope encouraged the Catholic Monarchs in their plans, allowing the collection, from the clergy, of the *cruzada* tax to finance the war. Jews also made contributions. Because both monarchs became involved in the practicalities of the war, for example Isabella controlling supplies and Ferdinand directing the campaign, the soldiers fought more enthusiastically than they might otherwise have done. Isabella played a leading role despite giving birth to her third child during the conflict. Ferdinand was given a large silver cross by the Pope which was carried in front of the troops to inspire them. As the war continued, the army became less of a **feudal** force and was organised more fully by the monarchs. The army was small by modern standards, but large by the standards of the day with approximately 50,000 foot soldiers and 10,000 mounted soldiers. A Muslim who observed the fighting described some of their weaponry: 'The Christians disposed of cannons with which he launched fire bombs … These projectiles were one of the causes for the abandonment of the places on which they fell.' Much of the fighting actually took the form of old-fashioned sieges generating a great deal of destruction of property and loss of life.

A significant victory took place in 1483 for Ferdinand and Isabella when large portions of Andalusia were taken; this was both an important military gain and also helped to weaken the local economy that was based on the silk industry. The war then fell into a phase of skirmishes and raids and a period of stalemate. One important event, however, was the capture of Boabdil, the young prince of Granada. His release was eventually gained by taking an oath of loyalty to Ferdinand meaning that, ultimately, Granada could become a vassal state.

This 'surrender' caused divisions in Granada and weakened the state. However, by 1485, the Catholic Monarchs and their armies were still feeling the pressure. They found the warriors of Granada to be persistent opponents, constantly developing their tactics and avoiding set piece battles. Towns became fortresses and the war developed into a series of sieges. Had the monarchs' appeal for more forces not succeeded, the outcome would have been very different. Hopes rose when they gained Marbella. The next significant event was the successful four-month siege of Málaga in 1487; this was the first large city to be attacked from both land and sea.

The Moors overall were unable to sustain a lengthy resistance; there was limited support from other Muslim states, such as those on the North African coast. Also, Kamen concluded that, despite the widely differing backgrounds and origins of the monarchs' troops, an important factor was that the army of the Catholic Monarchs worked together 'in harmony and obedience, like members of one family' operating as a national army. However, this was not a permanent standing army. Armesto believes that the oath of loyalty that Boabdil had sworn to Ferdinand in 1483 was the real deciding factor, giving strength to the Catholic Monarchs and ultimately allowing Ferdinand to seize Granada. The Spaniards also seemed to have reached the point where they wanted to 'rub out' Granada totally. Armesto suggests that Boabdil had been fooled into an alliance that would lead to 'the division and perdition of the kingdom of Granada'.

For the Catholic Monarchs, a very serious issue was raising money to fund supplies and more troops. It was fortunate that, at dawn on 1 January 1492, Granada surrendered after extended negotiations. The lands of the Catholic Monarchs were now, by far, the largest proportion of the Spanish peninsula and Portugal was the only independent kingdom remaining.

The Muslims were soundly beaten. Approximately 10,000 died in the conflict. Source 1 is a description of a meeting between Ferdinand and Boabdil, son of the Moorish King of Granada, at the end of the struggle.

> King Ferdinand, dressed in his royal costume and his splendid garments, headed for the castle. Soon after came the Queen, their children, the grandees, arrayed in brocades and fine silks. Boabdil (the Moor), the prince, came out to meet them accompanied by 50 men on horseback. He indicated that he wished to dismount to kiss the victor's hand , but the King would not consent to it. Then, looking gravely at the ground, Boabdil said, 'Yours we are, invincible King; we deliver this city and this kingdom to you, trusting that you will treat us with mercy and moderation.' Having said this, he gave Ferdinand the keys of the castle.
>
> The King, kneeling with great humility, gave thanks to God for the empire of those wicked people having been uprooted in Spain, and for the banner of the cross being raised in that city, where for so long impiety had prevailed with such force and with such deep roots.

1   *Quoted in J. Cowans (ed.), **Early Modern Spain: A Documentary History**, 2003*

As a consequence of their victory, Ferdinand and Isabella were given the title of the 'Catholic Monarchs/Kings' by the Pope. He called them 'the athletes of Christ'.

Outcomes of the war

The conquest of Granada was a glorious piece of publicity for Ferdinand and Isabella. It suggested that they were powerful and it also brought Castile and Aragon closer together in their triumph. Their success was applauded, particularly by royalty, in the rest of Europe, as well as in Spain.

On 2 January, Ferdinand and Isabella were given the keys of the city of Granada; on 6 January 1492, they officially entered the city. This day was a Christian feast day, thus emphasising their victory over the Moors. Up to 100,000 Muslims had died in the conflict. The Moorish

Key terms

Feudal: a form of government that was widespread in medieval times. In this system, the monarch is not only the ruler, but also deemed to own all the land in the kingdom. He distributes land to his magnates or lords, whilst owning and retaining a good proportion himself. His 'vassals', who receive the gifts of land, in return, will have to provide certain services to the lord, for example, military service. In their turn, the lords retain some land for their own use and divide the rest of it amongst the lesser orders, requiring military service and/or produce of the land/ payment for the grant of land. Each person in the chain owes loyalty to those above him. In this way, kings gained armies and income.

Exploring the detail

Moors originated from North Africa. In the 8th century, they invaded and settled in approximately two-thirds of the land later to be known as Spain. They established an empire that incuded Christians and Jews living in *convivencia*. The Moors introduced new foods such as oranges and rice; they were cultured and produced many books. Nevertheless, Christian reconquest began; one famous example was the conquest of Valencia by El Cid in 1094. By 1252, Ferdinand III of Castile had regained land in the east and south from Murcia to Cadiz. By the 14th century, the Moors had been pushed into Granada and *convivencia* began to break down.

Activity

Thinking point

To what extent do you consider the description of Boabdil's surrender in Source 1 to be reliable? Explain the reasons for your conclusion.

Activity

Challenge your thinking

Why would the Pope use the particular phrase 'the athletes of Christ' to describe Ferdinand and Isabella?

Fig. 3 *Boabdil's surrender document. Granada is given back to the Catholic Monarchs in 1492*

inhabitants were given the opportunity to leave if they wished and approximately 200,000 did so, with a similar number staying in Granada. Over time, it was expected that those Muslims who stayed in Granada would become Christians. There were mass baptisms and a mosque was converted into a church. Such forcible conversion resulted in a revolt in 1499 in the Muslim quarter of Granada; opposition continued into 1500 and 1501. Although most Muslims eventually conformed outwardly, resentment against the situation fermented slowly over time.

Some other unintended consequences occurred, for example, the need to provide the royal army with food and other supplies created shortages and a consequent rise in prices. Nevertheless, the emergence of what could almost be called a national army, as men from all over Spain fought together, was seen to be a positive factor.

The raw facts of the victory over Granada would suggest that the Moors became second class citizens. However, there were some interesting terms included in the Treaty of Granada of 1491 which ended the conquest. Here are some of them:

At the end of forty days, all the Moors shall surrender to Their Highnesses freely and without coercion ... And to assure secure conditions, they shall offer as hostages the minister, with five hundred persons, children and siblings of the leading citizens ... once all is surrendered they shall be freed.

The Moors shall be judged under their own laws and courts by the Islamic law they are accustomed to observing, under the authority of their judges.

Their Highnesses shall give free and safe passage to those Moors who shall want to go live in the Berber lands or any other place they wish.

Neither their Highnesses nor their son, the prince Don Juan, nor those who succeed them shall ever order the Moors who are their vassals to wear signs on their clothing as the Jews wear.

They shall not allow any Christians to enter in the mosques of the Moors where they pray, without the consent of their officials, and anyone else who enters otherwise shall be punished for it.

Their Highnesses shall not permit Jews to have any power or authority over Moors, nor shall they be allowed to collect any kind of rent from them.

Legal disputes that arise amongst Moors shall be judged by their Islamic law … and if a dispute shall arise between a Christian and a Moor, judgement shall be made by one Christian and one Moorish official.

No Moor shall be obliged to become a Christian against his will.

Their Highnesses and their successors shall not ask or inquire of King Abdilehi or any other person covered by this agreement about anything they have done, no matter what it is, previous to the day of the surrender of this city and its fortress.

The Moors shall not be compelled or forced into any kind of military service against their will.

Christian slaughterhouses shall be kept separate from those of the Moors and the supplies from one shall not be mixed together with those of the other.

2   *The Treaty of Granada, 1491. From the Surrender Treaty of the Kingdom of Granada, 1491; quoted in J. Cowans (ed.),* **Early Modern Spain: A Documentary History***, 2003.*

Activity

Source analysis

Study the text of the Treaty of Granada in Source 2.

1 Why did the Catholic Monarchs apparently give so many concessions when they had won the war?

2 What would be the likely impact of these concessions in view of the multicultural nature of Spain?

As a result of the conquest, the *Mudéjars* (Muslims) found themselves living in a Christian-governed state. Archbishop Talavera was a believer in conciliation and he tried to ensure that feelings were considered and some balance achieved. For example, Muslim music was allowed, but Muslims were also taught about Christianity. The Inquisition was not allowed in Granada. The archbishop learned Arabic and encouraged the clergy to follow his example. A converted Moor became Talavera's confessor.

Talavera's successor, Cisneros, was less willing to allow concessions and after a minor revolt in 1500, he claimed that the Moors should be converted and used as slaves because then they would be 'better Christians; the land will be made safe forever, for they are nearer the coast … and are numerous'. The reference to safety was a suggestion that the *Mudéjars* might try to collaborate with the Moors of North Africa, possibly inviting an invasion. By 1500, forced conversions and mass baptisms became the norm; in 1501 Arabic manuscripts and books were being burned. *Mudéjars*, by 1502, had a choice of conversion or exile.

Most contemporaries certainly saw the conquest of Granada as a significant event. An eye-witness declared it to be 'the most distinguished and blessed day there has ever been in Spain'. A Muslim pronounced it to be 'one of the most terrible catastrophes to befall Islam'. Europeans in general saw the conquest as a triumph. Ferdinand declared, 'After so much travail, expense, death and bloodshed, this kingdom of Granada, which for 780 years was occupied by infidels, has been won to the glory of God, the exaltation of our Holy Catholic Faith, and the honour of the Apostolic see.'

Kamen believes the terms of the surrender to be 'generous' and that the treaty 'reflected the medieval traditions of *convivencia*'. Overall, a limited amount of land was given away, for example to nobles, but many Moors emigrated to North Africa and a wave of immigration occurred as landless peasants, mostly Christian, arrived. However, Kamen also states that conversion to Christianity was compulsory, generating considerable opposition in 1499, and a revolt in 1500, suggesting that *convivencia* was just as much under threat as it had been before the conflict. The Christian Moors were now singled out with a new name, *Moriscos*.

Cross-reference

For more information about the Moors and *Mudéjars*, see pages 80–1.

■ **Key profile**

Archbishop Talavera

Hernando de Talavera (1428–1507) was initially Isabella's confessor and became the first Archbishop of Granada. He was a humanist scholar and interested in Arabic studies. He was positive in his attitude towards the Moors, whom he saw as generous and charitable people. He did not approve of the forced conversion of the Moors to Christianity, but preferred preaching and persuasion. He said, 'We must adopt their works of charity, and they our Faith.'

It could also be argued that the aftermath was both peaceful and well within the spirit of *convivencia.* For example, services were delivered in Arabic and Castilian as well as in Latin, and some Muslim music was introduced. Muslims were taught about Christianity.

A significant contribution to harmony in the province was Talavera's success in persuading Isabella that the Inquisition should not be allowed to operate in Granada. However, his successor, Cisneros, was less tolerant and reversed some of these concessions, e.g. by introducing the Inquisition and requiring conversion. The revolt in 1500 provided some retrospective justification for his actions. Isabella, in particular, listened to this argument and, although there was no immediate change in policy, religious issues began to have some precedence.

Despite the fact that the Catholic Monarchs were generally conciliatory, Armesto considers that their main aim was to encourage Muslims who would not convert to emigrate. By 1501, following a rebellion that lasted several months, emigration was forced upon those who would not convert, particularly in Castile. This policy would not only reduce religious clashes, but would also bring another benefit; Castilians could settle on Granadan lands. They were offered help to do this through the provision of transport and the cancelling of tolls and taxes that were usually raised on emigrants. For those Muslims who remained, the situation worsened with greater pressure exerted to encourage conversion.

However, Ferdinand was more conciliatory with the considerable number of Muslims already living in Aragon, making up at least one-third of the population of the province of Valencia. Although there was some friction later between Muslims and non-Muslims, Muslim customs were protected, but emigration was limited. This approach may have been significant in maintaining peace overall in Spain. The difference between the two states was probably a consequence of Isabella's extreme piety; Ferdinand was more practical and saw politics as the overriding principle in dealing with religious divisions.

These early moves to acquire control in Castile and Aragon, and particularly the conquest of Granada, might be seen as a 'crusade' rather than politically or economically driven. Ferdinand and Isabella gave their justification of the war in Source 3.

■ Activity

Group activity

What do you think was important about the outcome of the Granadan War for the Catholic Monarchs and the Muslim population of Granada? In small groups, list positive and negative points and compare these with other groups.

We neither are nor have been persuaded to undertake this war by desire to acquire greater rents nor the wish to lay up treasure. But the desire which we have to serve God and our zeal for the Holy Catholic faith has induced us to set aside our own interests and ignore the continual hardships and dangers to which this cause commits us; and thus we can hope both that the Holy Catholic faith may be spread and Christendom quit of so unremitting a menace as abides here at our gates, until these infidels of the kingdom of Granada are uprooted and expelled from Spain.

3   *Quoted in F. Fernandez-Armesto, **Ferdinand and Isabella**, 1975*

However, the outcome was politically important; the conquest of Granada further consolidated the influence of the monarchy of Ferdinand and Isabella over the Spanish peninsula. It was also economically significant because the law said that land gained by conquest could be used and disposed of as the conqueror saw fit. So, Granada became a prime target for use in rewarding loyal subjects, or those who might be tempted to be disloyal. Having brought their own kingdoms together through marriage, it is possible that the political imperative of the Granadan War was just as important as the religious; and the economic possibilities were clearly a potential advantage.

■ The role and suppression of the Holy Brotherhood (*Santa Hermandad*)

The **Santa Hermandad**, meaning brotherhood or company, probably developed from early vigilante style units in Castile, which became more organised and permanent as a result of the upheavals of the mid-15th century. Units of the *Santa Hermandad* were linked together in a 'holy union'.

The *Hermandad* had a strong peacekeeping role both as a police force and as judges. Its members were paid by tribute from the provinces and local committees in the towns. One of its specific tasks was to maintain order on the roads, which was vital for traders who often found themselves the victims of attacks by local landlords. Criminals who tried to run away were chased and shot at with bows and arrows. When the *Hermandad* reached the boundaries of its own community, the next community would take up the attack. The *Hermandad* could execute criminals without trial; this was done by shooting with arrows. However, it also ran tribunals or courts that were staffed by unpaid officials, similar to magistrates and known as *alcaldes*. There was one of these in every village containing up to 30 families and two in larger communities. They dealt with crimes such as murder, rape, theft and wilful damage. They could sentence offenders to death or mutilation. One contemporary stated, 'There was much butchery, with the cutting off of feet, hands and legs'. For less serious issues, fines were imposed; some of this revenue was used to fund the voyages of Christopher Columbus.

The *Hermandad* also played a particularly important part in controlling the 'overmighty' nobles who often employed private armies, controlled huge amounts of land and considered themselves invincible. Its actions provided greater security for the monarchs, especially in the early days when nobles were a significant challenge, and especially to a female monarch in Castile.

However, the *Hermandad* was so successful that the organisation was eventually disbanded officially in its current form. It had achieved its

■ Activity

Revision exercise

1 List the factors which indicate that Ferdinand and Isabella had strengthened their authority as rulers of Spain by 1500.

2 List the factors which suggest that there were issues still outstanding.

3 Write an essay on the following: 'Religious peace rather than political unity was the most important motivation for the Catholic Monarchs in their conquest of Granada.' How far do you agree with this view?

■ Key terms

Santa Hermandad: an organisation set up in 1476. Groups were set up by some towns, usually of more than 50 inhabitants. Units were expected to produce a quota of troops of approximately one horseman to every 100 householders. They also recruited ordinary soldiers and crossbowmen, later playing a significant part in winning the war against Granada and the conquest of the Canary Isles. They funded their own activities and raised large sums for the war effort through their national assemblies or juntas.

Activity

Thinking point

Make a list of the strengths and weaknesses of the *Hermandad*. Based on your answers, why do you think it was suppressed?

specific purpose and the monarchs were concerned that it could become a threat to the crown. Nevertheless, it still survived in some local communities in a more limited form. The punishments were now less harsh, appeals to ordinary local courts were allowed and its officers became more like a local police force with fewer powers. They demonstrated that the new state of Spain was to be an orderly one. Fernandez-Armesto comments that: 'The *Hermandad* excellently illustrates how the emergency conditions in which Ferdinand and Isabella seized the crown promoted the creation of strong institutions of government and so in the long run increased royal power.' Elliott seems to agree, saying that it was 'the perfect medieval institution revived to meet new needs'. A stronger survival was the *Hermandad de las Marismas*, which protected shipping and trade.

The establishment of the Inquisition, 1478

The Inquisition has always had bad publicity and is associated with secrecy, punishment and death by horrible means. Its name is derived from the Latin word for 'investigation' or simply 'inquiry', which translates as *inquisición* in Spanish. The name describes its purpose; a thorough inquiry into a person's beliefs and actions.

Inquisitions in Spain were not new; they had operated for many years before the reign of Ferdinand and Isabella. These earlier bodies were linked

Commissioners: these were usually parish priests and they did most of the paperwork.

Lay workers/familiars: these were often seen as informers and spies. They were not priests but were members of a brotherhood called the Congregation of St Peter the Martyr. They could carry arms. Many were nobles.

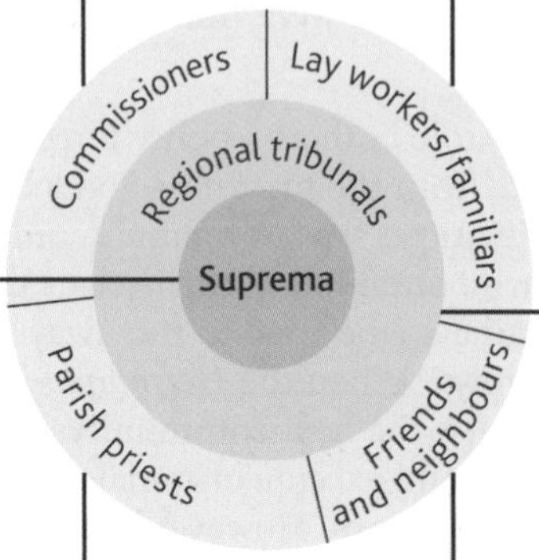

Suprema: this was the central council of the Inquisition. Its members met regularly. They were appointed by the monarch and generally coordinated their work through the Inquisitor-General. Its duties were to investigate cases of deviance from accepted religious beliefs and activities, particularly *conversos*, and to give instructions about punishment. One such case occurred in 1500, when 130 victims were burned on charges of Judaism. The Suprema had been independent of the papacy since 1483 and owed ultimate loyalty to the monarchy.

Regional tribunals: these were linked to and supervised by the Suprema, they collectively became a powerful body with authority throughout Spain. In 1498, Torquemada decided that each tribunal needed two inquisitors, a constable and a prosecutor. Inquisitors were usually trained in the law.

Commissioners / Lay workers/familiars / Regional tribunals / Suprema / Parish priests / Friends and neighbours

Parish priests: they could denounce individuals in the same way as any other member of the community. They also acted as 'comisarios' and received statements from witnesses. They usually represented the Inquisition in the countryside.

Friends and neighbours: these could denounce individuals to the Inquisition. For example, in the case of Pedro de Villegas in 1484, Antonio the cloth maker, who had known Pedro for five years, stated that he had seen Villegas eat meat on Fridays. In this case, Villegas was released as he had spent time in prison whilst his case was being investigated.

Fig. 4 *How the Inquisition worked*

to some degree to the growing hostility towards Jews and their financial activities, although not so much in their role in the medical field.

However, the Inquisition initiated by Ferdinand and Isabella was continued by their descendants and was to become one of the most firmly established and feared aspects of late 15th and early 16th century Spain. Even today, more than 500 years after its foundation, the word 'Inquisition' conjures up pictures of fanaticism, torture and death. Many critical accounts of its work have been written generating what is known as the 'Black Legend', suggesting a brutal and horrific institution persecuting innocent people. This view was often the work of Spanish Protestant exiles and of contemporaries such as Bartolomé de Las Casas, who was actually referring to treatment of Indians in the New World. John Foxe, also a contemporary Protestant English writer, highlighted 'the extreme dealing and cruel ravening of these Catholic Inquisitors of Spain'.

In order to understand why the Inquisition was created at this point in time and why it was to become such a significant aspect of the religious (and political) systems of Spain, it is important to appreciate that Spain had never been religiously united, just as it had never been politically united. The three major faiths, Christianity, Judaism and Islam, had traditionally exercised freedom of worship. However, Christianity was now perceived as being under threat and Ferdinand and Isabella were determined to rectify this – uniformity would be a strength, whereas diversity could be a weakness.

Appointments and regulations required the agreement of the Pope but, significantly, tribunals were responsible to Ferdinand and Isabella, although this did not stop the Pope attempting to interfere on occasion. Ferdinand, for his part, made his jurisdiction very clear when the Inquisition was set up in Aragon. He is reported to have said, 'Although you and others enjoy the title of inquisitor, it is I and the Queen who have appointed you, and without our support you can do very little.'

Key chronology

Inquisition, 1478–92

1478 Isabella petitions the Pope for an Inquisition, which is granted.

Ferdinand agrees to introduce it in Aragon.

1482 Inquisition set up in Seville (Castile).

1492 Inquisitorial tribunals are based in 13 Spanish cities, seven in Castile and six in Aragon.

Did you know?

The Catholic Monarchs were praised by the Pope for dealing enthusiastically with 'those matters which contribute to the praise of God and the benefit of the orthodox faith'.

Numbers of burnings:

1484	30
1492	32
1485–1501	250

Condemned to death but absent:

1491	220

Fig. 5 *A tribunal of the Inquisition*

The Inquisition was the only body whose authority ran through all the territories of Spain, although its authority was not always accepted. Conflicts occurred in a number of towns, such as Saragossa, Valencia and Barcelona, and were often caused by the presence of large numbers of *conversos*. The *converso* was seen as a significant threat to the authorities.

Activity

Talking point

Research/discuss why the tribunals might have been sited in these particular towns and provinces. Use the map (Fig. 6) to help you.

Table 1 *The establishment of tribunals of the Spanish Inquisition in Castile, Aragon and the Mediterranean during the reigns of Ferdinand and Isabella*

Castile	Date of establishment	Aragon	Date of establishment
Seville	1482	Zaragoza	1482
Córdoba	1482	Valencia	1482
Toledo	1485	Barcelona	1484
Llerena	1485	Sicily	1487
Valladolid	1488	Mallorca	1488
Murcia	1488	Sardinia	1492
Cuenca	1489		

*From H. Rawlings, **The Spanish Inquisition**, 2006*

Only those who were clearly of Old Christian/Jewish ancestry were legally able to occupy positions of importance. Despite this, some Castilian bishops had Jewish (*converso*) ancestors, for example the Bishop of Segovia. Even Ferdinand himself was thought to be from *converso* origins, although this was never proved. Gradually, as more efficient checks were carried out, those of Jewish ancestry were less likely to gain such posts.

In order to coordinate the work of the Inquisition, the *Suprema*, or Council of the Inquisition was created. It typically had five or six members meeting regularly every day of the week except Sundays, either in the morning or the afternoon. It heard appeals, made decisions and gave out instructions (*cartas accordas*) to the provincial tribunals. In 1492, tribunals operated in 26 different towns scattered throughout Spain. A complex network of officials of different kinds ensured that the Inquisition worked with reasonable efficiency. Regional tribunals were usually staffed by law graduates or previous employees of the Church, helped by other officials such as notaries, constables and prosecutors. Figures quoted by Kamen show that out of 57 inquisitors of Toledo in the entire period 1482–1598, all except two had degrees and doctorates linked to legal studies.

Fig. 6 *Tribunals of the Inquisition, 1492*

In order to ensure conformity to Christianity amongst Christians, by 1500 regular inspections were in place, although there were some areas which were never reached. Regional tribunals relied on parish priests, particularly in remote areas, to provide information about suspects and the results of interrogations. There were also commissioners, often clergy or aristocracy, who carried out investigations with the help of lay workers called *familiares*. These posts were prized, despite lack of pay, because they were perceived as prestigious. They eventually formed a brotherhood or *Hermandad* called the Congregation of St Peter the Martyr. Although often regarded as spies and informers, the evidence shows that initial denunciations were usually made by friends and neighbours of the accused and not by the lay workers.

Overall, the Spanish Inquisition appears to have been little different from the medieval version that had operated in Languedoc (France) and Aragon. Although the basic rules had been put together between 1484 and 1498, they were still being developed. The key official of the Inquisition was the Inquisitor-General; the first appointee in Spain was Tomas de Torquemada.

Key profile

Tomas de Torquemada

Torquemada (1420–98), a Dominican friar, was appointed by Pope Sixtus IV as Inquisitor-General of Castile, Aragon, Valencia and Catalonia, and in post from 1488 to 1498. He was praised by the Pope for 'having directed your [sic] zeal to those matters which contribute to the praise of God and the benefit of the orthodox faith'. Torquemada's Inquisition was itinerant and on occasion other Inquisitor-Generals had to be appointed so that work could be carried out in other parts of Spain. In 1494, for example, four bishops were promoted to the post at the same time as Torquemada. The Inquisition was the only body with authority throughout Spain.

We would expect that the primary motive for the establishment of this Inquisition would be a religious one, for example, to ensure that those of other religions such as Jews or Muslims converted to Christianity and remained adherents to their new faith. However, the Catholic Monarchs were not particularly anti-Jewish, but were concerned about those who had converted and become *conversos*. Ferdinand simply saw the Inquisition as a means of extending and consolidating royal authority. Financial motives could have been more important; for example, *converso* property could be confiscated by the crown and this would clearly cover some costs of government. The papal bull setting up the Inquisition in 1478 had given the Catholic Monarchs power over both appointments and confiscations. Kamen is not fully convinced about financial motives, but evidence that those who had their goods confiscated were often the richer *conversos* supports it. Contemporary comments such as, 'They burn only the well-off, because they have property; the others they leave alone' and 'Don't be afraid of being burnt, they're only after the money' are useful evidence. It was also the case that punishment could often be converted to a cash payment.

Another motive could have been to extend the monarchs' political authority; a charge usually placed against Ferdinand rather than Isabella. However, it was in Castile, not Aragon, that the *Suprema*, or Council

Fig. 7 *A Spanish Jew before the Grand Inquisitor*

of the Inquisition, first came into existence in 1488, emerging as a part of Isabella's overall reforms of government structure. It was seen as a 'natural' development for the monarchs to create 'a separate council for the Inquisition', which was quickly becoming an essential tool in the battle against heresy and religious deviance.

It is important to appreciate the possibility that the Inquisition was initially never seen as a body with authority stretching across most of Spain. It was at first confined to Andalusia, and even there, only in specific areas such as Seville. There were also variations; for example, in Cuenca, the Inquisition (established in 1489) was organised in the same way as the limited body that had operated in Aragon as early as the 13th century. This suggests it had been a response to particular circumstance, rather than a major policy. Nevertheless, the initial growth of the Inquisition confirms that it was seen as a useful tool. Reductions made in the numbers of tribunals in the early 16th century, however, suggest either a considerable element of success in dealing with identified 'heretics', i.e. fewer heretics, or possibly financial factors.

Furthermore, the Inquisition, although set up by the monarchs as a result of the papal bull of 1478, was still subject to the oversight of the Pope. All bulls of appointment, decisions about the regulations and where the Inquisition operated, had to be negotiated with the Pope. The Inquisitor-General was the most important figure in the Inquisition; his role had to be authorised by the Pope. At one point in this period there were five Inquisitor-Generals. On the death of Isabella, there were two Inquisitor-Generals, one for Castile and one for Aragon. By 1518, the two posts merged again.

The rules of the Inquisition were drawn up in 1484 and continued to be added to until 1500. They were known as the *Instrucciones Antiguas*. Kamen considers that they were 'unsystematic, had to be regularly modified, and led to variation of practice between different tribunals'.

The tribunals of the Inquisition travelled around Spain; by 1500, there were 26 of these itinerant bodies. Each tribunal consisted of two inquisitors, an assessor, a constable and a prosecutor. Inquisitors could be laymen and had mostly studied law at university; however, the majority were clerics. Many of them subsequently became bishops. The tribunal was supported by 'familiars' who protected the inquisitors; many of the familiars were nobles.

■ The expulsion of the Jews, 1492

Jews were the smallest religious group, varying in number from c.80,000 to 200,000. Undoubtedly, however, their numbers were much larger than in most other European states where Jews generally were less valued for their skills. In Spain, many Jews were doctors, financiers, traders and artisans. Their importance fell to some extent, particularly after the Black Death; their natural state of segregation in Spain, combined with their cultural rules, seemed to result in fewer deaths from the disease than in other groups in the population.

Isabella had once declared, 'All the Jews in the realm are mine and under my care and proection.' This may or may not have been a sincere statement. Jews were, in any case, frequently subjected to persecution. Those who converted to Christianity to avoid such persecution were called *conversos* but were always suspect; their conversion was not fully accepted. This perception was often supported by evidence that they kept many links to their Jewish culture and continued to practise their Jewish faith in private but were 'Christians' in public. *Conversos* were therefore seen as a significant threat by the authorities. This was confirmed by a number of enquiries conducted by the clergy, for example, the Archbishop of Seville. Constant rumours also circulated about the reality of their commitment to Spain and Jews continued to be mistrusted.

Evidence for negative attitudes towards Jews can be seen in a range of ways, for example:

- Very flimsy evidence was often used to convict Jews of heresy, for example one accusation was made on the basis that lamb had been cooked on a Friday; this was unlikely to be true as Friday was a day of fasting.

- Only those who were clearly not of Old Christian/Jewish ancestry could legally occupy positions of any importance. Some Castilian bishops had Jewish ancestors, for example the Bishop of Segovia; even Ferdinand himself was thought to be from *converso* origins, although this was never proved. Gradually, as more efficient checks were carried out, those of Jewish ancestry were effectively excluded.

- Unbaptised Jews tended to live in ghettos and were, in Castile, ordered to wear distinctive red and yellow badges.

- Jews were heavily taxed; some had been expelled from Anadalusia as early as 1483, athough they were subsequently allowed to return.

Fig. 8 *The expulsion of the Jews from Spain, c.1492 (19th century illustration)*

- Although many Jews had important professional roles in society, particularly finance, medicine and education, the crown clearly saw their conversion to Christianity as highly necessary and significant for its own authority in Spain.

- Refusal to convert could lead to severe punishment; Seville and Córdoba regularly hosted **autos-da-fé**. By 1490, 2,000 Jews had been put to death by the Inquisition. Other penalties included exclusion from participation in government at both local and national level, a ban on joining the army, forming trade guilds or working in universities.

Key terms

Auto-da-fé: literally, an 'act of faith' usually, in the Spanish context, the burning of a heretic after sentencing by the Inquisition.

An accepted explanation for the treatment of Jews is that there was a financial motive; Jews were a potential source of wealth, providing both income and goods; in the latter category, land was the most coveted as it could be used as a resource for the crown, sold on or given as a reward to other enterprising subjects.

Key profile

Juan Falcón the Elder

Falcón is an example of the way in which *conversos* were dealt with in this period. As a converted Jew, Falcón was liable to be seen as a target. In his trial, 39 witnesses gave evidence. They claimed that he was guilty of a range of crimes such as eating unleavened bread, saying prayers in Hebrew and observing the Jewish Sabbath. Other crimes were the slaughtering of animals in the manner prescribed in Jewish law. A total of 29 witnesses came forward to comfirm these activities. Although his trial took place after his death, his remains were still burned in an *auto-da-fé* held in 1485.

When the two monarchs inherited their respective thrones, the legal status of their Jewish subjects had remained largely unchanged for several centuries. Jews, like Muslims, were treated as separate communities although they were not necessarily confined to separate quarters. They were allowed religious freedom and their own leadership, which was responsible for collecting the taxes which they owed, but their religion excluded them from many of the essential institutions of late medieval Spanish society, such as national and local government, the Church, the legal system, trade guilds and the universities.

4   *From J. Edwards, **Ferdinand and Isabella**, 2005*

Following a ruling issued by the Cortes of Toledo in 1480, they, (Jews) were forced to live a segregated existence, confined to urban ghettos where they were the victim of various forms of social and fiscal discrimination. In Segovia, Jews were not allowed to buy food during working hours or to eat fish on Fridays, while in Medina del Campo they were prohibited from participating in commercial activity in the local market. In Burgos, Jewish midwives were not permitted to attend to Christian women in childbirth.

5   *From H. Rawlings, **Church, Religion and Society in Early Modern Spain**, 2002*

Activity

Source analysis

Consider Sources 4 and 5.

 1 To what extent had the position of the Jews deteriorated during the reign of Ferdinand and Isabella?

2 What would you consider to be the most unacceptable restriction on the Jews?

The eventual consequence of changing attitudes towards Jews was the recommendation by the Inquisition in 1492 that all Jews should be expelled. In fact, they were presented with a choice, which was not really a choice at all. They had four months in which to decide whether to leave the country or to convert. The ruling applied to mainland Spain and to all territories of Spain, excluding Naples, where the introduction of an inquisition had been strongly resisted. This policy is the basis of what came to be called 'The Black Legend'.

Possibly this expulsion was threatened, not just for religious reasons, but as a good way of swelling the royal coffers, particularly in view of the expenses of the war against Granada. The suggested figure for those who left permanently is in the region of 50,000. Although exact numbers are difficult to confirm, up to 200,000 Jews offered significant sums of money to the Catholic Monarchs to allow them to stay. Many Jewish families who did leave eventually returned to Castile; they were even able to buy back their land provided they could prove that they had become Christians. Those who later returned as converts were able to work in their professional roles and, therefore, continued to contribute to the growing wealth and development of Spain.

Source 6 contains a description from a modern historian.

> After the King (Ferdinand) had captured the city of Granada from the Muslims, he ordered the expulsion of all Jews in all parts of his kingdom … even before that the Queen had expelled them from Andalusia. The King gave them three months in which to leave. The number of the exiled was not counted, but after many inquiries, the most generally accepted estimate is 50,000 families. They had houses, fields, vineyards and cattle, and most of them were artisans. The King did not allow them to carry silver and gold out of his country, so that they were compelled to exchange their silver and gold for merchandise of cloths and skins and other things.
>
> One hundred and twenty thousand of them went to Portugal; the King allowed them to stay in his country six months. After the six months had elapsed, he made slaves of all those who remained in his country and banished seven hundred children to a remote island, and all of them died.

6   *From A. Marx, 'The Expulsion of the Jews from Spain', **Jewish Quarterly Review**, 1908*

Activity

Thinking point

How consistent was the attitude of the crown towards the Jewish population in Spain? Why might there be differing attitudes? Write down some ideas individually, and then put your ideas together to make a class list.

There was no doubt that many Jews lived in dread of the Inquisition; even *conversos* were not exempt from the fear. A contemporary, a tanner from Segovia, expressed his concerns about the potential consequences of the arrival of the Inquisition. Another Jew from Cuenca said, 'I would rather see all the Muslims of Granada enter this city than the Holy Office of the Inquisition which takes away life and honour'.

Religious and social implications of the expulsion of the Jews

Every territory of Spain, except Naples, was involved in the policy of expulsion of 1492. Altogether, the Jews who left Spain were approximately only three per cent of the total population. Although this seems a small loss, the impact will have varied from place to place, both on society and in religious affairs. There were particular concerns about skills gaps in the population. Although there were other groups that could step into their commercial role, such as the *conversos*, this was not the only concern. Many Jews were doctors and professionals; others were tax collectors, financiers, artisans and traders and their contribution to the economy was highly significant.

There is evidence that some contemporaries did not seem to think they could be replaced; an Aragonese historian, Jeronimo de Zurita, thought that the King was making a mistake 'to throw out of his realms people who were so industrious and hardworking, and so outstanding both in number and esteem as well as in dedication to making money.'

■ A closer look

Convivencia and expulsion

In social and ethical terms, the loss of the Jews could be seen as a disaster. Arguments that support this view are as follows:

Expulsion gave the lie to the concept of *convivencia*, which was a cornerstone of the regime and enabled Spain as a whole to develop.

It raised the question of who would be the next to receive the same treatment; would it be the *Moriscos* or the *Mudéjars*? The Inquisition clearly had the power to expel other ethnic groups, if it were to expel the Jews.

Some families could be split up, particularly those families that were part-Jewish and part-Christian.

Meanwhile, however, there was also an underlying ethical concern should the Jews remain: should the use of, for example, arrests without trial, torture, secrecy, etc. have been allowed to continue? Woodward argues that some of this behaviour might be warranted in a war situation but not in peacetime. He quotes, for example, the cases of 250 burnt at the stake from 1485 to 1501 and 400 people imprisoned over a nine-year period in Córdoba. There would also be the problem of instructing *conversos* in the Christian religion; the Church authorities in Spain were frequently accused of not making adequate efforts to assimilate the *conversos*.

Kamen offers some support to Woodward in suggesting that even the Inquisition itself was concerned about the persecution of Jews and certainly some Spaniards were antagonistic, although for different reasons. Kamen quotes the Inquisitor Luis de Paramo as saying that 'first, those who had been baptised by force had not received the sacrament (of baptism) properly and therefore remained essentially pagan; secondly, the expulsion was an implicit invitation to annihilate the Jews, which would be contrary to scripture'.

Fig. 9 *Ferdinand and Isabella being petitioned for mercy for the Jews*

The extent and end of *convivencia*

It is important to understand the concept of *convivencia*; it was a 'state of co-existence' and religious tolerance between different populations of Muslims, Jews and Christians in early modern Spain. It was not just a religious issue; it was also immensely significant, socially and politically. It worked in the early stages of Ferdinand and Isabella's reign because of the geographical separation of the differing communities; living together in the same country, but in different areas and in specific communities. As those communities converted and became more mixed, the situation became more complex; suspicions about the reality of the conversion grew on both sides.

There were more than 100,000 Jews in Aragon and Castile. In the early days of the reign, they were treated differently, for example they were expected to wear distinctive clothing, usually red or yellow badges; they could not use the best materials for their clothing; they were not allowed jewellery. By 1480, they had begun living separately from other communities in some towns, a policy called *apartamiento*; these distinctive areas were later called ghettos.

Muslims also increasingly found themselves under threat. Those who converted were called *Moriscos*; those who lived under Christian rule were known as *Mudéjars*. They formed a fair proportion of the population, for example, 20 per cent of the total population in Aragon. Those who lived in Granada were not subject to persecution initially, but when Archbishop Cisneros became the ruling cleric, forced conversions were the order of the day.

Forced conversions and the consequences

As previously noted, matters came to a head for the Jewish community with the 1492 decree of expulsion. However, in November of the same year, Ferdinand issued another document that suggested that those who had left could return if they agreed to be baptised as Christians. The monarchs also seem to have set up a scheme that would allow *conversos* to pay to be absolved from any religious offences.

Jews were probably the first group to experience difficulties as many of them decided to convert to Christianity and become New Christians. Tension grew within the Jewish communities but also among Christian populations. The very naming of the different groups highlighted the differences and created ill feeling between them. Conversions were not always seen as 'real' by either Christian or Jewish communities.

For the Muslim community in Granada, their difficulties also came to a head in 1492 when their land was conquered by the Catholic Monarchs. As far-sighted monarchs, Ferdinand and Isabella had already formulated plans to introduce Catholicism and consulted with the Pope. The change was rolled out almost in military fashion, started by Archbishop Talavera and extended by Cisneros. The programme is shown in Table 2 on page 40.

Archbishop Talavera, Edwards claims, was personally responsible for the conversion of more than 100 people. He is also credited with the building of around 100 parish churches and establishing a seminary to train priests to support Christians and convert Muslims. He encouraged his clergy to learn Arabic; he contributed on a social level, caring for abandoned children; his motives were also clearly religious, hoping to draw these young people into the Catholic Church.

Exploring the detail

The Holy Child of La Guardia, 1490

This incident illustrates the way in which Jews were perceived and treated, even when they had converted. A *converso*, it is said, was found with some of the unleavened bread (called the host) used in the Catholic mass, in his luggage. This was treated as sacrilege; the individual was thought to be under the influence of the devil. Further charges suggested that a small boy had been kidnapped and possibly crucified. Ten *conversos* and a Jew were questioned by the Inquisition. The child's body was never found but all the accused were found guilty and put to death by *auto-da-fé* in 1491.

Table 2 *Programme for the introduction of Catholicism into Granada*

Introduction of Papal Bull 1492	Work to be carried out by the archbishops of Toledo and Seville.
New cathedrals	Granada, Málaga, Guadix, Almeira.
Conversion of Muslims	Selection of missionaries.
Support from Ferdinand and Isabella	Funding of church furniture, especially objects such as altars, candles, texts, etc. Also allocating captured lands and goods which would provide income.
New churches	c.100 parish churches to be built.
Seminary	Training priests for their new congregations; this included learning Arabic.
Social care	Orphanage; nunnery; hostel for women; *Morisco* children to learn to read and write (so they could recite Catholic prayers); hospital.

However, Cisneros is usually perceived as being rather more hard-hitting than Talavera and, as Edwards claims, this led to 'the introduction of far more drastic and brutal techniques'. The resulting riot in December 1499 led to an even more vigorous campaign by Cisneros to convert the Granadans. For example, he set out on a campaign for mass conversion and claimed that 3,000 were baptised into the faith. However, outright rebellion ensued. Ferdinand had to intervene militarily, supported by some of the nobility. Cisneros was replaced by Talavera and other lesser clergy were drafted in to help. By 1501, copies of the Qu'ran were being confiscated. A final ultimatum was issued in 1502 that conversion or exile was to be chosen. Those who chose to leave could not go to the Ottoman Empire or North Africa. Penalties were also to be imposed on Castilians who tried to help these Muslims.

Fig. 10 *A Spanish monastery*

The beginnings of Church reform

Cardinal Cisneros is the individual most linked to Church reform outside Granada in this period. He was particularly interested in reform of the religious orders and set up specific inspections or visitations. As a consequence, the Dominicans, Franciscans and female orders were ordered to improve their conduct to give them greater credibility. Education was also enhanced, for example, by the foundation of the College of Santa Cruz in 1484, enabling priests to understand the scriptures better and be more authoritative in the guidance they gave to their flock.

The monarchs were more able to influence religious reform than their predecessors because the Pope was eager for their support. In return, he was willing to give them more freedom in running the Spanish Church. This was particularly useful in appointing offices in new lands, for example Granada, as well as overseas territories. It did not apply to Spain itself. The monarchs were also able to ensure that foreigners were not placed in Spanish benefices.

Despite all these measures, there were still faults to be found, for example, Isabella wrote to one of her bishops in 1500 about the lack of discipline, i.e. 'the greater part of the clergy are said to be and are in **concubinage** publicly, and if our justice intervenes to punish them, they revolt.' Another group of clergy was warned about gambling, fighting, singing and dancing.

Key terms

Concubinage: the practice of cohabiting outside marriage. In this period, women who lived with men and were not legally married were seen as promiscuous. Clergy were not allowed to marry having taken a vow of celibacy. Such behaviour, therefore, was sinful and an extremely serious matter.

Key profile

Francisco Jimenez (Ximenes) de Cisneros

Archbishop of Toledo from 1495 and Inquisitor-General from 1507, Cisneros (1453–1517) was a key figure in support of progress and learning, and a significant influence in the Church. He founded the University of Alcalá, which was renowned for its humanist studies. He instigated the production of the Complutensian/Polyglot Bible in 1522. This was a significant enterprise as it contained four versions of the Bible: the Hebrew, Greek and Chaldean originals and the Latin Vulgate.

Summary questions

1. Explain why the Inquisition was concerned about the persecution of Jews.
2. Explain why the conquest of Granada was a significant achievement.

3 Economic and financial issues, 1492–c.1500

Fig. 1 *Map showing ships departing to trade in the Mediterranean and the New World*

In this chapter you will learn about:

- the role of the Cortes and other groups in raising royal finance

- taxation and the extent of crown debt

- the strengths and weaknesses of the economy and finance in the early years of Ferdinand and Isabella's reign.

In 1489, the **financial** demands being made on the people, particularly to support the war against Granada, generated substantial opposition. This attack on the crown continued and intensified. Source 1, a verse written by an unknown critic, spells out one of the factors in this situation.

> If you should your intent declare
> The better for your sheep to care
> Or to exalt your law more high
> Or make your pastures broader lie
> And call well spent the wealth employed
> To see the mountain realm destroyed
> We'd say, 'What good's this extra land
> With our herds dying by your hand.'

1

*Quoted in J. Edwards, **Ferdinand and Isabella, Profiles in Power**, 2005*

The role of the Cortes and other groups in raising finance

Spain is generally regarded as having been a poor country in the 15th and early 16th centuries, despite some of the developments identified in the previous section, with conditions varying considerably between the states. Income was variable but taxes, one of the main sources of income, were wide-ranging. Figure 2 shows the most common of these taxes.

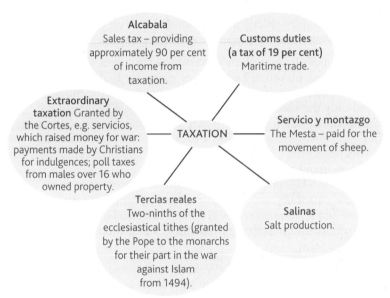

Fig. 2 *Sources of income*

In financial matters, the issue of debt was significant. The discovery of gold and silver in the Americas did not immediately benefit the country. As money poured in, prices rose. The main source of revenue for the government in Spain itself was the *alcabala* or sales tax, which was first introduced in the 14th century. It had to be paid by all but, as it became an agreed sum paid in one regular payment by some towns, it was more difficult for the monarchs to increase the rates. This was a limited issue in the reign of Ferdinand and Isabella, but was to become more significant in the reign of Charles I.

Taxation and crown debt

Despite what appears to be a wide range of sources for raising taxes, the crown often found itself in debt. This was paid off with the use of *juros*, which were a kind of state loan, offered to known and reliable supporters of the crown, and repaid at 10 per cent interest. Furthermore, the monarchs had to accept that there was a ceiling above which they could not expect their subjects to pay taxes; eventually the clergy were excused the *alcabala*. This was the crown's biggest source of revenue, first introduced in 1342 and initially

Cross-reference

For information about other contributions paid by the Church over time, see Chapter 6 (page 85) and Chapter 9 (page 133).

Key terms

Finance: relates to the management of money and, in Spain, especially to taxation.

Alcabala: a sales tax, levied in Castile. The rate of taxation was 10 per cent of the price of the goods, This was a version of modern-day VAT (Value Added Tax) imposed by the government and paid by buyers of specific items on top of the price of the goods. If the price of the goods was 10 *excelentes*, then the *alcabala* tax would be an additional 1 *excelente*, making the total cost to the customer 11 *excelentes*. **Customs duties** were paid on goods brought into the country and on goods that moved between the different states. **Sheep taxes** were paid by the Mesta to the crown on each sheep.

Fig. 3 *The crown receiving taxes collected by royal officials*

Table 1 *Examples of the costs, in maravedis, of some of the Catholic Monarchs' policies*

	1480	1504
Residences for ambassadors	8 m	34 m
Militia and royal ordinance	20 m	80 m
Military expenses	*	500 m

Income also rose through increased taxation:
1481 = 150 m
1496 = 269 m
1510 = 320 m

*No figure available
H. Kamen, **Spain, 1469–1714: A Society of Conflict**, 1991

collected by tax farmers, but later devolved to the nobles. It accounted for up to 90 per cent of the crown's income. Cities could pay a lump sum (instead of individual citizens' contributions), which was called the *encabezamiento*. These changes meant that the crown lost a regular flow of income which, in turn, meant it was less able to regulate its finances in a systematic manner.

From 1482, the crown became involved in wars both in the Spanish peninsula, for example with Granada in 1492, and outside Spain. As costs for the war rose, ordinary income was not sufficient. Some subsidies came from the military orders, the *Hermandad* and, on the occasion of the Granadan War, from papal grants for obvious reasons.

Ferdinand and Isabella have been described as surviving 'without major financial problems', although Kamen does recognise that they were in a condition of 'constant debt'. Woodward believes that the monarchs considered only the short term and did not anticipate the eventual outcome of some of their policies. There was, undoubtedly, an increase in military expenses, particularly as a result of the war in Granada. During this period the Cortes were rarely called and household expenses grew as the monarchs developed their court to demonstrate their status. Nevertheless, if the Catholic Monarchs were to demonstrate their fitness to rule politically, they had to pay for the court, and ultimately for the army and for foreign policy. The last item was particularly important in terms of preserving their thrones and their status abroad as well as internally.

Figures quoted in G. Woodward, 1997, suggest that income for the crown in this period was increased. On their accession, Ferdinand and Isabella were struggling; the income of 11 million maravedis they received in 1474 was approximately one-seventh of the expected amount. This had, however, increased to 269 million in 1496. Despite these later increases, the crown was still not financially strong; some nobles had greater incomes than the crown.

Administrative failures

Officers were negligent or often simply guilty of embezzlement, which is diverting money from the taxes for their own use. This could be done by altering figures on the records. It was noted that in 1497 'the crown had lost 20 million maravedis by the deviousness of officials in the treasury'. An investigation was launched that suggested many taxes had just not been collected. This was a particularly significant issue at a time when money was most needed as the monarchs attempted to assert their authority both in Spain and overseas.

The monarchs' problem was not unusual in one sense; early in the reign it was clear that income did not meet expenditure. Part of the reason for this was tax farming; a system whereby individuals bought the right to collect taxes. They then charged more when they made their collections so that they could make a profit. In addition, the tax system was regressive; the wealthy paid less than the middle and lower classes.

Despite attempts to improve the situation, for example by keeping more detailed records, changes were marginal and slow. The nobles continued to collect *mercedes* (royal grants) even though they were not entitled to them, and many of the profits of other taxes still did not reach the treasury.

There were other factors in this shortfall in income for the crown. It is worth remembering that a large number of potential taxpayers, i.e. the clergy, were exempt from the *alcabala* sales tax. In addition, some towns paid a sum that had been fixed in 1495 and not changed since, and the nobility carried out a form of self-assessment that was unlikely to be realistic.

Strengths and weaknesses of the economy, 1496–c.1500

Agriculture and trade

The issue of crown finance is closely connected to **economic** change and development. As the **economy** of Spain grew, it provided the monarchs with the finances to fund their policies. The economy was largely based on agriculture, trade, commerce and industry. There were variations throughout Spain, but Castile, which was four times as large as Aragon, was the most productive area. Elliot describes Ferdinand and Isabella as being 'as active in legislating for the national economy as they were in religious and administrative reform', but also as 'content to build upon already existing foundations'. He sees the nobles benefiting from the land made available to them and from the right to 'establish entails', thus being able to pass on their land and possessions to their heirs. As a consequence, 97 per cent of the land in Castile belonged to three per cent of the population.

Exploring the detail

Juros

A significant factor that compromised the government's finances was the issuing of *juros*. These were government bonds on which a fixed rate of 10 per cent interest was paid. However, costs rose to 112 m maravedis to pay the interest in 1504. As the crown got into more debt, higher rates of interest were paid to encourage more purchasing of *juros*. This eventually led to using a substantial part of government income to cover the debt.

Key terms

Economy/economics: terms used to indicate the ways in which a country or state produces and distributes its wealth, for example through agriculture and/or industry and trade.

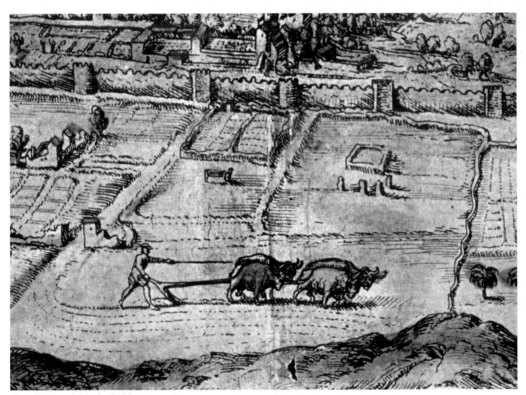

Fig. 4 *Ploughing the fields*

There were many other aspects of Spain's economy that had potential: silverware, silk, leather and ironwork. Soap, cloth, ceramics and wine were all existing trades. However, they remained fairly small-scale and

Fig. 5 *Iron mining*

Vives' interpretation

Vives' work has been reassessed by later historians such as Kamen who suggest that there was some moderate expansion in trade. Alongside, or because of this, the population expanded and there was 'modest prosperity', which coincides with similar changes in the rest of Europe. In some aspects of the economy, our knowledge is more limited, but it is important to understand that the size of Spain means that it cannot be seen as a whole; simple matters of change in climate across the peninsula or putting more land to the plough where possible made a difference.

were often hampered by regulations; for example, this applied particularly to Granadan silk which was often in short supply. Agriculture was much more central to the economy, and included both arable and pastoral farming, the latter largely sheep.

A positive but more long-term development began with the voyages of Christopher Columbus and his discovery of what was to be known as America. The papal bull, *Inter Caetera,* in 1493, had given Spain rights to territory in South America and was significant later as trade developed more fully.

Commercial rivalry between Aragon and Castile continued and, as such, was a healthy activity; Castile sought to improve methods of communication and transport by, for example, giving privileges to the carters' guild. Aragon developed a successful postal operation at Barcelona, but suffered from a large number of internal customs barriers and merchants had to pay tolls when they left or entered the country. However, this was balanced to some extent by progress in cooperation between the two monarchs, which brought a degree of peace to Spain and allowed the economy to develop and flourish.

Trade was controlled by the monarchs through licensing and they encouraged it through fairs. However, tolls on bridges, ports and frontiers remained between the different kingdoms. This led the historian Vicens Vives to state that 'Ferdinand and Isabella did not aspire to the attainment of an effective (economic) unity in Spain'.

Sheep farming – strengths

Sheep farming was big business, particularly in Castile, and was largely supervised by the Mesta. This was a kind of guild or trade union, formed originally in the 13th century, which controlled the grazing areas. A royal councillor was appointed as the president of the Mesta in 1500, demonstrating how important the monarch considered sheep to be as part of the economy. Understandably, not everyone agreed that this was the case. In 1501, sheep farmers in Castile were given the right to graze their sheep on any land where sheep had previously grazed. This often caused clashes between herdsmen and landowners; conflicts were usually resolved by the local magistrates, employed by the crown, in favour of the herdsmen. Farmers who tried to use land owned by the Mesta found they were quickly removed. In Aragon, however, sheep were not always allowed to move through cultivated land.

Sufficient wool was produced by Spanish sheep to generate a regular export trade with other European countries such as England and France.

A trading organisation was formed, the *consulado*, to carry out and regulate the trade, and the port of Burgos was given the monopoly in the export of wool. The *consulado* acted both as a guild (or merchant trade union) and a court where complaints could be brought. The Mesta gave the monarchs a monopoly of the wool trade overall, which allowed them to extend the tax on a herd of sheep into a tax per sheep. The monarchy benefited from this as wool became Castile's main export.

Overall the Mesta controlled approximately 2.8 million sheep. The Catholic Monarchs were able to encourage the wool trade's development through their influence abroad, for example by appointing agents in European cities such as Bruges who would then liaise with the Mesta to promote trade. Spanish towns such as Burgos and Bilbao, and to some extent, Santander, became rivals in competition for this trade. The wool was sold in Flanders, England and France. In return, Spain imported textiles, In addition, the wool was sold at trade fairs in Castile; one of the most important of these was at Medina del Campo.

Sheep farming – weaknesses

In contrast to the apparent strengths of the wool industry, it could be argued that reliance on wool as the basis for trade demonstrated that Spain was economically weak and that arable farming suffered at the expense of sheep. The emphasis on sheep and wool sometimes had a detrimental effect on agriculture, causing shortages of food and creating an imbalance in the economy. This was particularly so in Castile where approximately 90 per cent of the land was owned by less than three per cent of the population. Kamen challenges this negative view by suggesting that farmers responded by taking over the common land and waste lands. Also, the Mesta could not allow its sheep to feed in cornfields, vineyards, fruit crops, hayfields and other pasture for livestock. These were known as 'the five forbidden things'. The huge investment in sheep created uneven economic development; other activities such as the silk trade were hampered by customs duties, and the infrastructure, especially the roads, was poor. Vives, in opposition to Kamen's view, declares in an article entitled 'The Economy of Ferdinand and Isabella's Reign' that this situation resulted in a 'wilful sacrifice' of Castile's long-term requirements to more immediate considerations. The issue of the Mesta's privileges was not easily settled; their contribution to the economy of Spain overall resulted in benefits for the ports of northern Spain, such as Santander and Corunna. It was also a good source of revenue for the crown. However, it initially led to a high level of unemployment, only easing later as manpower was required in the New World.

Did you know?

The origins of the Mesta go back to the 13th century when the crown created the organisation in return for money grants/donations. In addition to controlling the wool trade, the Mesta had the positive effect of stimulating the economy and encouraging trade in Spain's northern ports, for example Santander, Coruna and San Sebastian. Trade with the Netherlands was particularly significant.

Exploring the detail

Medina del Campo

This was an important commercial centre, attracting merchants and financiers. They set up banking facilities and the town rapidly became a prosperous community. Trade fairs were held regularly and were some of the biggest in Spain. It was the home of a *consulado* or trading body, which held a monopoly of trade in northern Europe.

Key chronology

State intervention in the economy

1494 Burgos becomes the centre for the wool trade.

1497 The three principal coins are all given the a value of 375 maravedis. Each kingdom continues to mint its own coins.

1498 Import duties are imposed on cloth from France.

1500 All local trade guilds are made responsible for the upkeep of roads in their area.

Fig. 6 *Farming in Granada*

Food production and policy

In the period up to 1500, gradually more food was produced as waste pastures and common land were brought back into use as arable land. This was needed as the population increased. In 1500, the monarchs also agreed to free up trade in grain, indicating that, 'our subjects exploit their holdings and work with a greater will in agriculture'. This agreement was part of what was known as the Sentence of Guadaloupe of 1486 and was the consequence of a peasant rebellion in the same year.

- Peasants were given ownership of their land following payment of a considerable sum for the privilege.
- Produce could be sold freely with the exception of wheat sales to Muslim territories, although this stricture was relaxed in 1500.
- Taxes could be suspended when, for example, harsh weather conditions hindered crops growing.
- Exports were allowed when crops were plentiful.
- Even so, as the population grew, the increased demand was not always met and, at times, there were serious food shortages that became worse in the early years of the 16th century. This provoked tensions that sometimes overflowed into conflict.

Historical overview

Different historians view the development of the economy between 1492 and 1500 in different ways. One view is that it developed along mercantilist lines. This theory suggests a highly organised system run by the government with clear ground rules, for example promoting national industries rather than importing goods, regulating producers, prohibiting the export of gold and silver and imposing customs duties on goods coming into the country. For example, duties were imposed in 1498 on French cloth imported into Spain. An alternative view, however, describes development as more piecemeal and inconsistent, for example there were still many internal tolls to cross bridges or take goods through ports; these impositions clearly increased the price of locally produced goods. Nevertheless, there was one positive development in that an attempt was made to standardise the currency across the territories of the new monarchs.

Learning outcomes

Throughout this section, you have learned about the unification of Aragon and Castile and the workings of the new regime. You have examined the conquest of Granada and have come to understand the importance of religion in the lives of the people. Your understanding of the concept of *convivencia* will have allowed you to appreciate the ways in which this affected the structure of society. You have also examined the economic and financial state of Spain and should be in a position to reach a judgement about the strengths and weaknesses of the new state.

Activity

Group activity

Working in groups, make a large poster or chart to illustrate the strengths and weaknesses of the Spanish economy c.1500. Discuss what different views about finance and the economy held by historians you can find in this section. Think of three reasons why historians might differ in their views about particular issues.

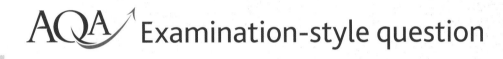

AQA Examination-style question

'The expulsion of the Jews in 1492 was a serious error on the part of Ferdinand and Isabella.' Assess the validity of this view.

(45 marks)

The question focus should be clear, but the notion of a 'serious' error and not just 'error' is important. This means that the process of expulsion and its outcomes need to be evaluated in a range of aspects. Consideration should be given to the number of Jews in the country before expulsion and their contribution socially and economically; this could be set against the religious issues that divided Spain. Understanding of the issue of *conversos* should also be shown. The concern of the monarchs for stability within Spain would also be worth discussion.

This could then be followed by an evaluation of the expulsion largely in religious, social and economic terms. For example a discussion of the impact of the loss of the Jews as entrepreneurs and in the professions; judgement about the impact on unity of the removal of one religious group and the concept of *convivencia* could be made; the impact on towns and communities across Spain; the fact that the expulsion was not total; the issues of those who 'converted' and remained in Spain. Can any improvement in terms of religious unity really be proved when the Inquisition was seeking out Jews throughout the reign?

Consideration of such factors should lead to a supported judgement about the concept of 'error', particularly a 'serious error'.

4 The dual monarchy in action

Activity

Thinking point

What are Martyr and his contemporary really saying about the reign of Ferdinand and Isabella?

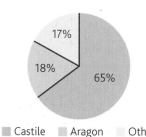

Castile ■ Aragon ■ Other

Fig. 1 *Size of Castile and Aragon as a percentage of the Iberian peninsula*

'There can be no monarchy in Spain as there was then,' said one contemporary about the reign of Ferdinand and Isabella. Peter Martyr, a humanist scholar, expressed a similar sentiment about the reign of Ferdinand and Isabella when he said: 'If ever it was permitted among mortal men to say that one spirit might infuse two bodies, these are the two bodies which by one spirit and one will are ruled. They have disposed that the Queen should govern in such a fashion that she shall be seen to govern jointly with her husband.'

Key profile

Peter Martyr

Martyr (1457–1526) was a significant humanist scholar and a lecturer at Salamanca University in 1488. By 1492, he was entrusted with the education of young men at court. In 1501, he successfully went on a diplomatic mission to Egypt and by 1504 he was Prior of Granada. In 1511, he was promoted to chronicler, publishing the first accounts of Spanish discoveries in the New World, especially of Columbus and Balboa. He later wrote about Cortes and the conquest of Mexico and Magellan's circumnavigation of the world. Most of his information was first-hand from the explorers and state papers.

The dual monarchy and personal rule

As the strength of their partnership grew, the monarchy of Ferdinand and Isabella, up to Isabella's death in 1504, is often known as the 'dual monarchy'. This term emphasises that their authority was more than just their individual, personal authority in their own states. They would not tolerate any limitations to their rule. Historians confirm this by pointing to the fact that they were able, on occasion, to ignore the law. This power was aided by the commonly held view during this period that monarchical authority extended from God and therefore its might was divinely sanctioned. Kings were the temporal or earthly leaders of their state 'at the summit of a mountain shaped society', despite the fact that the Pope also had considerable influence as the head of the nation's spiritual welfare. Ferdinand and Isabella, however, were absolutely clear that the Pope's power in their kingdoms was limited to matters of faith. Although Ferdinand and Isabella were both pious people and anxious to promote the faith, they did not want a third party in their partnership and were not prepared to tolerate papal interference in their political position. This is a further example of their establishment of direct and personal rule. Together they were the sovereigns and 'natural lords' of their lands and peoples. Dual monarchy is the term often used to describe this partnership.

The concept in this period of a dual monarchy, i.e. a strong and an equal partnership had not been forced upon Ferdinand and Isabella. Although female, Isabella was entitled to rule in her own right, just as Ferdinand could in his kingdom. The succession of a female was perfectly acceptable in Spain, and Aragon and Castile could have remained separate states. There was no need for Isabella to marry in order to rule if she did not personally wish to do so. However, the need for a legitimate heir was strong, in order to prevent Isabella's inheritance becoming the target of other unscrupulous and ambitious royals. Whilst a marriage did not necessitate a union of the two states which the royal couple represented, the practicalities of the situation did suggest that Ferdinand and Isabella would need to cooperate.

The concept of a dual monarchy, rather than a more informal partnership, placed a particularly strong emphasis on the decline of **feudal ties** as the main form of social and political organisation and, as a historian puts it, 'strengthening of centralised royal authority, at the expense of traditional social groups such as the military aristocracy and the Church'. In other words, power and authority were focused on the two monarchs rather than shared or delegated to other potentially powerful individuals. After the death of Isabella in 1504, this focus on the monarchy and its officers became even more noticeable, for example, in the membership and authority of the Council of Castile. Nobles were allowed to attend, but they were not able to vote; the business of the realm became the province of a small number of **caballeros**, or gentlemen, members of the higher clergy and a larger number of *letrados* or lawyers, rather than aristocrats. Increasingly, legal training was essential if a gentleman wished to participate in governmental activities at a high level.

The extent of the partnership

Isabella on her accession, instructed her chroniclers always to report government actions as having been done by both herself and Ferdinand. This was, of course, not always true; they were bound to have differing obligations at certain times. The concept was ultimately taken to extremes by the chronicler Hernando del Pulgar who wrote that 'the King and Queen on such and such a day, gave birth to a daughter'.

Common aims

As separately governed states with differing laws and traditions, there were bound to be differences in institutions and processes in Castile and Aragon. These differences would not be easy to reduce and it would seem that the young and inexperienced Ferdinand and Isabella did not deliberately set out to unify their kingdom and become King and Queen of 'Spain'. Indeed, their marriage contract indicated that their territories were different and separate.

However, the fact that some issues were addressed in both states would suggest that Ferdinand and Isabella had some common aims. One of these was the aim of restoring law

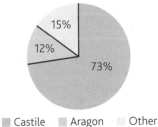

Castile ▮ Aragon ▮ Other

Fig. 2 *Population of Castile and Aragon as a percentage of the Iberian peninsula c.1500*

Exploring the detail

Government and plural kingship

Ferdinand and Isabella did not make any fundamental changes in government despite or because of the plural nature of their kingship. Within each state of Spain, the crown had the greatest authority, although there were variations from one Spanish state to another; beneath the Catholic Monarchs, authority was exercised by specific bodies that had gained their privileges from the crown, for example town councils. Below them, was the authority of the 'seigneurs' or lords who had rights over land and their vassals. In principle, this was very much like the feudal system.

Key terms

Feudal ties: in the feudal system, peasants were subject to their landlords through a wide range of requirements, for example to work on the land, play a military role in their overlord's forces. Nobles owed allegiance to the King as the highest civil and military authority. The system operated variably between the Spanish states; it was more limited in Castile but strong in Catalonia. Kamen considered that it gave the nobility too much control and the crown too little.

Caballeros: a reference to a person equivalent to an English knight; he would have a title equivalent to 'Sir' and be skilled in riding, horse management and own some property, etc. It was part of Ferdinand and Isabella's policy to use these people in local government; this would prevent them feuding amongst themselves.

Cross-reference

Look back to pages 17 and 19 to refresh your memory about the *letrados*.

Cross-reference

Look back to page 25 to remind yourself of the basic definition of 'feudalism'; the information in this chapter places the system in more context.

Key terms

Feudal dues: payments in kind (goods) or in cash to their overlords by those, usually peasants, who worked the land for the local seigneurs or lords. The peasants were often housed on the lord's land and provided with a small plot of their own. This system dated from medieval times; although some aspects were more relaxed, it was still the basis of landholding in most European states.

Cross-reference

Look back to Chapter 2 to remind yourself of the complexity of the religious situation and the treatment of non-Catholics in the period up to 1500. More information will also be found in Chapters 5 (pages 76–81) and 8 (pages 124–31).

Fig. 3 *Coat of arms of Queen Joanna of Castile*

and order following the civil war that had erupted on the death of Henry IV.

In Aragon, there was a move to abolish some **feudal dues**, allocate posts in government by lottery and establish a system that allowed royal power to be held in check.

In Castile, order was initially reimposed through the *Hermandades*, which maintained a peacekeeping role in the towns and provinces. There was no similar body in Aragon.

The judicial system was another area in which both sovereigns wanted significant improvement. An attempt was made to ensure that laws were common throughout Castile: permanent law courts were also established in Madrid, Seville, Santiago and Valladolid in Castile. There was also a court in Granada. However, this did not mean that the same laws operated throughout their two kingdoms.

There also seemed to be no desire to develop a common administrative body shared by the two states; instead, the Council of Aragon was created to govern in Ferdinand's frequent absences. There was no specific body to oversee foreign affairs. If new territory was gained, it seemed to be given on an ad hoc basis to the two states; for example the Indies were allocated to Castile and Naples to Aragon. When Isabella died in 1504, Ferdinand was regularly based in Castile not Aragon. This suggests that Aragon was seen as the junior partner and Castile as the more powerful state.

In their views on religion, Isabella and Ferdinand clearly wished for an all-Catholic Spain. In addition, they wanted to ensure that the Catholic Church was unchallengeable in its devotion to the faith, and that its servants, the clergy, set the appropriate standards for ordinary people to follow.

Royal justice

Justice is key to a fair and orderly community. Kamen stresses this when he writes that changes in the system in the reign of Ferdinand and Isabella were 'at the heart of the policy of pacification'.

In judicial matters, the authority of the monarchy was initially weak; the power and influence of the nobility and the Church combined was stronger. An example of this can be seen in Salamanca where over 60 per cent of the population owed their primary allegiance to the nobility and 6 per cent to the Church. In addition, the nobles of Castile, rather than the monarchs, were the main authority in 258 towns and villages; for example, they chose the public officers who directly governed these towns.

A closer look

How powerful was the crown?

Kamen says that weaknesses developed because the crown had needed to make alliances with the nobles in the period before the accession of Ferdinand and Isabella. However, as monarchs, Ferdinand and Isabella now personally travelled around the country dealing with criminal activity and general law-breaking, settled disputes and dispensed judgement. Kamen comments that 'the firm use of direct personal authority … was the essential aspect of the power of the Catholic Kings.' The chronicler Hernando del Pulgar wrote that Isabella was 'much inclined to do justice'.

However, Kamen is clear that the Catholic Monarchs were not exceeding their authority in this respect. Hunt also agrees that Ferdinand and Isabella were firm and decisive in this period of their rule and that the establishment of the *Santa Hermandad* 'ended many opportunities for noble brigandage'. On some occasions, the monarchs had to be very proactive, for example by seizing estates as in the case of the port of Gibraltar, which was taken from the Duke of Medina-Sidonia in 1502, and Cartagena, which was taken from Don Pedro Fajardo. Both of these were significant naval bases.

Despite Ferdinand and Isabella's aggressive actions in such cases, the nobility involved were usually compensated with other property. In this case, Cartagena became one of the most important naval bases in Spain and had, therefore, been a judicious choice for the Catholic Monarchs.

Key profile

The Duke of Medina-Sidonia

The Duke of Medina-Sidonia (1464–1507) was a grandee, i.e. a member of one of the oldest dukedoms in the kingdom. He could be very dangerous to the new dynasty; he had enormous assets, for example he controlled posts, owned mills, wine and olive presses, banks and brothels. He loaned large sums of money to the Catholic Monarchs during the war against Granada. At one point he owned Gibraltar, but it was removed from his control by Ferdinand and Isabella in 1500.

As the responsibilities of the Catholic Monarchs grew, time for travelling was more limited. Thus, permanent courts were established, for example in Santiago de Compostela in 1504 and Granada in 1505, to deal with disputes. The Royal Council met regularly as the highest court of appeal twice each week. In addition, the Cortes were used to regulate some very specific issues, for example, in 1505, at the Cortes of Toro, Ferdinand dealt with disputed succession to noble lands. Nobles were encouraged, from this point on, to prevent the division of their lands to their heirs through the application of entail. The new rules also prohibited the sale of the land.

Following unsatisfactory attempts in earlier reigns, Ferdinand and Isabella began to **codify** the laws in 1503 and 1505. By the latter years of their reign, however, Hunt points out that Ferdinand's costly wars meant that there was a greater reliance on the nobles to help both in person and through financial contributions. As a result, there was less likelihood of nobles who did ignore the rules being severely punished. For example, the crown was unable to prevent free villages in northern Spain being taken over by predatory nobles and, moreover, made no offer of redress from the crown; this was one of the issues that later led to the Comuneros Revolt.

Financial union

Financially, the traditional view is that Ferdinand and Isabella refilled the royal coffers. Although their financial affairs were largely kept separate, there were some limited similarities in the financial supervision of Castile and Aragon: in both states, Gonzalo Chacon

Cross-reference

Look back to Chapter 1, page 20 for a definition of 'entail'.

Key terms

Codify: this refers to the collecting together of all the laws of the kingdom, so that there can be no doubt about the law and what is expected of the people and the punishments that may ensue if the laws are broken.

Cross-reference

For detail on the Comuneros Revolt, see Chapter 8 (pages 114–20).

Activity

Thinking point

In what ways were Castile and Aragon reformed under the leadership of Ferdinand and Isabella? Did the reform improve the two states or not?

Cross-reference

For more information on revenue and taxation during this period, see Chapter 6 (pages 84–6).

was the mastermind under the supervision of the monarchs, and the coinage, although different in name for each of the three kingdoms, was worth the same. Total income in 1474 had been 900,000 reales; this had increased dramatically to 26 million by 1504.

Key profile

Gonzalo Chacon

Chacon (1429–1507) was the chief accountant, head of government finances and a royal steward. He was also one of Isabella's closest confidantes, having worked with her before she became queen. He was also, significantly, a *conversos*.

Did you know?

There were originally no coins of common value in the kingdoms of Spain. Maravedis were exclusively Castilian coins. Three hundred and seventy-five maravedis equalled one Castilian ducat (that is the equivalent of 33 pence in our money). Aragon used *libras*, *sueldos* and *dineros* (pounds, shillings and pence). Catalonia used the *principat* and Valencia the *excellent*.

By 1497, however, the Catalan *principat*, the Valencian *excellent* and the Castilian ducat had the same value, despite their different names. The maintenance of their different names is both a recognition of the partnership/cooperation of Ferdinand and Isabella and an indication that they did not regard Spain as a single unity.

It is important not to exaggerate the state of Spanish finances during this period. Although revenue had doubled by 1500, as time went on, the policies of the Catholic Monarchs were increasingly costly.

Table 1 *The Catholic Monarchs' policy expenditure in maravedis (million)*

Activity	1480s	1504
Maintenance of crown residences and ceremonial activities, e.g. hosting ambassadors	8 m maravedis	35 m maravedis
Royal militia and ordinance	20 m maravedis	80 m maravedis
Military expenses		500 m maravedis

For ease of comparison, Table 1 showing expenditure has been set out in maravedis. One issue that had to be resolved was that of the currency; there were different currencies in different kingdoms. Aragon worked in pounds, shillings and pence; Castile in ducats, reals or maravedis. This did not make joint financial policies easy to implement and control. Elliott remarks that: 'Just as the crowns of Castile and Aragon were politically united in the person of their kings, so their monetary systems were similarly united only at the top, by a common coin of high value, a mocking reminder that the policies of the Catholic Kings were no more than a faint beginning. Economically as much as politically, Spain existed only in embryo.'

Activity

Thinking point

What do you understand by the statement that 'Spain only existed in embryo'?

Figures for Castile suggest that revenue rose from 11 million maravedis in 1474 to 320 million in 1510, although inaccuracies and fraud are likely to have obscured the real situation. Furthermore, it was also just as important for monarchs to spend as to collect money. To maintain influence abroad 75 million maravedis in total was spent on ambassadors and, to keep the nobility 'on side', only limited taxation was imposed upon them. Much of the pacification in the early years created debts and the beginnings of income from overseas was not enough to generate huge surpluses. Nevertheless, neither Ferdinand nor Isabella were in debt at the end of the reign. Their treasuries were organised more efficiently with officials handling different aspects of the collection and accounting processes were refined.

Despite the evidence of rising costs, the monarchs appeared to remain in credit, suggesting that increased expenditure could be met by increased income. The fact that there was an increase in law and order in the kingdoms suggests that most of the revenue collected actually reached the government. A significant further source of income was in the form of payments by the Mesta in return for increased privileges: upwards of 5 million sheep roamed the *canadas*. However, the increase in sheep farming continued to have a detrimental effect on arable farming. The need, on occasion, to import corn eventually incurred more expense.

There is no doubt, however, that there was an increase in revenue at this time, whether it came from taxation or other sources. But, there was also an increase in prices that began around 1501, albeit in a fairly moderate way. This increase in prices is usually explained by a theory proposed by E. J. Hamilton in *American Treasure and the Price Revolution in Spain, 1501–1650*. He identified the cause to be silver from America flooding into Spain and encouraging rising prices. This can be questioned as the largest amounts of silver came into Spain earlier in the century, but the biggest price rises were in the second half. The figures reflect this, for example from 1551–55 imports were at a total of 11,838,63 – vastly greater than the rates in 1503–15. Nevertheless, large imports of silver at any time, over a period, were bound to have an effect on both the economy and finance. The impact of increased circulation of coinage would not necessarily have been immediate, but would certainly be incremental.

Table 2 *Imports of bullion from the New World, 1503–15*

Period	Royal	Private	Total
1 1503–5	116,660	328,607	445,266
2 1506–10	256,625	722,859	979,484
3 1511–15	375,882	1,058,72	1,434,664

Figures are shown in ducats (each ducat equals 375 maravedis)

Activity

Source analysis

Study Table 2.

1. What are the overall totals for royal and private imports over the period 1503–15? Can you offer any explanation for the difference?

2. Calculate the increase between period 1 and 2, and period 2 and 3 in ducats. Which period shows the biggest increase?

3. Which group has the highest level of imports – royal or private?

4. What conclusions can you draw about imports of bullion from this information?

Another issue for Ferdinand and Isabella was the problem of **inflation**. Inflation was caused by a number of factors, for example:

- Population growth: one town alone, Burgos, had a population rise from 8,000 to 21,000 in the first half of the century. Therefore this growth in population created a higher demand for goods and pushed up prices.

- Failing harvests, mostly from about 1502–09, increased the price of grain. Elliott states that the government dealt with this by importing vast amounts of grain and setting a maximum price of grain; this did not necessarily benefit the economy nor encourage greater grain production in Spain itself. The power of the Mesta seemed to indicate that the situation was unlikely to improve.

Key terms

Inflation: often identified when a sharp rise in prices occurs. In the late 15th and early 16th century, this was the result of a large increase in the quantity of money in circulation in relation to the goods available. This situation occurred in Spain as a consequence of the gold mined in the Americas. Retailers ask for more precious metal (coin) for their goods and so prices go up, although the item paid for may be no larger, better, etc. than it was before inflation began.

- Higher spending among the Spanish aristocracy.
- The crown's borrowing.

Although the causes of the price rise have sparked intense debate among historians over time; more balanced views are often now held, for example, that a range of factors such as those suggested above was responsible, particularly increased demand as population grew. The subsequent inflation is reflected in rising revenue in Castile: 315 million maravedis in 1504 and 320 million by 1510.

Activity

Challenge your thinking

Using the information above, decide what was the single most important factor in generating inflation in Spain in this period. You will need to consider each factor carefully and draw conclusions that can be supported by evidence/ effective reasoning. You could do this in small groups and compare answers and reasons for your answers.

This could be followed up by writing an essay in response to the following question: 'How far was the increase in bullion from America the explanation for the rise in prices during the reign of Ferdinand and Isabella?'

The economy across most of Europe was affected by this same issue of inflation, and so Spain was not in a unique situation. Nevertheless, Spain is often considered to have been the worst affected. Overall, in this period, Spain continued to be a largely agricultural country. However, industry did expand and the population increased gradually, around 5 million in total; not as much as other European states. Some analyses suggest an overall growth rate of no more than 20 per cent, possibly due to high infant mortality and deaths of older members of the communities. Growth occurred at different rates in different parts of the peninsula. Some factors promoting this growth were the lack of major epidemics and war with other states.

Cross-reference

Look back to Chapter 3 (pages 46–7) for more information on the Mesta and the wool trade.

Most industry was still agriculturally based; there was some limited expansion, i.e. more land being exploited; this did not necessarily improve the lot of the peasants. As already noted, sheep predominated and were either loved or hated, particularly after the law of 1501 that gave rights to pasture on lands which had been used, if only once before, for that purpose.

The emphasis on sheep can be seen as important, as it freed up Castilian manpower for military and colonisation purposes, but there were also concerns that it placed short-term goals ahead of long-term consequences. Agriculture after 1500 gradually became 'the Cinderella of the economy' as a result of the continuous growth in sheep farming and the Mesta. However, the impact of this, as a specific issue, was not readily recognised as it was masked by general economic expansion which encouraged freer trade in grain by 1500 to boost the supply. This was limited, not just by natural factors such as poor soil, and limited irrigation and fertilisation techniques, but also by heavy taxation. Despite some easing, as the early years of the 16th century continued, difficulties in agriculture remained and became more obvious as harvests failed. Grain prices were particularly high around 1502–09. The government had to set up a pricing structure to prevent traders making excess profit; at that specific point, ironically, one really good harvest in 1508 reduced prices so much that many farmers could not make a living. The government responded to this further crisis by setting a fixed maximum price for corn and, at the same time, allowing imports. However, there was little support for the farmers in the longer term.

Industry fared better. Textiles, mainly wool, remained important. There was also a key silk industry in Granada and other centres in Burgos and Medina del Campo. Soap was manufactured in Seville and shipbuilding was centred on Barcelona. To service the export trade, particularly with the New World, Seville, in the south of Castile, became a major city and its population grew steadily. In contrast, Madrid was never as strong in economic terms, despite being the capital city; Bilbao, however, prospered.

Nevertheless, overall, industry was quite limited. One factor in explaining this was the expulsion of the Jews in 1492, which particularly affected the cloth industry.

Another limiting factor was the issue of poor communications. The roads were in poor condition and distances between the place of production and the place of sale were often enormous. A further problem was an increasing emphasis on high-quality goods; many northern towns found that the quality of their product was not deemed good enough. For the wool industry, this meant that cheaper wool was often exported and better quality wool imported. By 1517, merchants were complaining that there were wool shortages and wanted the government to ban exports. For home-produced goods, the further they had to travel to market, the greater the cost of those goods. Some effort was made to improve roads, and some tolls and dues were reduced or abandoned entirely. In Castile, in 1505, a new postal system was created.

However, economic unity was still limited. There were restrictions in parts of Spain, for example Catalan merchants had only limited trade concessions in Castile and were not allowed to trade with the Americas. Aragon was less productive than Castile. Despite these issues, the monarchs were rarely seen to involve themselves in economic issues.

Cross-reference

Look back to Chapter 2, pages 34–40 for more on section on the expulsion of the Jews and the impact this had on the economy. This will help you to understand some of the problems of the development of industry.

Activity

Talking point

1. In small groups, decide what the major obstacles to the development of the economy were in this period.

2. Who suffered most as a result? Each person in the group could take on a role, e.g. as a noble, a merchant, a sheep farmer, etc. and give a short presentation to explain his or her difficulties.

3. Try to explain the problems of the economy from Ferdinand and Isabella's point of view. Does this perspective help to explain why they 'rarely took direct initiatives in economic matters'?

Policy making and *fueros*

There is no doubt that there was agreement in a broad sense about Ferdinand and Isabella's objectives and policies; for example, both saw law and order and increased control over the Church as essential to ensure stability. They both saw the need to impress their personal authority upon their subjects in order to ensure peace and obedience.

However, there were some occasions when Isabella and Ferdinand did not always deploy the same policies or consult in detail. Foreign policy was one of Ferdinand's main responsibilities and not a joint activity. He was very successful in this respect, for example he masterminded the capture of the Canary Islands. He also worked effectively with the Holy Roman Empire in Italy, gaining Naples in 1504. Navarre, which was significantly positioned between Spain and France, was acquired later in 1512.

 A closer look

Royal authority – a new monarchy or a medieval revival?

Centralised royal authority meant more than just having government in one place, vested in the persons of Ferdinand and Isabella. In the context of the 'new monarchy' it meant creating a more bureaucratic government run by appointees of the crown. Some of these were members of the Church and the nobility; many were royal secretaries. They were constantly in touch with the King and Queen and understood the monarchs' wishes. Their influence reduced the authority of the council. They had their own staff who could advise and support them. The secretaries drew up the documents for the monarchs to sign and used the 'secret' or court seal. Two significant secretaries were Hernando de Zafra and Luis de Santangel.

Nevertheless, some aspects of medieval government still survived in a different form. Pendrill claims that it was not new methods, but the commitment of Ferdinand and Isabella to their task which was different. This is confirmed by Edwards' view that the centre of government remained, as in medieval times, the royal household and the court. Often of noble descent, its officials would double up as both administrators and personal servants of the crown. This was a very subtle change in the evolution of the structure of the monarchy.

 Activity

Thinking point

'Dual monarchy' and 'new monarchy'. Is one of these descriptions more appropriate than the other? Make sure you explain the reasons for your view.

Clearly, however, if Spain was to become a strong state, and this was Ferdinand and Isabella's joint target, it would need to have a greater sense of overall unity than was evident in the early stages of the reign of Ferdinand and Isabella. Traditionally, the two states, Castile and Aragon, were hostile. In addition, Ferdinand's territories were rarely treated as a political whole; he spent time in each state – Catalonia, Valencia and Aragon, each of which had its own Cortes.

One common feature of the government in this period, however, was the continued appointment of the *corregidor,* operating in both Castile and Aragon.

 Activity

Thinking point

Why might a *corregidor* be chosen for his lack of connection with the town in which he was placed? You could refer to Chapter 1 to refresh your memory about the earlier development of *corregidores*.

 Exploring the detail

Cortes Generales

Each of the three separate territories in Aragon had a Cortes that met separately but could also meet as a whole body, known as the Cortes Generales. Each Cortes could put its grievances before the King. In Aragon, the official known as the justicia, whose role was hereditary, had the authority to question the King's decisions. Catalonia also had officials whose job was to protect the rights of the people. These officers were called *Diputats* and *Oidors*.

Joanna of Castile

Joanna (Juana/Joan) of Castile (1504–55) was sometimes called Joanna the Mad or Juana La Loca; Joanna was the eldest child of Ferdinand and Isabella. She was married to Philip the Handsome of Austria and was the mother of Charles, who was to become Charles I of Spain and V of the Holy Roman Empire. Despite the fact that Joanna was regarded as unstable, she and her husband were declared as King and Queen of Castile on Isabella's death in 1504. However, Joanna's husband died in 1506 and Joanna, who, it was said, was distraught, became too ill to continue her own role. Another version of events is that she was imprisoned for political reasons. Cardinal Cisneros acted as Regent until Ferdinand could take over. Ferdinand had the title of Governor of Castile and ruled all Spain until his death in 1516. Charles, Joanna's son, now Charles V of the Holy Roman Empire, came to claim the throne. His mother remained locked in a tower until her death in 1555. It is possible that she was schizophrenic or that talk of her madness was simply to enable Ferdinand, and eventually her son, Charles, to take up the crown. Charles remained King of Spain until 1556.

Fig. 4 *Statue of Queen Joanna of Castile*

Because the states that made up Spain at this time had evolved separately, each state had its own laws or *fueros* that were quite distinct. Castile probably had the edge in terms of influence as it was much larger and had more resources than Aragon. It boasted the biggest population and 'one Cortes, one tax structure, one language, one coinage, one administration and no internal customs barriers'.

However there were some strong similarities between the states. For example:

- their populations were growing
- both were ruled by monarchs whose powers were wide but not tyrannical.

Activity

Challenge your thinking

Study the list of similarities and differences between Castile and Aragon on pages 12–13 in Chapter 1. Compare it with what you have just read about policy making.

1. Can you think of any explanation why the differences between the states remained when Ferdinand and Isabella became the monarchs? You might need to reflect on information given in previous chapters to help you with this.

2. To what degree did these differences inhibit the government of Spain overall – strongly, only moderately, or not at all? Explain the reasons for your decision.

Common foreign policies

Foreign affairs were a significant issue. In terms of the peninsula of Spain itself, when Ferdinand and Isabella became the rulers, Granada, Portugal, Navarre, Cerdagne and Rousillon were all outside their jurisdiction. These additions were thus foreign conquests. Beyond the Spanish peninsula lay the rest of Europe; the closest neighbour was France, and beyond that the Holy Roman Empire. To the south across the Mediterranean was North Africa.

Despite their internal insecurities, both Ferdinand and Isabella thought it important to extend their territory where possible, not only for reasons of prestige but also for religious and economic reasons. Hence their involvement in the New World. However, Aragon's priorities were limited; its concern was simply to safeguard Aragon within the northern Mediterranean area. Nevertheless, southern Spain and Aragon were left exposed when the Turks established bases along the North African coast.

The New World

Isabella was a key figure in supporting Columbus and his discovery of Caribbean lands in 1492. By 1500, Spanish settlers, approximately 1,000 in total, were occupying Hispaniola, an island in the Caribbean now called Haiti. This encouraged other forays, resulting in the acquisition of Puerto Rico in 1508 and Cuba in 1511. From these Caribbean footholds, expeditions went further west: Columbus' last voyage in 1502–04 took him to the mainland of South America and the discovery of the Orinoco river. Although Columbus died in 1506, further land-based exploration led to the discovery of the Pacific Ocean by Vasco Núñez de Balboa. The name America was not used for the land he discovered until around 1507 when Amerigo Vespucci wrote an account of his own voyages to the continent.

Initial contact with the native inhabitants of these lands seems to have been relatively positive, albeit there was an ulterior motive for the adventurers. Columbus appears to have been genuinely interested in the natives as people, but was also aware that their lands would have value for Spain. This tension can be seen in a letter to Ferdinand and Isabella in which he comments:

> *They (the natives) believed that I came from the heavens. This does not happen because they are ignorant, for they have very sharp minds and are men who navigate these seas, but rather because they had never before seen men wearing clothing, nor ships such as ours ... As soon as I arrived I took some of them by force so that they might learn our language and inform me of what was around here. They are the most timid people in the world; the men I left there could destroy the entire land ...*

1

The Pope, who was of Spanish extraction, agreed to issue papal bulls that confirmed Spanish rights to these new lands. The most important was the bull *Inter Caetera* of 1493. In 1494, Spain came to an agreement with Portugal, also involved in exploration in South America. This resulted in the redrawing of the boundaries of Spanish territory, which enabled the Portuguese to claim Brazil rather than the Spaniards.

Did you know?

Papal bulls

A bull had the force of law when issued by the Pope; it was called a 'bull' because the Pope's seal had a bull on it and the Latin word for seal was 'bulla'. A bull could be used to denounce individuals who had disobeyed Catholic laws, to make important statements and also to confirm agreements of a more political nature.

Key profiles

Christopher Columbus

Columbus (1451–1506) was a sailor and explorer of Italian extraction, making four voyages to the Caribbean and South America between 1492 and 1504. The first trip was to San Salvador, where he captured some of the local inhabitants; he called them Indians believing he had reached India. On his second voyage in 1493 he established a base on Hispaniola (now Haiti and the Dominican Republic). His third visit in 1500 led him further south to Trinidad, eventually arriving at mainland America. His last voyage was to Central America in 1502–04. As a reward for his enterprise, Columbus was allowed a coat of arms. His body was eventually laid to rest in 1899

Fig. 5 *Christopher Columbus (1451–1506), Genoese explorer discovering America in 1492*

in Seville. There is a monument dedicated to him in Washington DC; Columbus Day is still celebrated in America on 12 October. Despite his achievements, however, it is clear from archeological work that the native population of the Americas was often treated harshly, and Columbus received some of the blame for this.

Vasco Núñez de Balboa

Balboa (1475–1519) was born in Spain but eventually settled in Cuba. He is known for his discovery of the Pacific Ocean. He stowed away on a ship to mainland America and eventually became the unofficial governor of Darien. On his travels around the area he was told about an ocean on the other side of the land. Hoping to win the approval of King Ferdinand, he set out on an expedition in 1513, sighting the Pacific on 25/26 September 1513. King Ferdinand gave him the title of Admiral of the Pacific. He planned to conquer Peru and explore more of the western coast and ocean. However, the new governor of Darien became jealous, accused him of treason and he was executed in 1519.

Amerigo Vespucci

Amerigo Vespucci (1454–1512) was a well-educated Italian who became a trader working for the prestigious Medici family. He helped Columbus in preparing ships for his second and third voyages to the New World and eventually became a master navigator. In a letter, Vespucci talked about the Mondus Novus, thus giving the name 'New World' to these new found lands. He particularly commented on the native population who were 'well formed and proportioned … They have hair plentiful and black; they are agile and dignified.' The Spanish monopoly on trade between Europe and America was managed by the House of Trade in Seville, and Vespucci, who gave his name to America, became the head of the organisation.

■ **Cross-reference**

To read about the impact of the discovery of America, see Chapter 6 (pages 92–7).

By 1510, Spanish settlements were developing in the Caribbean. As early as 1503, a central trading office was created in Seville to control trade between the Americas and Europe. In 1511, a Royal High Court was established in Santo Domingo on the island of Hispaniola.

Settlers were attracted to the islands and the South American lands believing that they might become rich, either through finding gold or possibly via the slave trade. Religious orders also sent representatives to convert the natives. Even in these early stages of the colonisation, there were concerns about the morality of these acquisitions and the status of the native inhabitants. This was because most of the *conquistadores* were not nobles; they were often lawless and ruthless as the occupying nation. It was said that even the best settlers were unwilling to accept boundaries. They were looking for fame, excitement, glory and riches. Hernán Cortés, who eventually claimed Mexico, arrived in Hispaniola in 1504 declaring his motive was 'to get gold not to till the soil like a peasant'. The conqueror of Peru talked about 'great enterprises … to conquer the unseen and the unknown'. Some explorers were inspired by medieval stories of chivalry and adventure.

There were two main groups in the indigenous population: the Canary Islanders and the Indians, and with the best of intentions, the structures of Castile were imposed on all these peoples. By 1512, the Laws of Burgos had been introduced to establish more appropriate regulations, for example the natives were to be treated as 'the free subjects of the King'. Ironically, they were also required to work for the colonists, given the opportunity to become Christians and also to swear allegiance to the Castilian monarch. This made little difference to their status.

Settlers followed the explorers in quite considerable numbers, possibly as many as 150,000. Later came the religious orders such as the Franciscans and, eventually, the Jesuits.

North Africa

As early as the 14th century, Alfonso XI of Castile had been interested in North Africa as an area for expansion. He informed the Pope in 1345 that 'the acquisition of the kingdoms of Africa belongs to us and our royal right'. This assertion continued to be made by Castilian rulers throughout the next century and resulted in an attack on Gran Canaria in 1478. Their motives were probably both commercial (to gain money) and strategic (to gain influence). Gold, slaves and land would provide useful commodities, such as sugar and corn and the possibility of a linkage with the spice trade. The need to stem the influence of Islam, either by conquest or by conversion, was also seen as essential.

Europe

Ferdinand and Isabella, as new monarchs, were determined to make their mark in Europe. The biggest challenge was France, which had recently become stronger and was one of the most populated and wealthy European states. Isabella was less positive about her European neighbours, and described the French as 'a people abhorrent to our Castilian nation'. Ferdinand, however, was the chief architect of Spanish foreign policy after Isabella's death in 1504, despite the fact that the crown had passed to Joanna, his youngest daughter, and her husband Philip. Difficult relations between Spain and France continued and are not surprising at this time; they were close neighbours with ambitious rulers, developing their external as well as their internal strengths. In the years before 1500, they had clashed in Italy over Naples.

France and Spain eventually agreed to divide Naples between them, but problems continued and war was renewed. Two major battles in 1503, Cerignola and Garigliano, enabled the Spanish army to drive the French out. Spain's own ongoing internal reorganisation gave the country greater strength, despite the death of Isabella in 1504. Some ingenious diplomacy ensued and Louis XII of France passed his rights to Naples to his niece, Germaine de Foix. Ferdinand, now a widower, married her in 1505.

Conflict with France was once more resumed in 1512 over Navarre and Milan; once again Ferdinand succeeded in removing the French with some help from German troops. Over the next few years, Milan changed hands several times, but eventually remained the responsibility of Spain.

Other challenges came from Eastern Europe and the Ottoman Empire, thus generating a two-pronged challenge on both political and religious terms. The trick was to ensure that only one hostile state was engaged with at any one time.

Ferdinand was particularly proud of his achievements in foreign affairs, and foreign nations also recognised Spanish imperial expansion. Kamen comments that Ferdinand's policies gave Spain improved security on its northern border and greater influence over the Mediterranean. By 1514, Ferdinand himself said that 'the crown of Spain has not, for several hundred years, been as great or resplendent as it now is'.

However, Ferdinand's global view of the strength of Spain itself, i.e. Aragon and Castile were in a union but not unified, can be challenged. There were weaknesses that could prevent real development, for example the Aragonese were poorly represented in the diplomatic world and Castile had better resources such as manpower, money, etc. Effective unification of Spain and the creation of a stronger state with the potential for a real empire was still some decades away, despite these early beginnings.

Exploring the detail

In 1480, Louis XI of France inherited a claim to the kingdom of Naples, Cerdagne and Roussillon in southern France. This provided the French with easy access to the Catalan (eastern) coast of Spain and particularly threatened Aragon. Ferdinand wanted these lands back. He concluded a treaty with England (Medina del Campo). His youngest daughter, Catherine, would marry Arthur, heir to the English throne. The treaty allowed Henry VII of England to invade Brittany and Ferdinand to invade Cerdagne. The result was France gave Cerdagne and Roussillon to Spain in the Treaty of Barcelona in 1493.

Key chronology

Foreign and colonial affairs, 1492–1516

1478	Spanish take Gran Canaria.
1492	Columbus discovers islands in the Caribbean.
1493	Spain gains Cerdagne and Roussillon from France.
	Publication of the papal bull *Inter Caetera*.
1494	Spain and Portugal agree division of land in South America.
1503	Spain regains Milan from the French.
	Trading office (*Casa de la Contratación*) opens in Seville.
1505	Treaty of Blois is completed; France and Spain allied.
1508	Puerto Rico discovered.
1511	Cuba is conquered.
	High Court of Justice is set up in Santo Domingo, Hispaniola.
1512	Introduction of the Laws of Burgos.
1513	Balboa discovers the Pacific.
1513–15	Spain holds Milan.

Activity

Class activity

'Spain's colonies were a source of weakness rather than strength.' Divide into two teams of three. Appoint a chairperson to oversee the debate, and a spokesperson for each team. One team speaks for the motion and the other speaks against. The spokespeople from each team should present their team's arguments. The rest of the class should listen to the arguments and ask questions if they wish at the end of the speech. This should be done through the chairperson. A vote should be taken at the end to decide whether the motion is supported.

The effects of the death of Isabella in 1504

Isabella became ill in 1503 and died in October 1504 at the age of 53. Her will was a lengthy document and said much about the concerns she had for the future of her kingdom, and of Spain. It was clear that she wished Ferdinand to take on her role in Castile and its territories. Ferdinand, however, was not automatically her successor; the rightful heir was Joanna, their eldest daughter. Unfortunately, Joanna was considered unstable. Should she prove unable to take on the role of monarch in full, it had been decided that Ferdinand would be the Regent. Ferdinand would need the support of the nobles if he was to continue to rule Castile. The nobles, for their part, quickly seized this opportunity to make capital out of the situation and took over land without royal permission, for example, the Marquis of Maya appropriated large tracts of Segovia. Joanna's husband, Philip, was also resentful of the terms of the will.

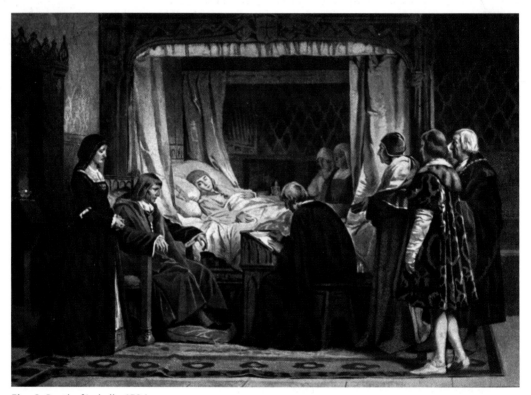

Fig. 6 *Death of Isabella, 1504*

Eventually, it was agreed by the Cortes of Toro in 1505 that Ferdinand would become Regent of Castile rather than King. He had made peace with France in 1505 and was to marry Germaine de Foix, the niece of Louis XII of France.

Hopes of an heir did not materialise (a son lived for only a few hours); although negotiations continued with Philip, Joanna's husband, and in the Treaty of Villafafila, Ferdinand surrendered his claim to the throne to Philip and Joanna. He kept the mastership of the three military orders and little else. However, he continued to plot to regain the crown. When Philip died, Ferdinand returned, spending the next few years regaining control of Castile from the predatory nobility. Joanna, by now, was incapable of ruling herself, having become entirely unstable after Philip's death. She kept her husband's body in an open coffin and refused to have him buried. Ferdinand therefore, remained as Regent. On Ferdinand's death in 1516, his grandson, Charles, was the heir to both Castile and Aragon.

Contemporaries and historians mostly suggest that Isabella, both in Castile and Spain, left behind a much improved state. Although contemporaries will usually speak well of a monarch on their demise whether they think it is deserved or not, it was certainly true that Ferdinand felt her death as 'the greatest hardship'.

Ferdinand's own death inevitably brought changes; Castile and Aragon were once again separate states and the spectre of division was further raised by plans to divide Castile and Aragon between Ferdinand's two grandsons, Charles and Ferdinand. However, Charles, the rightful heir, returned from the Netherlands where he had been brought up, to take up the throne. He was accepted as king by the Cortes of Castile in 1517, but there was also significant support for his younger brother Ferdinand who had spent most of his life in Spain. Ferdinand was therefore despatched to the Holy Roman Empire and Charles began his rule in Spain. In 1519, the death of the Holy Roman Emperor, Charles' grandfather, led to Charles' own election as Holy Roman Emperor. This was to be a 'body blow' for Spain, leaving the country with an absentee king. Revolution broke out in Castile.

■ Activity

Thinking point

To what extent was Isabella the driving force in the partnership of Castile and Aragon? Use the information here and your own research to draw your conclusions.

■ The extent of unification by 1516

Most historians use the term 'partnership' when they consider Spain in this period. Partnership is not the same as unification. Full unification demands the exact replication of systems, whereas partnership simply means working together in cooperation. Whilst Ferdinand and Isabella often followed similar policies within their separate states, they were not always identical. The monarchs played to their own personal strengths so that Isabella tended to be more influential in religious and financial matters, whereas Ferdinand dealt more with foreign affairs. However, despite what was only embryonic political unity between these two major Spanish states, there was some concept of 'working together', particularly in the intermarriage between families in the different states in the higher social levels, foreign affairs and in creating religious unity.

■ A closer look

Examining historians' views about unification

In many respects, Spain was more united in 1516 than it had been in 1492. Hernando del Pulgar, one of the King's secretaries, a *converso* and a chronicler, commented on the overall pacification of the country in which 'justice was (now) administered to certain criminals and thieves' and 'the citizens and farmers and all the common people, who were desirous of peace were very happy.' However, Woodward has suggested that there were still clear differences between the two kingdoms. Aragon had a separate legal system from Castile, whilst each kingdom had its own *audiencias* and it was much harder for the monarch to introduce reforms in Aragon than in Castile.

Pendrill suggests that a particular triumph for the monarchs was the conquest of Granada, which brought the Spanish peninsula greater unity. The emphasis on exploration and lands in the New World also gave Spain status in Europe. It also brought wealth and diverted the gentry and nobility of both states into less anti-monarchical exploits. In addition, the discovery of gold in the New World gave the crown an initial financial boost.

Kamen's view is that the monarchs also worked together, setting an example to their subjects, although this is not always well defined. For example, he suggests that:

Isabella seemed to represent the best of Italian virtues. Both monarchs ... were seen to be participating directly in the government of their subjects. Never again would Castilians be so directly and therefore so well governed.

2

*Quoted in H. Kamen, **Spain, 1469–1714: A Society of Conflict**, 1991*

However, this view could be erroneous; Woodward indicates that there were issues that continued to divide Spain, for example their policies towards the nobility were weak; the nobles were in effective control in the regions, not the monarchs. Although the monarchs forbade the building of fortifications, by 1504 only 84 castles had been destroyed and 265 had been rebuilt. This may well, of course, have been a product of the need to gain noble support rather than royal weakness.

In religious matters, Kamen also suggests that Ferdinand and Isabella's drive for religious unity was a strength in their lifetime, but 'at the expense of nurturing beneath the surface tensions and divisions which created within Spain a society of conflict'. The Inquisition was the chief architect of this development, but it came at some cost. This was therefore an issue that was likely to erupt again in the future.

In terms of unification, as opposed to joint rule, most historians generally agree that, by the end of the reign, there was little more real unity between the two states than there had been at the beginning. Hunt declares that 'the uncertainty at the end of the reign confirms that there had not been any real unification of the two Iberian kingdoms. Some policies had applied throughout the peninsula, intrinsic differences remained and there is little indication that Ferdinand and Isabella had any desire to turn their kingdom into a single unit.'

Cross-reference

For more information on religious reform and uniformity, see Chapter 5.

Whatever the views about the extent of unity during Isabella's lifetime, Ferdinand was based in Castile for much of the reign and especially after Isabella's death in 1504. Thus, he tended to deal with each state, Castile and Aragon, separately. The Council of Aragon had been especially created in 1494 to deal with the problem of governing in two places at once. Ferdinand also had no other option but to deal with the Cortes of Catalonia and Valencia as separate entities.

Another factor in the situation was the nature of the territory that Ferdinand and Isabella governed. There were great differences and consequently different demands on their stewardship. For example, Castile covered 65 per cent of the peninsula and Aragon only 18 per cent. This imbalance was reflected in the population; Castile had around 73 per cent of the total population and Aragon just over 12 per cent. This did not mean that there was less effective government in one or other state, just that there were differences. In fact, the differences had enabled Ferdinand to support Isabella and Castile more effectively because Aragon was geographically smaller; travelling distance between the governed and the governors was just as much a vital factor in early modern times as it is today.

Thinking of the peninsula as a united political entity under strong, joint monarchical control was, therefore, a significant leap of both faith and enterprise, and it is not surprising that this concept was never completely applied. Elliott agrees, suggesting that Spain, at this time, was 'a plural, not a unitary state' consisting of 'a series of separate **patrimonies**, governed in accordance with their own distinctive laws'. In other words, Spain was not perceived as one political entity, but as a group of different states.

However, both Ferdinand and Isabella, in more systematic and less dramatic ways, enabled the two kingdoms to adopt some signs and symbols that demonstrated their partnership rather than unity; for example both their images appeared on seals and coins and both their coats of arms were clearly represented on banners. They jointly signed royal decrees and were involved in making important appointments. In a less formal sense, cooperation was encouraged, for example marriages between families of the two kingdoms were supported. More specifically, Ferdinand gradually took on more control of Castile. Neither was there any attempt to join the states together on the death of Isabella in 1504: in accordance with her will, Joanna was to rule Castile. Ferdinand could be involved as 'governor and administrator' should she be unable to rule, for example through illness. However, Joanna and her husband, Philip of Burgundy, preferred to rule without Ferdinand's help and the two states went their separate ways for a time. Ferdinand certainly spent more time in Castile than he did in Aragon, employing teams of officers who worked constantly to keep him informed of issues in both states. Ultimately, both states were able to be governed by Charles I on Ferdinand's death.

Patrimonies: property, i.e. land inherited from parents, usually the father (from the Latin, *pater*) to the son. This was the accepted route by which property was passed between the generations. This is reflected in the comment of Lovett in *Early Habsburg Spain* that 'The parties to the marriage contract (Ferdinand and Isabella) thought in terms of their own pressing needs not of a permanent union of the Iberian kingdoms and a united Spain.'

Fig. 7 *Philip I, son of Maximilian I, Holy Roman Emperor, husband of Joanna the Mad*

Activity

Revision exercise

1. What were the main obstacles to political unity in Spain after 1500?

2. Which of these obstacles do you think was the most difficult to overcome and why?

3. How do you define 'dual monarchy'? Give some examples of the way it worked to support your view.

Summary questions

1. Which of the Catholic Monarchs, Ferdinand or Isabella, do you think had the greatest impact on Spain?

2. Which of the policies outlined in this chapter was the most successful for the Catholic Monarchs?

5   Overcoming the challenges to the crown

Alfonso de Palencia, the historian and royal chronicler, contemporary of Ferdinand and Isabella, was anxious to emphasise 'the disorder of the recent past and the peace and order of the present' in order to suggest that progress was made. However, Palencia did not approve of women rulers and commented on 'the arrogance and massive power of Lady Isabella, in no way disposed to accept the rules of government which, since the most remote centuries, have favoured the male' (quoted in Edwards, *Ferdinand and Isabella*, 2005). Ultimately, most chroniclers have tended to be positive about Isabella; even Palencia eventually decided that 'if anything worthy of praise was accomplished in Andalucia it seemed to be due to the Queen's initiative'. Pulgar, in his 'Chronicle of the Catholic Kings' joined in the eulogy saying, 'It was certainly a marvellous thing that what many men and great lords could not agree to effect in many years, one lone woman carried out in a little time.'

Isabella was a woman with a mind of her own, and she ruled the larger Spanish state. She was shrewd and very careful to ensure that she was seen to work closely with Ferdinand: after her death, Ferdinand took on Castile as well as Aragon. Both as a team and as individuals, the challenges faced were many, but their achievements are often described as 'great'. Despite this, they are often also perceived as a modest couple, working hard, governing directly and getting on with the difficult roles they had been given. This is encapsulated in the wry comment of a Flemish noble, writing in 1501: 'on the dress of the king and queen, I shall say nothing, for they wear only woollen cloth'.

Challenges to the crown

The challenges to the crown in early 16th century Spain arose out of the context of the earlier period of political disorder, religious division, extremes of wealth and poverty, and the changes that had already begun to take place in religion and society. However, historians have often focused on only one or other of these issues, for example, Kamen explores the relationship between Catholics, Moors and Jews, Fernandez-Armesto considers the interplay of political and personal issues and Elliott has concerns about the social and economic factors that underpinned other developments. Ferdinand and Isabella, by 1500, had garnered some experience from their earlier years. The question outstanding was whether they could now put that experience to full use and allow Spain to move forward.

The military orders

A major achievement of Ferdinand and Isabella was in generating peace and order in Spain. One way in which they did this was to take over the military orders that comprised the five Orders of Chivalry, founded in the 12th century.

Fig. 1 *Ferdinand and Isabella receiving the Embassy of the King of Fez*

Ferdinand, by 1500, was the master of each of three orders: Alcantara, Santiago and Calatrava. The papacy only confirmed this in 1523. There were also two other orders based in Aragon: the Orders of Montesa and St John. Each order had several hundred members and owned land, towns and fortresses. By this time, they no longer had to live a celibate life and were able to marry. Although members of the orders took vows rather like monks, their main purpose in medieval times and in the early 16th century was to act as crusaders and regain land taken by Muslims. During the war against Granada, the Order of Santiago alone had organised more than 1,750 cavalry and provided the Catholic Monarchs with weapons, horses, etc. to support the campaign. One-sixth of the cavalry used in the campaign overall was provided by the orders. It is estimated that the orders had authority over approximately 1 million **vassals**. These were workers who were dependent upon the Order for their livelihood and accommodation. Many nobles were involved in the orders and, as such, were able to control their strongholds and use the members as private armies. The orders were very wealthy; the annual rental income from the lands of all the orders was 145,000 ducats. They held towns, fortresses and large amounts of land or *encomiendas* on the Castilian borders. Consequently, they presented a potentially serious challenge to the crown and to each other as there were frequent internal disputes. However, the orders were possibly not as powerful as the nobility who were not taxed, owned much more land and controlled regional politics.

Nevertheless, taking over these orders was a great achievement for Ferdinand and Isabella: it made a statement about the Catholic Monarchs' authority and it brought them wealth and property. It also was significant in ending the risk of the nobility having a power base in the orders.

Revenue from this source grew over time and was useful as collateral when the crown wanted loans from bankers. A council was established that regulated their activities. When Ferdinand found himself in conflict with Philip and Joanna over the throne of Castile after Isabella's death, he eventually had to accept defeat. Although he lost Castile at that point, he retained the masterships of the orders.

The privileges of the aristocracy

By the early 16th century, the Castilian aristocracy, in particular, were a very wealthy group of individuals and from this stemmed their privileges. Estimates suggest that a total of 13 dukes were worth 565,000 ducats in annual income; 13 marquises had between them 330,000 ducats a year, and a range of other nobles had 414,000 ducats per annum. They had privileges such as being able to keep their hats on in the presence of the monarchs, who called them 'cousins'. If accused of a crime, they could not be tortured or imprisoned. Even the lesser aristocracy had large town houses displaying their coat of arms and became governors of the town. Some of them also had estates in the country.

Isabella, however, is particularly noted as having eventually 'destroyed' or 'tamed' the aristocracy of Castile, replacing them with well-educated bureaucrats.

Nobles who could invest time and capital were able to move into industry. The honorary Admiral of Castile, for example, was given a dyestuffs monopoly by the monarchs; another duke had his own fleet of trading ships; others invested in sugar and other similar commodities.

■ Key terms

Vassals: term used to indicate a worker who is not free; in the feudal system, the lords and monastic orders owned land that was worked by the peasants. In return, these workers were housed and would have a small plot of land to grow some food for themselves. They might also be liable for other duties as required by their lord. They could not leave their lord under pain of death.

■ Activity

Revision exercise

Make a list of the strengths and weaknesses of the military orders. Did their strengths outweigh their weaknesses? Make sure you justify your view with reference to the information given here. You may wish to find out more about these orders using the internet and/or your school/local library.

■ Activity

Revision exercise

As you work through this section, gather information about the nobles to help you decide how important they were. You could present your conclusions in writing or use them as part of a class discussion.

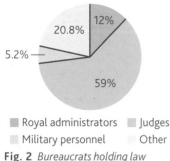

Fig. 2 *Bureaucrats holding law degrees in Castile*

- 12%
- 20.8%
- 5.2%
- 59%

■ Royal administrators ■ Judges
■ Military personnel   Other

■ **Exploring the detail**

Hidalgos

The lowest level of the nobility were called the *hidalgos*. They were of variable wealth and social standing; some were from noble families and others had recently been granted titles. They usually had a coat of arms, built impressive town houses and played a part in local government. Some were tax farmers or involved in commerce. They had legal privileges as well as social rank, for example they could not be imprisoned for debt. Elliott comments that it was not unknown for genealogical tables to be forged to enable individuals to claim this status.

These projects increased their contribution to the state, but also added to their wealth. Ferdinand and Isabella began to see the nobles as potential and necessary allies; thus noble influence had grown.

The nobility were often supported by other officials. For example, although the nobility were the representatives of the crown in frontier areas like Granada, most of their functions were often actually carried out by lawyers. Fewer than 12 per cent of royal administrators had degrees in law in 1500, but for judicial appointments the percentage of those with a law degree was 59.3 per cent. Only 5.2 per cent of those given military appointments had degrees, and of those serving in the royal household, almost none had qualifications, although there was unlikely to be a requirement for qualifications for such a post. *Corregidores* were seldom trained as lawyers but, if they had no qualifications themselves, they had to appoint one to their team.

The nobility could still be a threat in other ways; they usually had retainers and often fortified homes; in 1504 there were at least 265 of these properties that had been repaired and/or rebuilt. In comparison, only 84 had been destroyed. Although all castles had to be licensed by the crown, the government had difficulty in enforcing this.

Controlling the nobles

The extent of their power and the loyalty of some nobles therefore became suspect. They risked arrest and having their castles destroyed or their land confiscated; this enhanced the crown's finances. Other naturally arising factors also led to some reduction of their income and power, for example the growth of towns, and the movement of peasantry into those towns, deprived the nobles of their armies and workforces. This change was linked to the growing trade with the New World, which stimulated employment in the towns in trade and in manufacturing.

There were other positive ways of neutralising the nobles:

- *Letrados* were given posts in local government rather than the nobility; appropriately trained, they were often more reliable than the nobility.
- Churchmen were recruited less frequently from the nobility.
- Nobles were given grants of land in Spain or in newly discovered territories; this removed their feuding away from the centre of power and/or to another continent and gave them an opportunity to build up their fortunes.
- Nobles could attend the meetings of the Royal Council but not vote; the royal secretaries had the most power despite the fact that three members of the council signed all the official documents.
- Nobles were encouraged to participate in the war in Granada; many of them did this enthusiastically.
- They were encouraged to attend the royal court, although this was not a permanent or fixed institution.
- They retained their titles, for example of Constable or Admiral, but their power was very limited – they were 'empty dignitaries'.

Fig. 3 *The Duke of Alba, a member of the privileged aristocracy*

A closer look

The 'taming' of the nobility

Fernandez-Armesto seems to be divided in his view about whether the establishment of the royal court contributed much to the taming of the nobility. He quotes from the record of one of the monarch's university-trained councillors that: 'they (the monarchs) kept a great household and court accompanied by grandees and leading barons whom they elevated according to the quality of their degree, keeping them occupied in ways wherein they could be of service ... The monarchs were most careful to place men of prudence and ability to serve, even though such were of the middling sort rather than the great men from the noblest houses.'

But Armesto adds that 'the local power of the aristocracy was little impaired by their increased attendance on the royal persons.'

Woodward suggests that part of the problem in dealing with the nobility was the peripatetic nature of the court. Nobles were 'tamed' in other ways, for example they were encouraged to attend university (although relatively few did). Woodward also suggests that Ferdinand and Isabella used the concepts of 'opulence' and 'splendour' to display their own wealth, and, most importantly, their potential power. This policy of 'magnificence' gave them an aura of authority, portrayed them as cultured and knowledgeable as well as wealthy and powerful, and therefore superior to the nobles.

Examples of this tactic can be seen in the building of palaces, hospitals and universities, often copied by some of the nobility. The courts also became more influenced by the ideal of the perfect courtier, encouraging better standards of behaviour and a more industrious approach to life. There were time filling rituals for everything, for example dressing, undressing, eating and washing. Hunting, bullfighting and jousting were also popular. The monarchs, particularly, dressed handsomely to emphasise their status. On one occasion, Isabella declared that she had worn 'only a simple dress', but it was 'of silk, with three gold hem-bands'.

Prince John, the young son of Ferdinand and Isabella, also became part of the means of control. Just washing his hands before his evening meal required the help of the royal chamberlain who was of noble origin: sometimes it was the Duke of Medina-Sidonia, or a marquis, who helped him. Although relatively few new titles were created, the future of the aristocracy was still safeguarded by the right of entail, which meant that estates were not divided but passed on to the eldest son. Once exploration of the New World began, they also profited from grants of land. Old families did not disappear, they simply developed new roles, whilst retaining some of the old privileges.

Taking part in cultural activities further occupied the nobles. A German visitor to Castile was impressed by a Latin class he saw, run by Peter Martyr, which was full of dukes and other noblemen. 'All these are awakening in Spain the taste for letters', he said. Classical languages were studied at the University of Alcalá and printed books began to be imported in increasing numbers. Popular culture also developed, for example a book of verse was published in 1511. Art also became important as the influence of the Renaissance reached Spain.

Did you know?

Don Fernando de Velasco was a specific example of the nobility who needed 'taming'. He was the brother of the Lord Constable, which was an important post. Fernando burned to death a number of drunken young men who had been abusive and mistakenly thought he was a rent collector and a Jew. Ferdinand, the King, appeared to support Don Fernando, saying that, 'he had acted nobly in exacting satisfaction for the outrage they had committed against him.'

Did you know?

The Renaissance

This was an intellectual movement, a 'rebirth', which began in Italy and spread across Europe. It developed into a broad cultural movement, influencing scholarship, the visual arts, literature and music. Many scholars and artists had rich patrons who supported them. Some famous individuals in the Renaissance were painters such as Botticelli and Michelangelo, writers and philosophers such as Machiavelli and architects such as Alberti and Bramante. The discovery of America by Columbus was a direct result of the growth of curiosity and new knowledge about the world.

■ Key terms

Humanism: a movement that was strongly linked to the Renaissance. Humanism was about having an open mind, breadth of knowledge of civilisations, peoples and cultures, etc.; also understanding that people could have control over their actions and lives rather than believing all was ordained by God.

■ Cross-reference

For more information about Peter Martyr, see Chapter 4 (page 50).

■ Exploring the detail

Noble privileges

Despite attempts to reduce the political influence of the nobility, for example by keeping them at court, there was little attempt to reduce their privileges or incomes. A total of 13 dukes had combined annual incomes of 565,000 ducats. The Constable of Castile had an income of 60,000 ducats alone; the lowest income for a duke was 25,000 ducats and for the 13 marquises, 30,000 ducats per anum was not unusual. All those who fought in Granada were given houses, land and vassals (servants/workers who were tied to the lordship). Marriages often resulted in even larger blocks of land being created.

Isabella was herself interested in the Renaissance and the arts, and an important figure in civilising the nobles, who were increasingly willing to follow her lead. She was interested in **humanism**; she patronised several poets, scholars and writers and invited Peter Martyr, a famous Italian scholar, to visit the Castilian court to promote noble interest in learning and cultural developments. Obtaining a law degree opened the door to important posts and two universities were founded, at Alcalá in 1508 and Cuenca in 1510. If nobles were not interested in the literary arts, they were encouraged to turn their energy to building projects. An 'Isabelline' style of architecture developed and palaces, monasteries and libraries were constructed.

Noble courtiers also indulged in jousting, hunting, and bullfighting. Jousting was particularly favoured as it was practice for war. In the evenings there was music and dancing. The court moved around the country keeping the monarchs in touch with their subjects. The cost of entertainment, in these circumstances, was the responsibilty of the hosts.

Despite their wealth, status and attendance at court, some nobles found their influence weakened as other factors arose naturally to limit their power, for example the growth of towns and the movement of peasantry into these towns. These changes deprived the nobles of their armies and workforces. Overall, however, they remained loyal and sometimes looked to more civilised pursuits, in commerce or the arts, rather than war, particularly whilst Isabella was alive.

Fig. 4 *Gonzalo de Córdoba, the great captain, scholar and soldier, in his library*

The nobility after Isabella's death

When Isabella died, however, Ferdinand really needed the support of the nobles, especially in Castile. He had to rely more on loans from the nobility to pursue his foreign policy. Consequently, some nobles took advantage of the situation and began to revert to their previous behaviour, seizing land from towns and villages, and they were not called to order by the crown. One example was Andres de Cabrera, the marquis of Maya. He occupied large stretches of Segovia and turned the population into his tenants. Some nobles conflicted with local towns and villages for other reasons, for example over tolls for crossing bridges and land rights. A number of them became very wealthy, such as the Mendoza family.

Unfortunately, Ferdinand did nothing further to stop this excess of privilege. It eventually became a factor in the revolt of the Comuneros in 1520. The majority of the nobles remained very much as they always had been; a military class who would challenge the crown or other sectors of the population if they chose, but overall remaining loyal to the monarchy when times were good. By 1516, 1,000 patents of nobility had been issued and, although the monarchs had issued orders that no new fortifications were to be built, at least 265 had been rebuilt or repaired by 1504. Only 84 had been destroyed.

Woodward comments that the monarchy had to 'forge a partnership with the nobility if it was to survive; the monarchy would retain its political supremacy in central government and the nobility its social dominance in local administration'.

The role of the justicia

Law and order were major problems. The monarchs' authority to intervene and make laws, deal with infringements, etc. varied between the two states. In Aragon, all laws had to be approved by the Cortes of each of the three constituent assemblies. Sometimes the three Cortes met together as a single group, making them a more powerful body. The monarchy naturally disliked this situation and was often reluctant to summon the Aragonese Cortes. One of Isabella's civil servants, Guicciardini, said about this situation, 'Aragon is not ours, we shall have to conquer it again.' Each individual Cortes had distinct privileges, for example, in their ability to impose taxes or raise an army; this limited the power of the monarchs, particularly in Castile where the crown could not introduce or abandon laws without having to consult the Cortes.

When they first became the Catholic Monarchs, Ferdinand and Isabella dealt with judicial matters in person. As the reign continued, this became less practical, especially in Aragon, particularly as Ferdinand spent most of his time in Castile. There already existed an official called a justicia appointed by the King. The justicia's role was to see that the liberties of the kingdom were protected. He could not be removed from office, as the role was hereditary. In addition, the justicia could question the decisions of the King, ensuring that he, and not just the nobility, did not infringe the laws. The justicia's authority and the attitude of the Aragonese state to their liberty is clearly seen in the oath of loyalty taken by officials: 'We, who are as good as you, swear to you, who are no better than we, to accept you as our sovereign king and lord, provided that you observe all our liberties and laws, but if not, not.' However, as early as 1493, Ferdinand had gained agreement that the justicia could be advised by five *letrados* or lawyers, appointed by the crown, thus giving some leeway for a level of monarchical influence in criminal cases.

The development of the Cortes

In Aragon and Castile, the Cortes operated differently. See Table 1, which identifies some of these differences.

Despite the fact that the Castilian Cortes appears to be quite weak, Kamen says that Isabella 'never ceased to maintain that she was absolute,

Cross-reference

Look back to Chapter 1 (pages 15, 20–1) to refresh your understanding of the broader threat posed by the nobility, and refer to Chapter 8 (pages 114–20) to find out about the Comuneros Revolt.

Activity

Challenge your thinking

Ferdinand and Isabella set out to 'tame the nobility'. Why did they not achieve this aim completely? You should be able to think of a number of reasons, but you should also consider what was the most important factor. Make sure you give reasons for your judgement.

Did you know?

Catalonia, one of the kingdoms of the crown of Aragon, also had an official who acted very much like the justicia. He had a standing committtee of three *Diputats* and *Oidors*. They were, initially, financial officers who had oversight of tax collections. Their additional role was as a 'watchdog', ensuring that the rights and liberties of the people were recognised.

Activity

Class activity

Look back over the contents of this chapter so far. Your task is to decide how effectively Ferdinand and Isabella maintained order in Spain. You could judge this by a comparison with the situation on their accession (outlined in Chapter 1).

- Work in two teams: one looking for the positive points; the other for the negative points.

- Each team should give a brief presentation of their findings to the rest of the class.

- Finish with a whole-class discussion to agree the balance between the positive and the negative; were they very successful, successful, limited in their success or had they made no progress at all?

but yet took care to pass all her laws inside the Cortes.' This decision could have been a function of the issue of *servicios*, i.e. money granted for the running of the state. If the Cortes granted money, Isabella was prepared to put her legal proposals to them for acceptance.

Table 1 *The similarities and differences between the Cortes of Aragon and the Cortes of Castile*

Aragon	Castile
The three kingdoms had different Cortes.	One Cortes for all of Castile.
All laws had to be approved by each Cortes.	The Cortes was weak and could not control the monarch; laws could be made without the approval of the Cortes.
The Cortes could refuse to grant money; it was essential that the monarchs were present when this was requested.	The main role of the Cortes was to approve grants of money (*servicios*) to the monarch to run the government, but the crown had other sources of income and so was not dependent on the Cortes.
The monarchs had to gain the consent of the Cortes to amend laws or introduce changes in administrative activities.	The monarchs could dispense with the advice of the nobles and clergy at will; there was a tendency to rule by decree.
The Cortes were infrequently summoned; more emphasis was placed on the *Diputacio,* which consisted of people entitled to sit in the Cortes – this group could investigate and punish the shortcomings of royal officials. This system was clearly impacting on the power of the monarchy. There were, in later years, accusations that this body was trying to turn Catalonia (a province of Aragon) into 'a free republic under Your Majesty's protection'.	18 cities were normally represented, i.e. 2 burgesses per city = 36 delegates; this was often all the attendance in the Cortes. This made it easier for the monarchs to achieve their own outcomes with minimal opposition or discussion.

A closer look

Monarchs and the Cortes

Kamen's study of the parliaments of this period indicate that the Castilian Cortes were summoned 16 times, the Aragonese Cortes possibly seven times. In addition, the Catalan assembly met six times and that of Valencia, only once. There were three occasions when the Cortes of all three kingdoms of Aragon were summoned at the same time. Despite what seems to be a very limited opportunity for representatives to be formally involved politically, Ferdinand and Isabella often responded positively on the occasions when the Cortes was in session. Kamen gives some confirmation of this, citing the Cortes of Toro in 1505 when 83 laws were passed in the assembly. Ferdinand ratified/agreed them. Although Isabella, before she died, had largely approved these laws, it indicates Ferdinand's confidence in the Cortes to allow them to take this action without his presence. Some of this confidence might have been rooted in the fact that the nobles and clergy, who did not pay taxes, did not always attend; if they did so, it was certainly not in great numbers.

The infrequent meetings and limitations of the Cortes reflect the fact that, in Europe generally, the idea of governing through a representative body was anathema to monarchs. Even in England, where parliaments had been held since medieval times, it took until the 17th century for there to be a significant crisis that led to open warfare between monarch and parliament (the Civil War), and the eventual recognition that some kind of representation of the populace was required.

Law and order

Most 16th century monarchs had only limited rights to dispense justice. The reason for this was that so many different bodies and individuals claimed legal authority, for example the Church, the magnates or great lords, and merchant groups. However, in Castile and Aragon, despite the role of the justicia, Ferdinand and Isabella did dispense justice personally. At first, Isabella presided over a court held every Friday in a fortress in Madrid. Later, more courts were established, for example in Valladolid in 1489, and at Santiago de Campostela in 1504. Minor courts were also set up in Seville and Santiago. Fernandez de Oviedo, a contemporary chronicler, saw this as a very positive achievement.

A further important development was a proposal to codify the laws; administering justice is not effective if, for example, the meaning of the law is unclear, or there are differing views on punishments for the same crime. Alfonso Diaz de Montalvo, an authority at the time on the law, was enlisted to collect and publish all the law codes in existence. He produced an eight-volumed work published in 1485 that towns had to purchase. In 1503, a further collection of the legal judgements made by the Catholic Monarchs was also published. However, Kamen suggests that they failed to clarify the law overall; there was no attempt to reform the law or to reconcile any anomalies between laws dealing with similar offences, despite some initial work by the Cortes of Toro in 1505.

Nevertheless, the monarchs did make some effective changes:

- *Corregidores* were aided by two trained lawyers, one a civil lawyer and one a criminal lawyer; there were 64 towns with *corregidores* (increased from 49) by 1516; a ruling of 1500 ordered that no *corregidor* should remain in any one town for more than two years.

- Persons convicted had the right to a retrial. If this was not accepted, then the case moved on to the highest court.

- If this court's judgement was not approved, the case could go to the Council of Castile itself, where Ferdinand and Isabella were the judges; Fridays were set aside for this duty.

Punishments imposed by the courts could be very severe; the *Hermandades* would chase offenders on horseback and impose summary punishment. A physician at court commented: 'At first there was much butchery, but it was necessary because all the kingdoms had not been pacified.' The *Hermandades* became feared and resented and

Activity

Group activity

1. Draw up a list of the strengths and weaknesses of the Cortes in Spain during the reign of Ferdinand and Isabella.

2. Refer back to Chapter 1 and the section about the Cortes. Use this information and A closer look above as the basis for a class discussion/an essay entitled: 'How far was the authority of the monarch restricted by the Cortes in the reigns of Ferdinand and Isabella?'

Cross-reference

Look back to Chapter 1 (pages 13–16) for basic information about the role of the monarchy regarding law and order, and Chapter 2 (pages 29–30) for the involvement of the *Hermandad*.

towns complained about the cost of maintaining them. Local taxes funded the archers and the magistrates. Although they were formally dissolved in 1498, volunteers continued in Castile and the Basque provinces.

The monarchs were eager to see law and order well established in the towns and judicial officers or *alcades* served this purpose; in Burgos alone, six of them were appointed. The introduction of the *corregidor* was also a vital part of the judicial system, but, as crown representatives, were not always fully appreciated. Kamen comments that *corregidores* were most effective in Granada, where new systems were being put into place as a result of the conquest.

■ A closer look

Corregidores by 1516

There were approximately 64 towns with *corregidores* by 1516; short of Isabella's aim of appointing one in every town in Castile. Some towns actually rejected them. *Corregidores* had a two-year period of office and a report had to be published at the end of that time. Townspeople, however, often complained that the *corregidores* did not do their jobs properly and that they were more likely to deal with the nobility less harshly than they did with the ordinary people. The short period in office did not allow for consistency and continuity and the fact that they were not deployed in Aragon, where the Cortes refused to allow them to operate, weakened their overall acceptance. When Isabella died in 1504, there were signs that the system needed reform, but Ferdinand and his daughter Joanna could not always agree about the way in which Castile should be governed. Kamen notes that the Cortes were still complaining about *corregidores* as late as 1528 because 'the salaries of the *corregidores* have exhausted all the towns'. *Corregidores* did remain in some centres; some were still deployed as late as the reign of Philip II, but were perceived as being less effective than their predecessors.

■ Cross-reference

Look back to Chapter 1 (page 19) to remind yourself about the role of the *corregidores*.

Kamen indicates that the monarchs tried to act as mediators between rival groups in the towns, sometimes giving concessions as a result. On other occasions they might suspend the laws and/or suspend the council. The monarchs visited the towns on a regular basis, often staying for up to two weeks; throughout their reign, they visited every single town. If towns were in financial difficulty, assistance was offered, for example they might be allowed to collect the *alcabala* tax themselves and decide on its use.

This personal involvement was critical in the successful pacification of Spain. It was a significant achievement which brought together the interests of the people with those of the monarchs.

■ *Los Reyes Catolicos*

Ferdinand and Isabella were known for their piety and as *Los Reyes Catolicos*, or the Catholic Monarchs of Spain, they were determined to bring reform to a church which, in common with other European states, had become corrupt. In one diocese, clergy had to be requested 'to refrain from gambling or singing or dancing in public'.

■ Activity

Talking point

What do you think was the most important legal change made by the Catholic monarchs? Was it:

■ the introduction of the *corregidor*

■ the codification of the laws

■ the role of the *justicia*

■ the clarification of procedures and punishments

■ the personal involvement of the monarchs?

Discuss in groups, thinking carefully about the impact of these changes in relation to three sections of the population – the monarchy, the nobles and the ordinary people. Who benefited? Was anyone in a worse situation?

Isabella complained to a bishop in 1500 about the misdemeanours of the clergy in his diocese and that 'the greater part of the clergy are said to be and are in concubinage publicly, and, if our justice intervenes to punish them, they revolt'.

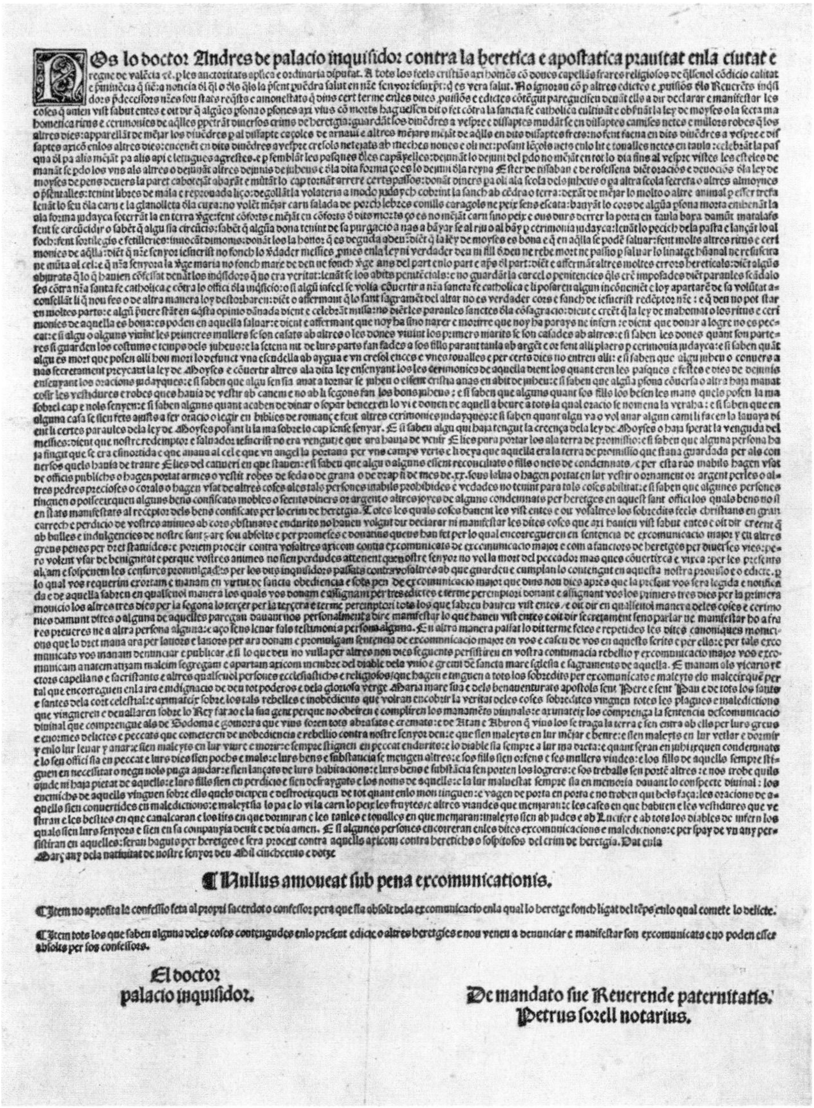
Nos lo doctor Andres de palacio inquisidor contra la heretica e apostatica pravitat enla ciutat e regne de valencia ...

Nullus amoveat sub pena excomunicationis.

Item no aprofita la confessio feta al propri sacerdot o confessor pera que sia absolt dela excomunicacio enla qual lo heretge fonch ligat del temps enlo qual comete lo delicte.

Item tots los que saben alguna deles coses contengudes enlo present edicte o altres heretgies e nou venen a denunciar e manifestar son excomunicats e no poden esser absolts per sos confessors.

El doctor
palacio inquisidor.

De mandato sue Reverende paternitatis.
Petrus sorell notarius.

Fig. 5 *Edict of Faith in Catalan. Published by the Inquisition in Valencia, 1512*

To encourage reform, the Catholic Monarchs set up colleges to educate the clergy. Men of non-noble origin were encouraged to train in the hope that they would be less likely to get involved in politics and conflict with members of the nobility.

By 1508, Cisneros had set up a university in Alcalá, near Madrid, although its first students did not arrive until 1518. The university became an important centre for theological training. It was here that the Polyglot Bible was published. This was a landmark event: it presented the scriptures in three languages in a format that allowed for comparison, encouraging debate and greater understanding. Rawlings says, 'It set the seal on the reputation of the university in terms of **humanist scholarship**.'

Did you know?

Concubinage

This is a term used to describe a man and woman living together, but not legally married. The female was regarded as being in concubinage; in some circumstances this related to situations where there was more than one wife.

Did you know?

The Polyglot or Complutensian Bible was in six volumes; biblical text was set out in Hebrew, Latin and Greek in parallel. It was produced in collaboration with a range of scholars from Spain and other European states. The project centred on the University of Alcalá. This was also the place where Erasmus' writings were printed.

Key terms

Humanist scholarship: usually seen as a study of logic, grammar and philosophy. It involved going back to the classics (Greek and Latin) and also understanding how the meaning of words had changed over time. One example of this was the definition of the Greek 'metanoeite', which had originally been translated as 'to do penance' but was translated by humanists as 'repent'; a different concept. This showed scholars how much distortion there could be in the ancient texts such as the Bible.

In addition, the Inquisition was allowed and encouraged to continue to work towards uniformity. In 1502, all non-baptised Muslims (Moors) from Granada, who had not converted to Christianity, were ordered to leave Castile and Leon. However, the majority remained despite the injunction. Overall, the number of persecutions fell in this period, but there were clear attempts to change the culture of the Moorish inhabitants. Talavera, the Archbishop of Granada, advised that they must conform 'in your dress and your shoes, and your adornment, in eating and at your tables, and in cooking meat; in your manner of walking, in giving and receiving, and more than anything, forgetting so far as you can, the Arabic tongue'.

However, the more important target for the Inquisition was the Jews. More than a thousand were arrested by 1505. Even Archbishop Talavera became a victim. Many were burned; in Córdoba alone in 1504, up to 134 *conversos* suffered this fate. In 1518, the Cortes of Valladolid reported that 'many innocent and guiltless have suffered death, harm, oppression, injury and infamy'. *Conversos* who formed part of the Comuneros Revolt, 1520–21, were also victims.

■ Cross-reference

See the later section on 'The extent of religious consensus' for more information about the Moors (pages 79–81).

Fig. 6 An auto-da-fé *in Madrid, in which those found guilty of religious offences were informed of their punishment. These sessions were held in public, often in the town square.*

Archbishop Talavera

Archbishop Talavera (1479–1546) joined the Dominican Order of monks in Salamanca. The severe discipline made him ill and he left to complete his novitiate (training) elsewhere. He studied at the University of Alcalá and later taught theology and philosophy. By 1518, he had become the General of the Dominican Order and ultimately became the Archbishop of Seville.

Juan Luis Vives

Vives (1492–1540) was a Spanish humanist and philosopher. His parents were *converso* who were reluctant to give up their Jewish faith. Vives left Spain in 1509 as a consequence of increased persecution by the Inquisition. His father was arrested and burned in 1524 accused of supporting Jews and his mother's bones were dug up and burned later in 1528. Vives studied in Paris but spent most of his time in the Netherlands. He never returned to Spain, despite being invited to take up an academic post. He became professor of humanities at the University of Leuven and wrote many books in the 1520s and 1530s on philosophy. He also wrote *The Education of a Christian Woman* and produced a Latin textbook. He was very interested in what we would now call psychoanalysis. This enabled him to understand more about how the mind works and receives and deals with ideas. Vives never returned to Spain and died in 1540. He wrote, on one occasion: 'We are going through times when we can neither speak nor be silent without danger.'

Monastic reform was also on the agenda, involving orders such as the Benedictines, Cistercians and Augustinians. Commissioners were sent out to reform the monasteries. The Pope agreed that appeals to Rome to allow exceptions to their Rule could no longer be lodged by the monasteries. The Rule identified the specific discipline of the Order, for example when or whether they were allowed to speak. These changes revived the strict observance of monastic life as orginally intended by the Rules of each Order.

The policies hit hard, but had some success in promoting the Christian faith. Nevertheless, there were still complaints as late as 1511 about clergy who had clearly not achieved their positions on merit.

Financial issues were also significant; one demand was the *tercias reales*, which was payment to the crown equivalent to one-third of the tithe; another was the *decima*, which was one-tenth of clerical incomes. Other taxes, such as the *subsidio*, were paid by the clergy on their incomes and owed to the monarchy and not to the Pope. These new taxes added to those already being paid by the Church from 1494; the *cruzada*, originally only collected to support action against non-believers, was now granted in perpetuity.

■ The extent of religious consensus

The Church continued to wield considerable influence, not only because of its guardianship of the souls of men but also because as an institution it was exempt from taxation. It had its own courts and even armies. The Archbishop of Toledo was small fry with an army of 1,000; others such as the Archbishop of Santiago had an army three times this size.

Key terms

Orders of Chivalry: wealthy organisations consisting of knights who had taken monastic vows (poverty, chastity and obedience). Ferdinand was in charge of all three orders; this meant that their income could be appropriated by the crown and was often used to ensure political allegiance from the orders.

Cross-reference

Look back to Chapter 2 (page 27) to refresh your memory about *Moriscos* and *Mudéjars*.

In addition, there were **Orders of Chivalry**, Santiago, Calatrava and Alcantara, which could also raise troops. These troops had been used on occasion against the monarchy; the orders' large estates and revenues meant that they could be a considerable threat. The Inquisition also had authority in both kingdoms; Ferdinand and Isabella, however, were clearly agreed that it was important for Spain to be united in religion.

This commitment to establishing the Catholic faith across their dominions, led them to be referred to as the 'Catholic Monarchs', a title suggesting that Catholicism was the only acceptable faith. Any Jews remaining after the decree of expulsion were expected to convert. Following the failure to convert all Muslims, they were now also faced with the option of leaving or of converting. Achieving and maintaining a religious consensus was not an easy matter in a state with the historical background of Spain.

The expulsion of the Moors/*Mudéjars*

For the Catholic Monarchs to achieve religious consensus, several tactics and rules were established that resulted in the expulsion of these groups (Table 2).

Table 2 *The process of expulsion*

Date	Change
1499	*Mudéjars* were to be compulsorily baptised, i.e. they 'should convert or be slaves' according to Archbishop Cisneros; this provoked a brief revolt. Another option was that they leave the country. Cisneros reported that, by January 1500, 'there is no one in the city (of Granada) who is not a Christian and all the mosques are churches.'
1501	In Castile, *Moriscos* (Christian Moors) or ex-Muslims had equality under the law with Christians, but were expected to forget their own culture and could not carry arms. *Morisco* children should be sent to classes to learn to recite the main Catholic prayers. Mass was to be attended on Sundays.
1502	*Mudéjars* in Castile could choose between baptism or exile; most chose baptism. Those who chose to leave, could only go to specified destinations, e.g. Egypt. Converted Muslims were not to leave the kingdom for two years, nor could they travel to Granada. Castilians were not to shelter Muslims and would be subject to loss of goods if they did so.
1511	A range of decrees limited cultural identities, e.g. speaking Arabic and the practice of circumcision were not permitted.

The process was not fully completed until 1526 when traditional dress, jewellery and the ritual slaughter of animals were forbidden.

Elliott describes Isabella's faith at this time as 'fervent, mystical and intense', promoting these harsh policies. Edwards comments that Isabella 'did not enter into the questions of the mechanism or sincerity of … conversions'. This might have been because she wanted to accept the situation at face value and use it to promote her achievement in 'unifying' the nation.

Ferdinand, however, had different views about the situation in Aragon. He was more positive about minorities: he saw the *Mudéjars* as hardworking and often cultured. They had not taken advantage of the war against Granada to rebel against the crown. Although Muslims still constituted one-third of the population, Ferdinand said, 'Our holy Catholic faith in the conversion of the infidels admits neither violence nor force but only full freedom and devotion.' He was reluctant to convert or expel them from Aragon, despite some sources of conflict in Valencia and the possibility that they might join with Spain's enemies if they felt themselves to be under threat. The Turks were one such potential enemy. On a much lesser scale, Muslim mosques and the five times a day call to prayer occasionally generated some ill-feeling. The atttitude of the Inquisition may have exacerbated this, but Ferdinand appeared to want to allow Muslims to continue this practice. He dismissed an attempt by the Inquisition to excommunicate anyone allowing Muslims to use a horn for the call to prayer. However, Ferdinand did make some rules – for example, he decreed that Muslims should live in specific areas and wear blue clothing. Open friction between the differing religious groups, however, appears to have been at a relatively low level in Aragon until the 1520s.

The Inquisition continued to operate in both Aragon and Castile and so provided an overall 'cloak' of commonality. Whatever the reality, the Council of the Inquisition continued its work long beyond the end of Ferdinand and Isabella's reign and the monarchy increased its control over the Church as the papacy increasingly required political support.

Catholicism had become the main religion of Spain and the crown was determined to keep it that way. Talavera, who had become archbishop after the conquest of Granada, spent much time and effort working with Muslims to convert them. It was slow work. Cisneros, the Archbishop of Toledo, wanted to speed up the process.

The work and role of Cisneros

Archbishop, and later Cardinal, Francisco Cisneros de Ximenes was a forceful character and often seen as intolerant. He had played a large part in the campaign in Granada, claiming to have baptised 3,000 into the Christian faith in 1499, and continued his work in maintaining the true faith in Spain into the early days of the 16th century. However, his policies did not fully settle Granada and there were more uprisings. Ferdinand and Isabella decided to intervene, although allowing Cisneros' proposal that more clergy from Castile should be brought into Granada to speed up the process of conversion. Further disruption, however, led to even more forceful measures introduced by Isabella in 1504. Subjugation of the Moors was ultimately a political rather than a purely religious process.

Cisneros played an important role in the period immediately following Isabella's death in 1504. Despite his warlike tendencies in defence of his faith, he also had a great interest in learning and was determined to raise standards in Spain. He set up the University of Alcalá in 1508 specifically so that theology could be studied and humanism promoted. Elliott sees him as the man who gave the Spanish Church 'new strength and vigour at the very moment when the Church was everywhere under heavy attack. Reformers (which included Cisneros) instead of rejecting the New Learning, used it to further the work of reform'.

Cisneros also championed the publication of the Polyglot Bible in 1522, which had the Hebrew, Greek and Latin texts side by side for comparison. As a hard line Christian, and Inquisitor-General from 1507, Cisneros acted firmly in 1506–07 when there was a noble-led attack upon the Inquisition's presence in Spain. However, he preferred to treat it as a military problem rather than a religious problem and used the army to defeat them. Cisneros also banned the preaching of indulgences,

Cross-reference

For more information about Cisneros, see Chapter 2 (pages 40–1).

Did you know?

Indulgences were significant in the development of the Reformation in the early 16th century. They were paper promises of forgiveness for sins that would shorten the time a person had to spend in purgatory after death, before being accepted into heaven. The recipient of an indulgence was expected to be sorry for his sins. However, by the 16th century, indulgences were sold and the money used to rebuild St Peter's Church in Rome. John Tetzel, a monk who sold indulgences in Germany, is reputed to have said, 'When the coin in the coffer rings, the soul from purgatory forth doth spring.'

Fig. 7 *Cardinal Cisneros directs the construction of the hospital of Sanctuary of the Charity of Illescas (Toledo)*

■ **Activity**

Revision exercise

Gather all the evidence you can find that suggests that, by 1516 the title *Los Reyes Catolicos* (the Catholic Monarchs) was:

a deserved

b not deserved.

which he saw as simple extortion committed by the papacy. This is an interesting aspect of his work; it was to be picked up by Luther in Germany in 1517 who went on to become the founder of the Protestant faith. Cisneros, although sharing the same attitude as Luther to indulgences, did not desert his faith. However, his ability to stand back and be critical was unusual at this time, and particularly in the Spain of the Catholic Monarchs.

For a brief period, Cisneros also had a political role, becoming the Regent of Spain, after Ferdinand's death in 1516 and until his successor, Charles I, arrived.

The right of *patronato* of 1508

In 1486, the Pope had given the Catholic Monarchs of Spain the right of *patronato,* that is, the right to appoint to all major ecclesiastical posts in Granada. In 1508, they were given the same rights to the Church in the New World in Spain. In other words, the crown was able to wield some of the authority of a pope dependent on the particular territory which the appointee supervised. This right was very significant as it enabled the monarchs to ensure that their clergy was Spanish. Not only this, appeals in clerical matters no longer had to be heard in Rome. Perhaps the most important benefit in the long term, however, was the financial gains this brought to Spain rather than to the Holy See. The nomination of bishops was not granted, but a certain amount of influence could be used.

The monarchs were careful to choose appropriately; often their nominee was Spanish and well-educated. It was also important that they were both pious and celibate; two qualities automatically expected, but not always delivered in this period. Talavera and Cisneros were their greatest appointments.

The closer cooperation between crown and Church that could result from this right of appointment did not always result in reform of the Church; much of that came from other sources and individuals, for example the Jeronomite Order, which had 14 monasteries by 1516. Kamen is quite clear that an effective reformation of the Church was not achieved in Spain, despite some attempts to achieve this by enforcing the rules more effectively within the Franciscan Order, which Cisneros strongly supported. There were orders made for records of baptism to be kept, but the result was rather piecemeal. Some clergy, like Archbishop Carillo, had children and others still maintained mistresses. The best example of a reforming cleric was probably Cisneros himself, but even he was personally involved in war. For example, at the age of 73, Cisneros led an army of 15,000 to capture Oran in Northern Africa.

Summary questions

1 How successful was the dual monarchy in addressing religious issues within Spain?

2 What do you think was the weakest aspect of government in this period? Explain your answer.

Finance and the economy

Open, open your ears.

Listen, listen shepherd

Because you are not hearing the clamour

That your sheep are making to you.

Their voices rise to heaven,

Complaining without consolation,

That you fraudulently shear them

So many times in the year

That now they have no wool to cover them.

1

*Quoted in Edwards, **Ferdinand and Isabella; Profiles in Power**, 2005*

Activity

Source analysis

In pairs or in small groups, read the verse in Source 1 and discuss:

1 What are the specific complaints made by the writer of this verse?

2 Why is the analogy to 'sheep' and 'shepherd' used?

3 Why would this be significant?

4 Why is the complaint in verse?

Compare your views with other groups.

This poem, written by Castilians in Andalusia, near the border with Granada, is an allegorical reference to the constant rise in taxes during Ferdinand and Isabella's reign.

Revenue and taxation

The collection of revenue in any form was crucial to the survival of the crown; it was essential to fund policies, particularly in war time, but also to maintain the royal court and its officers. By 1504, revenue had increased by 30 times the amount collected at the beginning of the reign; suggesting that the system was more effective and organised. Alternatively, increased demand for revenue as a result of changing systems of government, costs of war, etc. or rising prices could be the explanation.

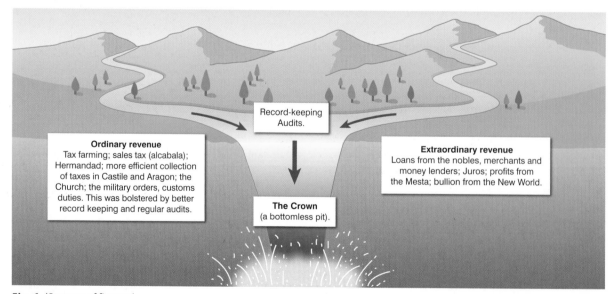

Ordinary revenue
Tax farming; sales tax (alcabala); Hermandad; more efficient collection of taxes in Castile and Aragon; the Church; the military orders, customs duties. This was bolstered by better record keeping and regular audits.

Record-keeping Audits.

The Crown
(a bottomless pit).

Extraordinary revenue
Loans from the nobles, merchants and money lenders; Juros; profits from the Mesta; bullion from the New World.

Fig. 1 *'Streams of finance'*

The main sources of revenue in both states were very traditional, employing taxation of differing kinds. The most important of these taxes, despite the fact that the clergy were exempt from it, was probably the sales tax or *alcabala*. First introduced in 1342, it remained a considerable source of income. It was raised by authority of the monarch, not the Cortes. In 1504, the *alcabala* brought in 284 million maravedis, and in 1516, 300 million, showing a marginal increase over this time period. However, the Catholic Monarchs were not solvent despite the fact that revenue overall had doubled since the turn of the century. The taxation system was a regressive system, i.e. the wealthy actually payed less pro rata than the poor. This seems to signify a weakness; the monarch's reliance on the nobility and a desire not to antagonise them. The **tax farming** system was also a weakness; tax collected directly would go more readily into the royal coffers. Tax farming provided opportunities for corruption and fraud amongst the collectors, meaning that both the crown and the tax payers were worse off.

Extraordinary income was usually raised via the *Hermandad*, Cortes and the Church. Woodward suggests that the tax on the *Hermandad* was the most reliable of these taxes usually amounting to about 18 million maravedis in any one year. However, this income was not always enough for the needs of the crown and other sources had to be found. Woodward pinpoints the largest **creditors** as being aristocrats such as the Duke of Cádiz who, on one occasion, loaned money in return for a village.

Financing large projects was achieved with the help of the Mesta, Genoese merchants and Jewish financiers; Jews were exempt from imprisonment for debt because they were so valuable as financiers. In Fernandez-Armesto's view, the Genoese merchants were more important than the Jewish moneylenders. Ferdinand renewed their contracts every few years seeing it positively as 'an advantage of my service and to the increase of my rents, levies and dues … that they do stay in these my said kingdoms in order to trade in their goods and articles'. *Juros* remained an important means of raising money. By 1516, repaying these loans at 10 per cent interest cost 131 million maravedis; one-third of ordinary income was being used to pay off the debt. Most of the loans came from the nobility, for example the Duke of Cádiz loaned 10 million maravedis and was rewarded by being allowed to take a village in Granada for his own property, as security for the loan.

By 1510, ordinary revenue from taxation had increased to 320 million maravedis; 90 per cent of this was raised from the *alcabala*. In addition, there was a lesser, but still important, increase in extraordinary revenue, largely because of increased efficiency in collection. Central records were now being kept and audits of tax collectors were carried out every two years. However, there were no further reforms of the systems and the monarchs were wary of asking for more from powerful landowners. Tax farming also continued and so, to some extent, did corruption and fraud. Finances were, however, in reasonable shape by 1516.

■ Cross-reference

For more information about a range of sources of revenue taxation and the extent of crown debt, refer to Chapter 1 (pages 18–9) and Chapter 3 (pages 43–4).

■ Key terms

Tax farming: a system by which the right to collect taxes was sold (farmed out) to individuals. This saved the monarchy from paying their tax officials, but meant that taxes were heavier than they should have been as tax farmers collected more than the government required to pay themselves. Possibly the monarchs gained less from taxes than they might have done using paid officials. However, resentment about taxes was focused on the tax farmers rather than the monarchs.

Creditor: someone who is owed a debt and expects the debtor to pay, usually within a defined period of time.

■ Did you know?

Credit bond of *juro*

This was a legal document in which it was stated that the holder expected money borrowed from them to be repaid at an agreed rate of interest at a specified time.

■ Activity

Challenge your thinking

Why do you think the crown retained this system of financing wars when it clearly only generated more debt?

■ Cross-reference

Look back to Chapter 2 (pages 29–30) to remind yourself of the role of the *Hermandad*.

■ Did you know?

Much of the Catholic Monarchs' income was spent on the war in Granada and by the early 16th century they were becoming more dependent on borrowing, usually at an interest rate of 10 per cent. They usually sold this debt on as *juros*; these were a form of credit bond but were only repaid annually. The crown, therefore, did not have a constant flow of income; Woodward comments that this hindered planning for the long term. The result was rising debt for the crown; by 1504, the total sum owed to the crown was 112 million maravedis, and by 1516, it was 131 million maravedis.

Fig. 2 *Elaborate stonework, which depicts the Castilian monarchs demonstrating the craftsmanship of stonemasons and the 'magnificence' of the monarchs despite mounting debt*

■ Activity

Thinking point

What were the strengths and weaknesses of the revenue and taxation systems?

Despite these various sources of ordinary revenue and taxation, there was no systematic analysis of need and of sources of income. If there was a change in circumstances, such as a failure in tax collection or rising military costs, such the 366 million maravedis for the Italian war, the monarchs had to resort to extraordinary sources of income. Those who were most likely to loan money were the nobility. Despite claims that finances were reasonably sound by 1516, they were certainly not as strong as they appeared to be.

■ Growth in population

Population figures are not easy to find in this period; there were limited means for government to keep track of such data. However, it is possible to look at some approximations and gain a reasonable concept of change and the issues that might arise. Although Spain was a large land mass with huge tracts of land, much was unsuitable for settlement, or used by the Mesta, and thus not available for agricultural/industrial development and settlement. This could place some limits on the growth of the population.

Overall figures suggest a population of 6.8 million in 1500 rising to 7.4 million by 1550. This averages out at 1–22 inhabitants per square mile. These figures may not be totally reliable, but are probably the best approximation as there was no specific, regular collection of such data. What figures there are suggest that any increase in population was comparatively slow, unlike our present 21st century population explosion. Castile probably had around 65 per cent of the total population of Spain; it was the largest single state covering about two-thirds of the peninsula. Table 1 shows a more detailed analysis of the situation near the end of the century.

Table 1 *Population figures for the Spanish states near the end of the 16th century*

State	Size in square kilometres	% of total area of Spain	Population	% of total population	Inhabitants per square kilometre
Castile	378,000	65.2	8,304,000	73.2	22.0
Aragon	100,000	17.2	1,358,000	12.0	13.6
Portugal	90,000	15.5	1,500,000	13.2	16.7
Navarre	12,000	2.1	185,000	1.6	15.4
Total	580,000	100	11,347,000	100	19.6

J. H. Elliott, *Imperial Spain, 1469–1716*, 1963

Kamen emphasises that most of the figures available for this period are limited; most are only from the mid-16th century. He also says 'there can be no dispute over the main pattern observable in most of the (Spanish) peninsula; a slow increase from the late 15th into the early 16th century with a marked and sometimes dramatic expansion in the central decades to about 1580, then a steep fall from 1590 into the next century. He links the expansion in the middle of the century with commercial development and suggests that numbers possibly rose by about 50 per cent in total. On the Mediterranean coast, a big population increase of around 75 per cent was thought to be the result of the arrival of French immigrants.

■ Economic disunity

Agriculture and developing industry remained the mainstays of the Spanish economy in this period. By 1516, Castile was the stonger state because of its size, resources and burgeoning trade with the New World. Nevertheless, there was a limited sense of economic unity through the similarity of the value of specific coins.

Pasture had originally been very important because of the value of the wool. However, agriculture was now growing more rapidly as the population expanded, leading to the use of wasteland and pasture to grow crops. In 1513, an important handbook, *Agricultura General* by Herrera, was published encouraging the trend in farming. There was also help available for farmers when the weather affected crops and incomes; for example, when an epidemic broke out in 1503, taxes were not imposed until production had recovered.

Balancing the economies of Castile and Aragon was a concern. Castile, on the whole, was a producer of grain and Aragon was an importer, but customs duties hampered the transfer of goods. By 1500, Ferdinand and Isabella had authorised much freer trade in grain between Castile and Aragon. This was extended throughout Spain in 1505.

■ **Activity**

Source analysis

1. What conclusions can you draw from Table 1? Think about differences and similarities between states and any factors that might explain those differences and similarities.

2. Why might these figures be unreliable? One reason has already been given, but there could be others.

■ **Activity**

Challenge your thinking

Keep the information on this page in mind when looking at the next few sections. Is the increase in population a cause or a consequence of social and economic developments in this period?

Fig. 3 *The port of Cádiz was a site of trade between Spain and the New World*

Exports to the New World were a good source of income, particularly wheat, which settlers could not yet grow in large enough quantities. However, irregular yields of grain meant Spain also often had to import. The agrarian workforce was also being diverted in other directions despite the monarchy wanting 'our subjects … to work with a greater will in agriculture'. Growth in population and bad harvests in 1502–07, caused by bad weather, also added to the difficulties. Setting the price for grain had limited success; fortunately by 1508, the danger of famine had receded.

Other tactics to encourage the economy included:

■ developing an international postal system in Aragon. Barcelona was the hub linked to Germany, France, Italy and Portugal

■ appointing an official in Castile to oversee the development of the post in Castile

■ decreeing that the Castilian ducat, Valencian *excelente* and the Catalan *principat*, all gold coins, would have the same value and could be used in all Spanish kingdoms

■ encouraging the sale of more goods within Spain, and to other states, for example Sardinia and Sicily could only import cloth from Catalonia; trade with Italy, Africa, Egypt and Rhodes was established and trade with America promoted. This trade gave the crown one-fifth of all its takings.

> ### ■ Did you know?
>
> The policies of the monarchs had some positive results, for example more bullion came into the country: from 1503–05 to 1511–15, bullion worth 166.9 million maravedis was imported and in 1511–15, the sum was 537.9 million maravedis. Internal trade increased and towns grew, for example Burgos, from 8,000 to 21,000 inhabitants. Seville and Cádiz also became rich as a result of the transatlantic trade.

However, the real consequence of rising prices was that it encouraged trade but inhibited manufacture of goods. This was not fully realised until the reign of Charles V. Other policies implemented before 1500 added to the problems. For example, war had caused a decline in the Granadan silk industry; the expulsion of the Jews in 1492 had decimated the textile industry; and wool was more valuable as an export than in Spain. Some difficulties were also caused by the **guilds**, which generally opposed technology and large-scale development.

By 1507, high prices and rising unemployment generated economic decline. Unemployment hit some towns in northern Spain extremely hard. The crown can bear the blame for the extent of these changes and, for example, problems with the wool trade and industries such as wine, shipbuilding and ceramics. Lead, copper and iron mining also suffered. Italians were beginning to take over the carrying trade. Native shipbuilders failed to get any support from the government unless they intended to build ships of 600 tonnes or more. Catalonia could not trade effectively with America because of the monopoly held by Seville; Catalan merchants were generally not welcome in Castilian towns.

In addition, Isabella is perceived to have been too concerned with religious issues to see the benefits that Jewish traders, expelled in 1492, had brought to the country by this time. The decision to promote a monopoly of trade with the Americas rather than generate competition was possibly mistaken. A further negative factor was the attitude of the nobility who were not always willing to invest in what they now saw as risky enterprises.

The idea that 'Spain still existed only in embryo' can be supported by the following arguments:

- Sheep farming had become more important than agriculture.
- The economies of the two states were kept separate.
- Some tolls were imposed between the two states.

Poverty

Poverty can be the product of a number of different causes, some external and caused by factors outside an individual's control. It can also be the consequence of specific actions taken by an individual or group. In Spain in the early 16th century, both factors were at work:

- Rising population – this put pressure on land, jobs, food, housing, etc. There were serious food shortages in Spain after 1504. Ninety-five per cent of the people were peasants; 80 per cent of the population of Castile were peasants.
- Movement of people from the countryside into the towns looking for work, but perhaps not having the appropriate skills.
- Sickness, leaving people unable to work and dependent on charity.
- Old age, which took experienced family members out of the workforce and made them dependent on relatives or other carers.
- Rising prices, which could mean less or nutritionally poor food; essential goods such as food rose the most, possibly by up to 100 per cent.
- Wages not keeping up with rising prices; wages rose by only 30–40 per cent in the same period.
- Failing harvests or poor farming methods that influenced and sometimes reduced the supply of food available.

Fig. 4 *'The causes of poverty'*

Activity

Group activity

1. In groups, organise the bulleted list of factors explaining poverty in order of importance. Discuss the reasons for your decision and compare with other groups.

2. How important was the issue of poverty?

Food shortages were one of the most common factors in the poverty cycle. After 1506, wheat had to be regularly imported to top up local supplies; this made bread expensive. Those in towns possibly suffered the most. The number of beggars increased substantially, leading to issues of law and order as they travelled in search of work.

Some charitable bodies could help the poor. Benefactors supplied money to build hospitals, such as the Hospital of Santa Cruz in 1514. The monarchs also had a hospital built at Santiago de Campostela for pilgrims and pauper children. Old and injured soldiers were catered for in Seville. Specialist hospitals for lepers were often built, usually outside the town walls for fear of infection.

However, not all peasants were poor; there was a small 'peasant aristocracy' in the countryside and some in the towns who had some land they could cultivate or they could work as traders. Nevertheless, it was easy to fall into debt lacking the means to pay tithes and taxes. Some peasants were more firmly tied to the land than others, for example in Galicia, and this factor clearly restricted their options.

The Mesta

The Mesta was often seen as a significant factor in food shortages and the rising food prices that were characteristic after 1504. Certainly their privileges increased throughout the reign, for example via the law of 1501 that decreed that any land on which sheep had fed, even if only once, was to be pasture always and could not be used for any other purpose. These privileges limited the growing of food, but nevertheless enhanced the growth of Burgos as a centre for the wool trade. Wool from all parts of Castile was sold to merchants at local fairs, transported to Burgos and then carried by pack mules to Bilbao and from there shipped to Antwerp. Although competition grew between Burgos and Bilbao, Burgos remained the centre of the wool trade.

The power of the Mesta was not easily broken. As late as the 18th century, it was still privileged, as commented on in Source 2 by an English cleric and geologist, Joseph Townsend, travelling in Spain.

> When the sheep are travelling they may feed freely on all wastes and commons; but, in passing through cultivated country, they must be confined within their proper limits. Hence, in such inhospitable districts (i.e. where the pasturage is poor), they are made to travel at the rate of six or seven leagues a day; but where pasture is to be had, they move very slow … The plowman and the grazier are here eternally at variance. Hence the land has been depopulated … This bishopric formerly contained 748 towns, but now it has only 333, the others being deserted, and their arable lands reduced to pasture.

2   *Quoted in J. Cowans (ed.), **Early Modern Spain: A Documentary History**, 2003*

If these were the observations about the Mesta written several hundred years later, it is not difficult to understand the problems in the 16th century when the institution was at its height. There were in the region of 1,100 law suits involving the Mesta provoked, in some cases, by what was seen as extreme favouritism.

Trade and commerce

Having done much to restore the power of the crown, Ferdinand and Isabella were also eager to extend Spain's wealth in the period 1500–16; trade and commercial activity were to be encouraged to achieve this. It is possible that they did not have specific plans, only a desire to improve commercially over time. However, lack of planning and forethought, as seen in the fact that there was no attempt to draw together the marketing and distribution structures of Aragon and Castile, hindered the very expansion they desired. Nevertheless, there was no shortage of legislation, with at least 128 ordinances issued to regulate systems.

Another obstacle to developing trade was that there were many tolls and taxes. They were often levied to help maintain roads, rivers and bridges, but, almost invariably, the money was taken by the nobles for their own use. Unsuccessful action was taken to make local guilds responsible for these works. In 1511, it was noted that 12 bridges had been swept away in one area alone and no attempt had been made to rebuild them. As a fusion of the two states had not occurred fully in political life, it is really not surprising that a 'joined up' economy was slow to develop. However, there were also other major hindrances, such as the expulsion of the Jews, in 1492, which removed a highly talented and enterprising community.

Cross-reference

Look back to Chapter 3 (pages 46–7) for more information on the Mesta.

Did you know?

In 1501, a decree had allowed the Mesta to use land at the same rates as when it was first leased; this was an enormous privilege in a time of rising prices and inevitably created some conflict with arable farmers. By 1500, a member of the Royal Council had become the president of the Mesta, indicating its signficance as a commercial body. New rules were drawn up in 1511. This change was significant particularly as the population increased and pressure to release more land for arable grew.

The one bright spot on the horizon was the government's decision to agree one coin, the *excelente*, common to both kingdoms. They now had exactly the same value that could usefully encourage trade.

However, trade and commerce did ultimately flourish. Wool remained the mainstay of Spain's internal and external economy. Most was produced in Castile. A *consulado* was set up in Burgos and *flotas* or convoys shipped the wool to other parts of Europe. Silk was also a significant export. A 1511 royal ordinance was generated to improve the quality of cloth manufacture, although little else was done to support this trade. Some traditional industries continued to do well, for example soap, leather and shipbuilding. However, the port of Barcelona began to decline because of the shift towards trade with America and the decline of the Mediterranean trade.

Fortunately, there was a good export trade in grain. A decree of 1505 was issued explicitly to encourage free trade across Spain as a result of the effects of a series of bad harvests from 1502–07. It also led to some control over prices to stop both hoarding grain and profiteering from the increased demand.

The impact of the discovery of America

Historians have claimed that the discovery of America was perceived by the Spanish initially as 'the least of Ferdinand and Isabella's achievements', maybe because, at first, they found little that seemed of value. However, this early assessment was soon revised. Spaniards quickly began to speak of these new areas as a *monarquia* and eventually as an empire.

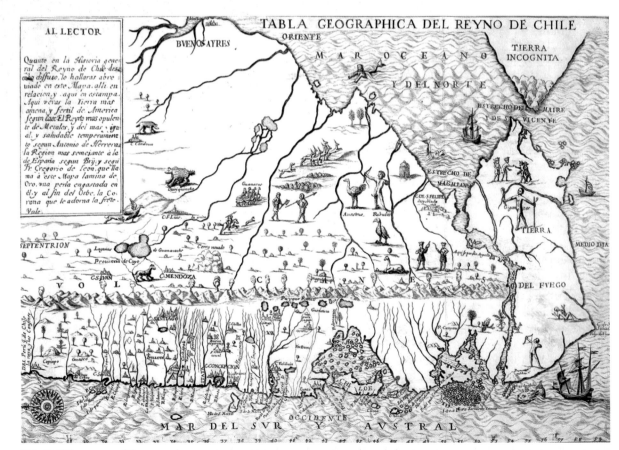

Fig. 5 *Chile – a map of the new colony*

Interest may also have been stimulated by the discoveries of Portuguese explorers, Bartholomew Diaz, who discovered the Cape of Good Hope, and Vasco da Gama, who was the first European to cross the Arabian Sea and reach India since the Roman era.

Columbus' exploratory journeys to America had touched some of the islands of the West Indies and the mainland of Central America.

■ **Cross-reference**

Look back to Chapter 4 (pages 60–2) for information on the process and extent of the Spanish discoveries in the New World by 1500, and for reasons why Spaniards emigrated.

Fig. 6 *Arriving in the New World*

One of the main activities for the new arrivals in these new found territories was to adapt Spanish systems to the new environment. This had a significant impact on the native population, particularly in the use of land which was parcelled out to Spanish settlers who were prepared to act as soldiers to defend it; each owner of a piece of land or *encomienda*, as it was called, had to protect his Indians, give them work and instruct them in Christianity. They were also to be paid. However, slavery also existed. Dominican friars who arrived in Hispaniola in 1510 wanted to abolish the *encomienda* system. Much discussion ensued, but did little to change the situation for the natives in the short term.

Encomienda was a system whereby native Americans were allocated to settlers in order to work for them. In return, their new masters were expected to protect them and convert them to Christianity. Although positive in their conception, in reality *encomiendas* resulted in many Indians living in almost slave-like conditions. Cortés is reputed to have placed 180,000 Indians in only 30 *encomiendas*. Many Indians succumbed to western diseases such as smallpox and influenza; living together in such close proximity did nothing to help the situation. It is estimated that almost 90 per cent of the indigenous population died as a consequence of these conditions.

Fig. 7 The old Merchant Exchange and *Casa de la Contratación*, Seville

Another consequence of Spanish colonisation was trade, which rapidly developed between Spain and New Spain, as the new lands were eventually called. New commodities and a workforce on hand helped to promote trade between Spain and New Spain. By 1501, foreigners, i.e. non-Castilians, were banned from travelling to the West Indies, and by 1503, the *Casa de la Contratación* was set up in Seville to oversee and control the trade.

Table 2 *The expansion of trade*

Period	Royal imports	Private imports	Total imports
1503–05	116,660	328,607	445,267
1506–10	256,625	722,859	979,484
1511–15	375,882	1,058,782	1,434,664

Relations between the settlers and the native population varied. Unfortunately, for the natives, many of these early settlers in America were Spaniards who had little education, were often unemployed and driven by their need to make a living for themselves and their families rather than by the potential of adventure. What some of them might have lacked in skills, however, they made up for in motivation; they wanted their children to have different opportunites and greater freedom.

However, many of the settlers found the native population puzzling; they were not sure if they were men or beasts. It was not until 1537 that the Pope decreed that 'the Indians are true men'. The differences in the Indian societies the Spaniards encountered were huge, ranging from cannibals, who were transients and had no real social and governmental structures, to people such as the Aztecs who built complex communities and had an architectural style of their own, as well as a religion involving human sacrifice.

Religion was also a significant issue at this time; Columbus wanted the profits of his voyage to be used to pay for a campaign in the Holy Land to free Jerusalem, currently in the hands of the Turks. More immediately significant was the desire to convert the native American population to Christianity. Every expedition had a priest, and Dominican friars were arriving in the New World from 1510. Unfortunately, the relatively brutal approach to this task promoted by the *conquistadores* only served to make the Indians extremely antagonistic. The Spaniards' aim to control, rather than to persuade, caused conflict. By the 1520s, however, greater numbers of Spaniards arrived with a more humanitarian approach.

A further concern for Spain was loss of manpower to the New World. After Isabella's death, Ferdinand allowed some emigration from Aragon and this right to emigrate became fully accepted in the latter half of the 16th century. Young men saw it as an adventure and tales of the New World inspired them. Women, however, tended to be less attracted to this new life, or deterred from emigration by societal expectations. They counted for less than 5 per cent of all emigrants. For most migrants, their most basic motivation, hopes of making a fortune, was not always fulfilled: Cortés said in 1504, 'I came to get gold, not to till the soil like a peasant.' Diaz echoed this complex mix of motives when he said: 'We came to serve God and His Majesty … and also to get rich.' For the New World, this influx of a different peoples was a mixed blessing; they brought new ideas and methods, for example of farming, but their aim was to exploit its wealth and gain control.

Fig. 8 Conquistadores, *with native allies, attack an Aztec temple in the New World*

The Spanish view of the New World and its inhabitants

As far as the government was concerned, the monarchs wanted to control the new territories, but had no wish to remove the native population; rather they wished to convert them to Christianity and use the manpower for their profit. A group of friars were commissioned in 1516 to study the Indians and see if they could live as Europeans. Their study suggested this would not be possible, provoking much discussion that continued until the 1540s.

The monarchs also were anxious to prove that the acquisition of the New World was morally right; a document called 'the Requirement', written by Juan Lopez de Palacios Rubios in 1513, indicates some of these concerns. It traces political development from the creation.

On account of the multitude which has sprung from this man and woman in the five thousand years since the world was created, it was necessary that some men should go one way and some another, and that they should be divided into many kingdoms and provinces, for in one they could not be sustained.

Of all these nations, God our Lord gave charge to one man, called Saint Peter ... And he commanded him to place his seat in Rome ... and to judge and govern all Christians, Moors, Jews and Gentiles, and all other sects. This man was called Pope ... One of these popes who succeeded Saint Peter, made donation of these isles ... Wherefore, we ask and require you that you acknowledge the Church as the ruler and superior of the whole world, and the high priest called pope, and in his name the king and queen, Lady Joanna, as superiors and lords of these islands, and that you consent and allow these religious fathers to preach before you.

If you do, you will do well, and we shall receive you all in love and charity, and shall leave you free without servitude, and they shall not compel you to turn Christians unless you yourselves, when informed of the truth, should wish to be converted to the holy Catholic faith ... And besides this, their Highnesses award you many privileges and exemptions and will grant you many benefits.

But if you do not do this, we shall powerfully enter your country, and shall make war against you, and shall subject you to the obedience of the Church and of their Highnesses; we shall take you and your wives and children, and shall make slaves of them, and as such shall sell and dispose of them; and we shall take away your goods; and we protest that the deaths and losses which shall accrue from this are your fault.

3   *Arthur Helps, **The Spanish Conquest in America**, Vol. 1, 1900. Quoted in J. Cowans (ed.), **Early Modern Spain: A Documentary History**, 2003*

Activity

Source analysis

Read Source 3.

1. What are the arguments put forward to support the act of conquest by the Spaniards?

2. How persuasive are their arguments likely to be for the local inhabitants? (You could also look back to the section on the New World in Chapter 3 to help you with this.)

3. Why do the Spaniards invoke God and St Peter?

4. What view of the Spanish and of Christianity is suggested in this document?

5. Why should the Spaniards argue that any 'deaths and losses' are the fault of the native inhabitants?

6. What were the consequences of the discovery/conquest of the New World?

In the reign of Ferdinand and Isabella, there seemed to be largely positive outcomes for the Spaniards. Here is a possible list:

- The discoveries of gold and silver resources initially boosted the wealth of Spain.

- Discontented Spaniards could go and seek their fortune.

- The peoples of the New World were potential workers and souls to be saved by Christianity; this became an important mission for the 'Catholic Monarchs', although it did not always have a good outcome despite the intentions of the monarchs.

- It improved the standing of Spain in Europe.

- There was a degree of rivalry with the Portuguese, for example Vasco da Gama sailed to India in 1502, Albuquerque siezed Goa on the the west coast of India in 1510 and in 1511 controlled the straits leading to China. By 1513, they reached Canton and eventually Japan.

Summary question

How strong economically was Spain during the reign of Ferdinand and Isabella?

Learning outcomes

Throughout this section, you have learned about the challenges that the crown continued to face in the period 1500–16. Awareness of the extent of changes that took place in political affairs should have enabled you to understand the reasons behind the growth of monarchical power. The strengths of Isabella as Queen and the impact of her death have been considered, as well as the influence of the conservative and deeply religious population and the fight for religious unity. The impact of issues such as a rising population, economic change and the effects of the discovery of America have been assessed and should be taken into account as you begin to analyse what made Spain such a powerful European state.

 Examination-style question

'The discovery of America was the most significant factor in changing the economy of Spain in the reign of Ferdinand and Isabella.' How far do you agree with this view?

(45 marks)

In this question, you are given a focus, 'the discovery of America', and an effect, 'changing the economy of Spain' within a context, 'the reign of Ferdinand and Isabella'. Each of these is useful to provide a framework for your answer. You should also be aware of the chronological context; it is the entire length of the reign. You should make sure you link only to the 'economy' of Spain; this excludes religious, political and financial affairs. In addition, you need to note that the question refers to 'the most significant factor'. This does not mean that you choose to write only about that one factor 'the discovery of America', but that you consider other reasons too and then make a judgement about 'the discovery' and its significance.

The discovery of America was obviously an important factor and a good answer needs to explain why, for example, it brought more money into Spain that could be used to generate wealth, business, etc. Not only gold, but other goods could be traded, for example sugar, potatoes, maize, etc. in exchange for domestic Spanish goods. In addition, there was land to be had and those who were allowed to go and seek their fortune could send money back home.

However, drawbacks also need to be discussed to provide a balanced response. One of the most important was the resultant inflation and price rise that did not benefit everyone, although the major effects of this were not felt until the latter part of the century. Another was the flow of migrants to America to seek their fortune, making production of some goods more expensive in parts of Spain where there were shortages of labour. In addition, other factors also need to be considered, for example Spain's own internal economy wavered in this period and American gold only added to inflation. However, this might be countered by an awareness that there was also trade with other European countries that grew in this period, for example wine and iron to England in exchange for wool.

Good answers will try to prioritise factors, for example: 'Ultimately, it was probably the export of people to the Americas that changed the economy in Spain the most, together with the development of a single common coin that could be used throughout Spain and freed up trade.'

In this chapter you will learn about:

- how Charles I set about establishing control and his relationship with the Cortes, the nobles and the other councils

- Charles' partnership with the nobility and the role of the *letrados*, Gattinara and Cobos

- the degree of change and continuity experienced between 1516 and 1529.

Fig. 1 *Joanna the Mad, daughter of Ferdinand II, mother of Charles I of Spain*

As the boat lurched through the mountainous waves, the passenger saw the rocks looming up through the mist and made for shore. He shivered as he tentatively stepped on to the rocky beach of a remote, uninhabited part of Spain. He was just 17 years old, cold, tired and apprehensive; bad weather had forced him to land in this unknown cove and his arrival was unannounced. There was no warm welcome or grand reception; only the boy and his entourage, all of them soaked to the skin and hungry but glad to be standing on firm ground. Charles Habsburg, the new King of Spain, now had no choice but to travel slowly by mule through the mountains to meet his new subjects.

From the early age of 6, Charles had significant responsibilites; he was the Duke of Burgundy and lived in the Netherlands. He was also a virtual orphan; his father, Philip the Handsome, died and his mother, Joanna (the Mad) of Castile, who never recovered from the loss of her husband, was unable to care for him. It was Charles' misfortune also that he had inherited the characteristic misshapen Habsburg jaw, which made it difficult for him to chew; his love of food often gave him indigestion from overeating. Elliott famously describes him as 'a gawky, unprepossessing youth with an absurdly pronounced jaw. Apart from looking like an idiot, he also suffered from the unforgiveable defect of knowing no Castilian.'

Charles I's arrival in Spain was delayed and caused bad feeling; He was seen as a reluctant monarch. The delay was caused not just by the storm, but also by a French threat to the Spanish territories in the Netherlands. Charles' sense of duty had meant he wanted to ensure peace before moving on; this was eventually concluded in a treaty at Noyon in 1516. Nevertheless, to his people in Spain, Charles was a reluctant foreigner, who knew nothing of the country, could not speak the language and brought with him foreign advisers. Furthermore, wishing to choose his own advisers, Charles dismissed, by letter, Cardinal Cisneros who had been acting as Regent. Unfortunately, Cisneros, who had been ill for some time, died on the same day as the letter arrived. The letter was seen as the cause of his demise. The scene was set for a potentially difficult reign unless Charles could charm his subjects, and also his ministers, quickly.

Unfortunately, even his confessor had his doubts, advising him: 'In your royal person, indolence is at war with fame. I pray that God's grace be upon you and that you will be able to overcome your natural enemies, good living and waste of time.'

Adding to Charles' difficulties, in 1519 he was elected Holy Roman Emperor as Charles V, on the death of his grandfather, Maximilian. This was a significant and weighty role in itself and increased concerns about the potential impact on his rule in Spain. No single person could hope to be a 'hands-on' ruler

■ Did you know?

The Holy Roman Emperor was chosen by seven electors. Often the election was decided in advance by the existing emperor persuading the seven electors to name his successor and give him the title of King of the Romans. Charles' grandfather, who was Holy Roman Emperor, died before he could do this. Consequently, Charles' election was contested by other rulers, for example Francis I of France. Charles resorted to bribery; borrowing from the Fugger family, German bankers. Once Charles had signed a statement agreeing to maintain the institution of the empire, he was duly elected.

■ Did you know?

Martin Luther was a German monk and professor at Wittenburg University. Through his study of the Christian scriptures, Luther concluded that salvation came though faith in God and not by doing good works. This started the Reformation making him an enemy of the Catholic Church. Although Luther was excommunicated, he still kept his beliefs. He clashed with Charles of Spain in his role as Holy Roman Emperor. Although Luther was eventually declared an outlaw, Charles abdicated from the empire in 1556, feeling he had failed. He was the first emperor ever to abdicate.

■ Did you know?

Charles spent only 16 years in Spain out of the 40 years of his reign, more time than he spent in any other part of his empire. He travelled around the country, but his visits were unevenly spread. Sometimes they caused major problems, as in 1527 when the crowds waiting to see him in Valencia were so great that a bridge collapsed and many died. Nevertheless, Charles was largely ignorant of Spanish affairs.

in all these possessions; Spain, as far as the Spaniards were concerned, would suffer.

Charles' extensive problems were:

■ rebels in the Netherlands wanting political and religious independence

■ issues in the Holy Roman Empire (now mostly modern-day Germany, Austria and Hungary), for example ambitious princes; Martin Luther and the Protestant Reformation; Ottoman Turks on the eastern border and in the Mediterranean

■ jealous French monarchs, threatened by the extent of Charles' territories

■ American possessions.

This was a heavy load for one young man who was just 19 years old, however effective and loyal his councillors might be.

One of Charles' advisers, Mercurino Gattinara, expressed his view of Charles' position in 1519: 'You are on the road towards Universal Monarchy, and on the point of uniting Christendom under a single shepherd.' However, although committed to his faith and with hopes for greater religious unity, Charles seemed to have no ambitions for creating an empire in which all states/components were governed from the centre. He is quoted as saying: 'There are those who say that I wish to rule the world, but both my thoughts and my deeds demonstrate the contrary.' He was probably acutely aware of the difficulties, tensions and opposition that could ensue, particularly in Spain, which was, like the empire, a collection of very different communities. Charles' lack of Spanish and mistakes made by his advisers created a tense atmosphere. The Cortes of Valencia even refused to recognise him as king until he visited the state. When he left Spain in 1520 to take up his role as Holy Roman Emperor, rebellion began. He did not return until 1522. When he did return, he spent the next seven years mostly in Castile and learned the language. Overall, he did spend more time in Spain than any other part of his empire, whilst constantly receiving a stream of reports from his other areas of responsibility, to which he wrote many replies himself.

First impressions clearly counted, yet Charles, over the years, was to prove, despite his failures, that he was dutiful and worked to try to ensure the security of Spain, defend his Catholic faith and destroy the Turks. He also pleased his Spanish subjects by his marriage to Isabella of Portugal. His son, Philip, born in 1527, settled the succession and provided some prospect of continuity. However, the period 1516–22 was one of great difficulty for Charles; he faced significant opposition and a range of political, financial and economic issues.

■ Key profile

Isabella of Portugal

Isabella of Portugal (1503–39) was the grandaughter of Queen Isabella of Castile, the elder daughter of Manuel I of Portugal and third in line to the throne of Portugal. Her marriage to Charles I of Spain was initiated in 1525 by proxy and finalised in 1526. Some records suggest that it was a happy marriage. Isabella acted as Regent in Spain during her husband's absences, demonstrating Charles' confidence in her ability to do so. They had five children, the eldest of whom became Philip II of Spain. Her death in 1539 was said to have devastated Charles, who never remarried.

Relations with the Cortes and the nobles

Charles I of Spain is usually seen as a ruler who followed and, when it seemed appropriate, developed the systems and policies of his grandparents, Ferdinand and Isabella. As Holy Roman Emperor, however, he was not always present in Spain even in the early years. His absences increased after 1529. Aragon, of course, had been used to an absentee monarchy.

A closer look

How effective was Charles I as King of Spain?

Hunt points out that, despite Charles' absences, he still made many decisions. For example, he was particularly interested in 'New Spain', i.e. the American possessions, and he assiduously read and dealt with the papers of the Council of the Indies, and even became involved in debates at the University of Salamanca about the ethics, or morality, of empire. Overall, Charles kept the nobles in line; they did not attempt to rebel, recognising that they relied on the Charles' government for their livelihood through payment for positions which were largely without responsibilities, and they were given tax exemptions.

However, Elliott is more critical, suggesting that Charles lacked initiative and saw his territories as 'a mere aggregation … almost fortuitously linked by a common sovereign', which led 'to a "freezing" of the various constitutional systems' and 'inhibited the development of any common institutional organisation for the (Spanish) empire as a whole'. These accusations of failure seem somewhat unfair; Charles' reponsibilities in the Holy Roman Empire would have made it difficult, in terms of time in particular, to impose constitutional reform and fully fuse systems in the kingdoms of Spain. In addition, there is no real evidence to suggest that such reform would have been greeted positively by the various kingdoms that would have had to implement the changes.

There was much, however, for Charles and his ministers to do; although the regency of Cisneros and earlier measures by the Catholic Monarchs had brought improvements, matters such as the roles and conduct of royal officials, corrupt officers and the power of the nobility were still areas ripe for change.

Relations with the Cortes

Relations with the Cortes were decidedly difficult at the start. In 1518, the Cortes held in Valladolid in Castile initially refused to recognise Charles as the King. It was vital for Charles to gain this acceptance of his royal authority. The Cortes wanted to extract as much from Charles as they could, for example they wanted him to respect Spanish laws, remove foreign advisers, learn Spanish (which he later did) and use Spanish officers in important posts. At one point, the Cortes of Castile declared: 'Most powerful lord, you are in our service.' Charles did eventually impose his authority on them, but not without a struggle. This is clearly seen when he was hoping to become Holy Roman Emperor and needed money. He summoned the Cortes at Santiago and Corunna; they gave him grants of money (*servicios*), but only after some stormy encounters and the application of a great deal of pressure and persuasion.

Activity

Talking point

What do you think was Charles' main strength as a potential King of Spain? What was his main weakness? Remember that you must be able to justify your decisions.

Did you know?

The Cortes of Castile met 15 times over the 40 years of Charles' reign. The Cortes of Aragon met 10 times. Although the number of times when the Cortes assembled was greater under Ferdinand and Isabella than in the reign of Charles I, Charles summoned the Cortes more regularly, on average every three years. In contrast, there was a gap of 18 years when Ferdinand and Isabella did not summon the Cortes at all.

In 1523, the Castilian Cortes met at Valladolid. Once in session, it began to discuss political issues. This was not the normal order of events and Charles had to step in and speak to them, asserting his authority. They would have to make the grant first. Source 1 is an extract from what Charles said.

> Yesterday I asked for funds; today I want your advice. Which seems to you better; that you should grant me the *servicio* at once, on my promise not to dismiss you until I have replied to and provided for everything that you must justly ask me, and that I should do so of my own free will: or that I should first reply to the petition which you bring me, and have it said that I should do so in order to get the *servicio*? You know that the custom had been to grant this first; thus it was done under my royal predecessors … Why try to establish an innovation with me? And since many evils have brought me to this necessity, you, like good and loyal subjects, will remedy them by doing your duty as I expect you to do.

1 *Quoted in J. Kilsby, **Spain: Rise and Decline, 1474–1643**, 1987*

Activity

Source analysis

Study Sources 1 and 2 carefully. Why do you think there was a differing response each time the Cortes was asked for money?

In 1525, at the Cortes of Toledo, in Castile, Charles proposed the idea of establishing a *Diputación* to get money from the Cortes. A *Diputación* was a committee that met in the absence of the Cortes to conduct business. This system was used in Aragon and allowed a permanent body to be set up to supervise the collection of the taxes and to ensure that Charles fulfilled his promise to the Cortes. This proposal was implemented.

In 1525, Charles described his views on the Castilian Cortes (Source 2).

> Since the *procurades* of the Cortes, who came at our command, are trying to serve us and to benefit our kingdoms, we are obliged to hear them benevolently and to receive the petitions, both general and special, and to answer them and do them justice; and we are ready to do this as our royal predecessors ordained; and we order that, before the Cortes are concluded, all the general and specific articles which may be presented on behalf of the kingdom shall be answered and that the necessary measures shall be taken as befits our service and the common benefit of our kingdoms.

2 *Quoted in G. Griffiths, **Representative Government in Western Europe in the Sixteenth Century**, 1968*

Cross-reference

For more information on revenue and financial issues, see Chapter 9 (pages 132–9).

In 1527, Charles was again in need of a special grant of money, this time to pay for campaigns against the Ottoman Turks. On this occasion, the Cortes of Castile refused and Charles, although he was given some private donations, got nothing else from them.

The Castilian Cortes was probably the most pliable of the Cortes, possibly because it was small; 18 towns sent two representatives each. There were usually no nobles or clergy present, which made it easier for Charles to make his demands.

However, the historian Maltby in *The Reign of Charles V* perceives that by 1525 Charles recognised that he could only go so far in using coercion to gain money grants or other rulings and developed an indirect means of managing the situation. He would send representatives to the town councils who would then discuss the matter and give reasons for their requests supported by personal letters from Charles. These letters also hinted at rewards that could include appointments that carried good salaries. Other honours might also be awarded. This process made it

Fig. 2 *Don Luis de Castello, a Spanish noble*

more likely that the government would then approve other legislation that the towns proposed.

Maltby also indicates that 'nearly half of the legislative edicts in his reign proceeded in the first instance from the petitions of the Cortes'. This view of the influence of the Cortes can be supported as Charles never tried to stop the members of the Cortes speaking freely; he recognised his duty to listen to their concerns. This is confirmed in the records of their meetings and can be seen in the comment Charles made to the Castilian Cortes in 1525 (Source 2).

Charles did, however, make some concessions, for example he allowed taxes to be paid by cities directly rather than through tax farmers.

There were, nevertheless, some confrontations with each of the three Cortes in Aragon over the period. For example, the Cortes suggested that Charles' brother Ferdinand become king and that Charles could be co-ruler with his mother Joanna, who was not of sound mind at this time. Although Charles was insensitive in his handling of the situation, this incident suggests that he was being influenced by some of his Burgundian/ Flemish advisers who were hoping for promotion. Charles subsequently appointed a Dutch bishop as Regent and a Piedmontese (Italian) diplomat and humanist as Chancellor. However, this particular incident occurred in the earlier period of the reign; opposition did reduce as time went on.

Relations with the nobles

The nobles disliked the fact that Charles I could not speak Castilian Spanish. Charles himself saw this as a problem. At the first meeting of the Cortes in Castile in 1518, he took a conciliatory approach and earned himself some breathing space by saying: 'To this request … I see the sense of it and I am in fact trying to learn Castilian.' Charles' 'foreignness' was also eased by his marriage to Isabella of Portugal in 1525. A further positive move was to exempt nobles from taxes and employ them in his government.

Another issue for Charles' administration was the appointment of foreigners to public office. When Charles returned to the Holy Roman Empire on the death of his grandfather, Maximilian, to stand for election in his place, Adrian of Utrecht was appointed as his Regent. He was clearly not a Castilian. This was one of the factors in the outbreak of the revolt of the Comuneros. Charles took note and later used members of his family, particularly his Portuguese wife, Isabella, to act as Regent.

Cross-reference

Look back to Chapter 6 (page 85) for a definition of tax farming.

Activity

Thinking point

How effectively did Charles I deal with the Cortes in the period 1516–29?

Cross-reference

For more information about the Comuneros Revolt, see Chapter 8 (pages 114–20).

Key profile

Adrian of Utrecht

Adrian (1459–1523) was born in the Netherlands, went to university in Louvain, France, and eventually became the equivalent of a modern-day Vice-Chancellor. He was tutor to the future Charles V when Charles was just seven years old. Adrian went to Spain as part of a diplomatic mission and then pursued his career there. He became Inquisitor-General of Aragon in 1516 and head of the united Inquisition of Aragon and Castile in 1518. In 1520, Adrian was appointed Regent of Spain. In 1522, he was elected as Pope, succeeding the corrupt Leo X, and set about reforming the papacy and the Church. However, Adrian was limited in his success. He controversially announced that popes could make mistakes in matters of faith, thus denying papal infallibility.

Only on one occasion did Charles attempt to tax the nobles. He suggested that they meet and discuss a proposal to tax food, which could have impacted significantly on their lifestyles. As might be anticipated, they were adamant that they had always been exempt from taxation and should remain so. This outcome was not surprising. What was remarkable was that Charles was prepared even to raise the question.

Royal councils and conciliar government

Ferdinand and Isabella had ruled successfully through councils and Charles I followed their example. Gattinara, Charles' chief minister, was the main channel through which policies were subsequently agreed.

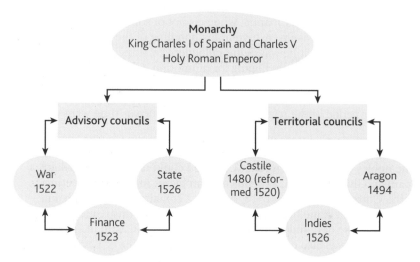

Fig. 3 *Councils established in Spain by 1556*

These advisory councils had no fixed base, as there was no confirmed capital city. They travelled around Spain and sometimes followed Charles to Europe, so that they could be available as required. However, over the reign, they were centred increasingly on Valladolid.

Their conclusions were usually presented in reports to the King, who would then decide whether to take any action or not. Most councils could not implement policies without the King's consent, particularly as there were not always enough officials out in the provinces to carry out the work. The councils can be seen as useful in keeping Charles informed about the opinions of the people and checking the power of the nobility. Charles relied on his secretaries who were professionally trained, competent and efficient. The overlaps between the duties/responsibilities of each council meant that good royal secretaries gained extensive knowledge of government policies and decisions. They were 'the power behind the throne'.

However, there were concerns about the Council of Finance; it had no authority to prevent Charles spending large amounts of money on foreign wars and sometimes on his own personal requirements. Payments, such as interest on royal debts, were not included in its calculations. Consequently, it was difficult for the King's secretaries to know how much money was available at any given time.

Table 1 *Royal advisory councils in the reign of Charles I*

Council	Role	Further information
1522 Council of War	An advisory council dealing with coordination of the military.	A new council; its members were largely the same as the Council of State.
1523 Council of Finance	Dealt with the accounts of the monarchy, as well as the finances of Castile.	A new council and often considered the most innovative. Set up by Gattinara. All members were Spanish. Cobos and Henry, the Count of Nassau, were significant members. It met daily to consider income and expenditure, oversaw borrowing, drew up budgets, etc.
1526 Council of the Indies	Jurisdiction over all American issues, including administrative, judicial and religious matters – a similar role to the Council of Castile in Spain.	Judicial authority was given to the six *audiencias* (courts of appeal) and viceroys who dealt with these issues. This separation of authority created an effective system of checks and balances to ensure that the crown in Spain remained the chief authority.
1526 Council of State	An advisory body; discussion of all matters and particularly foreign policy; oversaw the work of the other councils.	Members included Gattinara, the Count of Nassau and five others. Seen largely as a way of giving members prestige without the monarchy losing any power.
Royal Council of Castile (established 1480)	The highest administrative body in terms of internal matters; a Supreme Court of law; also gave advice, e.g. on relations with Portugal, the government of Spain and the empire.	Usually about 12 members, but grew over time along with its responsibilities; mostly staffed by churchmen and *letrados* with fewer nobles than previously.
Council of Aragon (established 1494)	Concerned largely with judicial matters and was the court of highest appeal in the state.	Members were mostly *letrados* rather than nobles and were usually drawn from the three kingdoms of Aragon. The treasurer in this period was Castilian.

The secretaries, who were the equivalent of modern-day civil servants, had significant authority. They decided, for example:

- who dealt with correspondence: Charles personally, or someone else
- to issue decrees in agreement with the King only, without consulting the council.

This meant secretaries had considerable influence on affairs of state. However, secretaries were not university trained. There were also frequent complaints about bribery and corruption. Cobos, who came from a poor family, had an annual income of 60,000 ducats when he retired; this was similar to, and possibly better than, some of the nobility. Secretaries often passed their role on from father to son (suitably trained). Although this ensured continuity, it also could limit innovation.

Cobos was important for his actions to try to streamline the system by creating an archive (record) of the work of councils for future reference. Papers initially tended to be kept in one of three places: Segovia, Medina del Campo and Valladolid, but were eventually all collected at Simancas.

 Cross-reference

For more information on Cobos and his role as secretary, see pages 109–10.

The members of the councils came from the same social strata as the secretaries, but were, usually, also university educated and had practised law or worked in the Church. Most achieved this status after working on *audiencias* (the High Court). This often meant that they knew very little about finance and the economy and were often rather elderly by the time they took up office. Like the secretaries, members of the councils were often open to bribery. Cobos' significant income of 60,000 ducats per annum was most likely as a result of bribes. Petitioners for titles and jobs often paid the councillors to speed up their request. Occasionally, nobles attended the councils in an honorary position but they were never permanent members.

Other important officials were the viceroys who operated in the Americas. They were very closely linked to councils in Spain, for example Francis of Toledo in Peru sent all of his reports to the Council of the Indies. The home-based council was expected to ensure there was no abuse of power by the viceroys in their distant territories. The process was:

- councillors read the report
- a document (*consulta*) summarised the views of members of the council on specific aspects
- the *consulta* was sent to the King
- the King made decisions or asked other groups for their views
- the King personally wrote the decisions on the original document
- a letter was sent to the viceroy for his action.

This system often slowed down processes, although it did provide safeguards and potentially prevent hasty and ill-advised decisions. However, it was more often viewed as a hindrance, as seen in the comment of one historian about the time taken and quantities of paper used to reach a decision. It was said that: 'No states were more governed in the sixteenth century than those of the King of Spain, if government can be measured by the amount of discussion devoted to any individual problem and by the quantities of paper expended on the solution.' In addition, all this bureaucracy often hindered rather than helped development of these new territories, and the sheer distance between them and Spain also meant long delays.

Partnership with the nobility

Ferdinand and Isabella had expended much energy and money in attempting to 'tame' the nobility. Noble rights and grants had generally been confirmed and many had been 'civilised', at least on the surface, by the courtly life. Rights to collected local taxes and grants of land from the war with Granada had done much to contain them. On Ferdinand's death, however, the nobles saw their chance and sabotaged attempts by the Regent, Cisneros, to maintain law and order.

Charles I, unfortunately, did not immediately endear himself to the nobility of Spain. For example:

- Burgundians and Flemings were given land in the New World, for example in the Yucatan and Cuba.
- Charles' tutor, Lord of Chièvres, gained the right to appoint to all vacant posts in America.
- Chièvres' nephew, at 17, was made a cardinal and granted the archbishopric of Toledo on Cisneros' death.

Activity

Talking point

What were the advantages and disadvantages of this conciliar system? In pairs, make a list of points and then consider how effective they were likely to be. Compare your conclusions with other pairs.

Exploring the detail

Emigration to the New World created demand for the trade of goods from Spain, for example wine, oil and grain. Soon the farmers in Spain found they could not keep up with the demand unless they brought more land into production. This led to significant borrowing at a rate of 7 per cent interest plus. Charles made the situation worse by refusing to allow the Catalans the right to trade in the New World. Inflation meant they could not match the prices of their foreign competitors and, consequently, their trading activities declined.

Charles himself, when elected as Holy Roman Emperor, put that title before that of King of Spain, suggesting that he regarded the kingship as an inferior role. This action played a part in generating the Comuneros Revolt. Once the revolt began, the nobles felt threatened by the scale of the movement in the towns and the countryside, fearing radical revolution against themselves.

These disturbances were significant but, overall, short-lived; after the battle at Villalar and the surrender of Toledo, the Comuneros collapsed. From this time onwards, the nobility were manoevred into seeking careers rather than power in the conventional sense; whether this really generated partnership or simply an uneasy alliance with the crown was not clear at the time. In addition, Charles also secured control over the towns. There was no further open antagonism to the monarchy, either from the nobles or the lower classes. Charles, however, remained in Spain for some time after the revolt, rather than returning immediately to his responsibilities in Europe.

Cross-reference

For more information on the Germania and Comuneros revolts, see Chapter 8 (pages 114–20).

A closer look

Interpretations of Charles' relations with the nobles

MacDonald argues that the nobility were 'one of the major pillars of his (Charles') success in ruling Spain. During the Comuneros Revolt, the nobility had proved their value to the crown in the maintenance of effective royal government.' The nobles were the government's shield against rebellion and riot in the countryside; peasants respected the local lord or churchman as the main agent of control. Consequently, Charles, was careful to avoid offending the nobles in case he should need their help again. Kilsby supports this view: the nobles' authority had been enhanced by their prompt assistance in defeating the Comuneros. Many of them were given rewards, such as employment in the Castilian government and exemption from many taxes. The Duke of Alva was given an honorary position in the Council of State. Some nobles showed their gratitude and loyalty in their action to repress the Germania Revolt. Kilsby also suggests that the victory cleared the way for Charles and Spain to take on a more high-profile role in European affairs. Mulgan makes the point that the issue of noble loyalty was not political but economic; the nobility would not oppose Charles as long as their tax exemption was untouched.

Activity

Thinking point

Which of the interpretations of the relationship between Charles and the nobility is most appropriate; were they his rivals or his loyal servants? Explain the reasons for your view.

The role of the *letrados* and the bureaucracy

Letrados, or lawyers, were fast becoming the new aristocracy in Spain. The best trained were those who studied at Salamanca, Valladolid or Alcalá University. After studying law for 10 years, they could take up posts in government. This raised interest generally in education and encouraged the idea of a trained bureaucracy. Kilsby agrees that they were well trained, but suggests that they often tended to have little independence of thought. For a role in government at the lower end, this may not have been always necessary.

Secretaries also had apprentices whom they trained and then used their powers of patronage to place them appropriately. This generated a powerful network amongst the *letrados* that could also be a potential security threat. A negative view of this consequence would suggest

Did you know?

The best *letrados* could rise to the rank of secretary. Their duties would be to:

- prepare agendas for council meetings
- countersign all royal documents
- distribute correspondence to the King or his advisers/councils
- issue royal decrees with the consent of the council
- recommend individuals for appointment.

■ **Cross-reference**

Look back to Chapter 1 (pages 16–18) for more on the Royal Council and conciliar government.

that it also perpetuated systems, inhibited change and encouraged the appointment of officials with few ideas or interest in change. There were also multiple opportunities for corrupt practices. In fact, this was to some extent encouraged by a policy which suggested that hard work could lead to favours; petitions from those who claimed to have done work for the King went to the councils and a select number were then passed on to the King. Councillors were happy to receive payments from the applicants to speed up and support their claims.

In addition to the *letrados* and secretaries, there were countless other officials, clerks, scribes, inspector and tax collectors who were seen as essential in making the system work.

The roles of Gattinara and Cobos

Both Gattinara and Cobos were advisers/secretaries to Charles I in the 1520s and Cobos also in the 1530s; although from very different backgrounds, they were to influence Charles' actions strongly.

Fig. 4 *Gattinara – cardinal, lawyer and statesman in the reign of Charles I*

■ **Key profile**

Mercurino Gattinara

Gattinara (1465–1530) was an Italian by birth and rose rapidly in both the Church and the administration. He became one of Charles I and V's main advisers. He began by reforming the Council of Castile, which remained the most important element of the government, and set up a new Council of Finance and a Council of the Indies. The restructuring of the Council of Finance (*Consejo de Hacienda*) was possibly the greatest of Gattinara's reforms; he took the idea from a similar institution in Flanders.

A longer-term project, not completed until the 1540s, was the setting up of an archive of official documents in the fortress of Simancas, near Valladolid in northern Castile. Papers that had been scattered were now kept in one place.

Whether through his own ambition or to promote Charles I, Gattinara encouraged the King to build a Christian empire that could dominate Protestants and Turks, as well as the native population of the New World. Whether it can be substantiated that Gattinara was the sole influence on this issue is not clear. MacDonald states that:

> ... the Emperor was often over-dependent on advisers and members of his family. In the 1520s there is evidence that he was somewhat in thrall to Gattinara. For long periods the internal affairs of Spain ... appear to have been guided not by the Emperor, but by his appointed deputies and advisers.

3
S. MacDonald, *Charles V, Ruler, Dynast and Defender of the Faith, 1500–1558*, 1992

However, it was obvious that Protestants and Turks should be challenged. The threat they posed to the religious and political stability of Europe meant that Charles would have responded eventually. His whole upbringing and education led him to see Islam as a threat to Catholicism. In addition, Gattinara was observant and saw Italy and the papacy as the key to the domination of Europe. In 1521, he officially became an adviser to Charles I. Charles did become involved in wars in Italy and even held the Pope hostage for a brief period.

Francisco de los Cobos is equally significant.

Fig. 5 *Francisco de los Cobos: councillor, adviser, financial secretary and servant of the King*

■ **Key profile**

Francisco de los Cobos

Cobos (1477–1547) had previously worked as an accountant for Queen Isabella. By 1510, he had experience of work related to the Indies and had invested a small amount in projects over there. He joined Charles I's court in 1516; by 1520, he was in charge of the administration of Castile. When Charles I decided to restructure his government, Cobos wrote criteria for the new councils, for example the Council of Finance, and also some job descriptions. By 1529, he was secretary of state and dealt with relations with Spain and Italy. He travelled widely with Charles I and V in this period, returning to Castile in the 1530s. He dealt with the affairs of Castile, Portugal, the Indies and, later, Italy.

Charles chose the best men to work for him; preferring the lesser gentry rather than nobility. Often those he chose had some training and had worked in small towns, but had no formal qualifications. They were hard-working, reliable and grateful for the opportunities he gave them. Cobos himself fitted these latter criteria well and set a good example, although he also made a personal fortune out of many of the 'gifts' he was given. He bought land and built palaces, collecting tapestries and fine pictures. His daughter made a good marriage to a duke and his son became a marquis. Despite this 'weakness', he continued to serve Charles V until his death in 1547.

■ **Did you know?**

The career of Francisco de los Cobos demonstrates the meteoric rise to power possible for hard-working, intelligent and ambitious, but often poor, young men in this period. Recommended by Zafra, Isabella's secretary, Cobos had previously worked as an accountant for Queen Isabella. His skills ensured that he continued to provide expert advice and support. Elliott suggests that 'the government of Spain ran so smoothly under the gentle guidance of Cobos that it almost seemed ... that the country had no internal history ... an unnatural calm had descended on Castile'.

Charles wrote to his son, later to be Philip II:

> Do not give him [Cobos] more influence than I have sanctioned in my instructions. Cobos is a very rich man, for he draws a great deal from the dues for smelting the bullion from the Indies, as also from the mines and other sources ... When I die perhaps it would be a good moment to resume these rights to the crown

4   *Quoted in J. Kilsby,* **Spain: Rise and Decline, 1474–1643***, 1987*

Despite this suggestion, Charles was effectively sanctioning this acquisition of wealth and other favours during an individual's lifetime. Charles is also reputed to have been suspicious of the influence of wives, particularly the wife of Cobos. This suggests how much power women had, even though it was not formalised. Sometimes Charles wrote personally to his ministers and ambassadors, possibly to avoid allowing his secretaries (or their wives!) to know so much. 16th-century politicians were obviously subject to the same potential problems as any modern-day politician. Cobos, however, was clearly an exceptional politician, although it is doubtful that he alone influenced the course of events in Spain.

Activity

Group activity

In small groups:

Either: Write a letter of application for the role of Royal Secretary to Charles I. Remember to point out your abilities and strengths in context, for example in devising systems of work, writing letters, running meetings, dealing with accounts, etc. Include some personal information and explain why you want the post.

Or: Set up an interview situation to decide who is the strongest candidate for the role of Royal Secretary. Choose some of the class as applicants who should produce an application letter with details about themselves for the interviewing panel. Other students can form the panel of interviewers. They should devise some questions to ask the candidates based on the requirements for the role of the secretary, but they could also ask some more personal questions to find out about individual strengths and weaknesses – is the candidate patient, do they listen well, are they someone who others could work with? Award points for the strengths of each applicant.

■ The extent of continuity with the reigns of Ferdinand and Isabella

Historians have often debated the idea of a 'revolution in government', in the reign of Charles I. There are some arguments for and against. The very fact that Charles was not from Spain himself, although partly of Spanish stock, might be significant. Although young and inexperienced, he came with no 'trappings' or preconceived ideas. In this latter respect, Charles was different to his grandparents and prepared to make changes. He was, like them, however, a peripatetic monarch, but more so, moving backwards and forwards between the Holy Roman Empire and Spain, and lacked the time to make many major changes.

Table 2 *Comparisons between the reigns of Ferdinand and Isabella and Charles I*

Some similarities with the reign of Ferdinand and Isabella	Some differences from the reign of Ferdinand and Isabella
They were both peripatetic monarchs; Ferdinand and Isabella travelled constantly round their territories; Charles I travelled between his Spanish kingdom and the Holy Roman Empire; when he was in Spain, he did spend time in both kingdoms.	The conciliar system of government aready existed in Spain, but Charles extended and revised it with the introduction of the Council of War and the Council of State.
Charles ruled through councils as did Ferdinand and Isabella; but he also added new ones, e.g. Finance, the Indies.	The Cortes met marginally more frequently under Ferdinand and Isabella: Aragon met 10 times and Castile 15 times in Charles' reign. Under Ferdinand and Isabella, the Aragonese met 17 times and the Castilian Cortes met 16 times.
Charles continued to summon the Cortes – he used the Castilian Cortes more than the Aragonese because of the traditional liberties of the Aragonese Cortes.	Charles used more advisers from the upper-middle and middle classes rather than relying on noble families.

Activity

Class activity

As a class, identify differences between the governments of Ferdinand and Isabella and Charles I, such as those outlined in Table 2. Refer back to Chapters 1, 3, 4 and 5 to help you. Discuss your findings as a class. Did any of these changes amount to a 'revolution' in government?

Summary question

'The role of the secretary was the critical element in the operation of Charles I's government of Spain.' To what extent do you agree with this view?

8 The growth and extent of opposition

The immediate reaction to Charles' arrival in Spain was not promising. Although he was granted the right to be king by his mother, Joanna, the Cortes were less welcoming. In Castile, the Cortes declared: 'Most powerful lord, you are in our service.' It was not a good omen.

Rady describes Charles as 'a lonely boy. Inarticulate and shy, he would often eat alone. He was pale, his eyes seemed to pop out; his jaw was large … Less charitable observers diagnosed mental retardation.' As the new and very young ruler of a large and complex country, Charles was also a foreigner. More positively, he had been brought up as a Burgundian prince in 'the loving care of his aunt, the Archduchess, Margaret of Austria'. Charles' tutors had trained him well, constantly exhorting him to remain true to his faith and to his subjects. He was devout, conscientious, considered advice carefully and tried to follow it. Nevertheless, he made mistakes, for example appointing a teenager, who was not even Spanish, to the Archbishopric of Toledo. Although thoughtful, he appeared dull. He never really revealed his true self.

The unity that had developed in the reign of Ferdinand and Isabella had succeeded largely because they were Spanish monarchs and always present in their territories; Charles, despite his Spanish origins, had spent most of his life in the Holy Roman Empire. He was now the ruler of both Spain and the Holy Roman Empire in an age with limited means of communication. His subjects in Spain were an unknown quantity and he was unsure how to deal with them.

Although King of Spain, Charles could not suspend his obligations to the Holy Roman Empire once he became the Emperor Charles V in 1519. The empire itself was a weak alliance of more than 300 states with differing constitutions; loyalties to the empire and its ruler were variable. The period 1516–22 was to be crucial for the establishment of his authority.

Fig. 1 *Catherine of Aragon: wife of Henry VIII, cousin of Charles I*

■ The causes and impact of the Germania and Comuneros revolts

From the start of Charles' reign, problems piled up. Two of these were the Germania and Comuneros revolts. The causes had grown over time. Dealing with them was a severe test of Charles' skills, and those of his advisers, in ruling Spain.

The Germania Revolt, 1519–21

The Germania were a Christian brotherhood, originally formed to protect the coast of Valencia from Muslim pirates. The Germania Revolt was an urban revolt and began first in May of 1519 in Valencia. Some of the factors generating the revolt were as follows:

■ The promised Cortes, to be held in Valencia, did not materialise because of the plague.

■ Nobles left the city to avoid the plague; the plague was seen by the Church as a punishment for immoral behaviour; ordinary citizens felt that the most immoral of all, i.e. the nobles, had not suffered.

- Members of the Germania were finding it difficult to get food as a consequence of the plague.
- Resentment towards the *Moriscos*/Moors; members of the Germania believed that the Inquisition was too lenient with them.
- The order to guilds to arm and prepare for raids by the Turks provided the residents with weapons.

The leader of the Germania was initially Juan Llorenc, a local weaver. He wanted Valencia to become a separate republic, modelled on Venice. He set up a committee of 13 (to represent Christ and the apostles) and this group generated the revolt. As it spread, local priests and the poor began attacking landlords and government officials. The unrest forced the governor, the Count of Melito, to leave the city, but he then raised an army, only to be defeated in 1521 at the Battle of Gandia. The next leader of the revolt was Vicente Peris, an extremist, who had seized control from Llorenc. Peris wanted to create an independent republic. He attacked nobles and forcibly baptised *Moriscos*, but was defeated in battle in 1521 and subsequently executed in 1522.

Key profile

Vicente Peris

Peris (1478–1522) was a member of the Council of 13 which governed Valencia and became its leader after the death of Llorenc. By 1520, he was almost at war with the Viceroy, Mendoza. A number of cities were taken over; property and goods were seized to pay to support the rebel troops. Many Muslims joined the noble armies, but were forcibly baptised as Christians if they were found by the rebels. Peris' most important victory was at the Battle of Gandia in 1521 during the Comuneros Revolt. Despite this, Valencia fell to the government in 1521. Peris was captured and executed in 1522. His head was put in a cage and hung up for all to see. His descendants were regarded as traitors down to the fourth generation.

Outcome

The Germania was a violent movement. The reaction to it played some part in the defeat of the less bloody, but larger scale, Comuneros Revolt. It alarmed the nobles and made them less sympathetic to the Comuneros Revolt. Resistance continued, albeit rather haphazardly, until 1524, when most remaining rebels surrendered. Many were put to death, fined or had their property confiscated. The nobility's authority appeared to be consolidated.

The Germania Revolt failed for a number of reasons:

- Too many of the poor and powerless, i.e. peasants, artisans and labourers were involved.
- The revolt occurred only in one place and so was easily quelled.
- It sprang out of the weakness of the crown at this time – a young inexperienced leader who had other major responsibilities – but one who was quick to learn the lesson and respond.
- Disagreement within the rebels, for example some were too extreme and wanted to establish independent city republics.
- The forces of the crown, aristocracy and Church combined were too strong for the rebels.

Exploring the detail

Llorenc and the guilds

Juan Llorenc (1458–1520) was the leader of a guild and saw the guilds as a counterbalance to the power of the nobility. Llorenc proposed that two representatives to the Council of Valencia be elected by the people of the city. When the votes were counted, Llorenc's candidates had clearly won, but the Viceroy refused to admit them. Riots ensued and the crown's administration of the city collapsed. Llorenc himself died shortly afterwards as the result of a heart attack.

Activity

Talking point

1 How would you rank the factors explaining the defeat of the Germania? Work in pairs and compare your views with the rest of the class to see if you achieve a consensus.

2 Are there any other factors you can identify as reasons for defeat?

Differing views of the Germania Revolt

Historians have disagreed about the Germania Revolt; it has been seen as radical, almost verging on a social revolution, despite its failure and, alternatively as a purely political revolt. MacDonald prefers political motivation for the revolt in Valencia; its focus was a clash between the crown and subjects rather than between workers in the towns and the nobles. 'Its origins lay in the distinctive racial, social and political circumstances of Valencia.' MacDonald also suggests that this revolt is far less important than that of the Comuneros, but agrees that it attracted broad support, largely because Charles was not 'the desired heir' and the fact that his mother, Joanna, was still alive, although incapable of taking over the crown. Charles' Burgundian advisers must also bear some of the blame. Kamen suggests they behaved 'as though they were in a conquered country'.

Both Kamen and Elliott, however, also propose deeper motives:

- Social divisions triggered by the new monarchy.
- Old rivalries between Aragon and Castile erupted; Charles spent longer in Aragon than he did in Castile, yet Castile was the larger state and was considered the centre of government.
- Charles' arrival polarised different interest groups, for example, in economic terms, wool exporters hoped to gain from a market in the Netherlands, but textile producers were afraid of growing competition with the Netherlands.

Kilsby considers the outcome:

- Suppression of the revolts suggested Charles was a strong, effective and potentially 'absolute' monarch.
- Leaders were executed; a general pardon was issued for other participants.
- Nobles continued to play an active part in local government.
- The powers of local officials such as *corregidores* were strengthened.
- The Cortes generally accepted all government proposals.

Kilsby suggests that Spain, from this time onwards, became an outward looking country; its monarch was a European monarch rather than a purely Spanish monarch defending Spanish interests. This last argument, however, cannot be fully supported. Charles' successor, his son Philip, was not Holy Roman Emperor. He devoted himself fully both to internal matters and to the defence of his state. His belief in the Divine Right of Kings, the control he exercised from his capital Madrid, his supervision of the Castilian Cortes that met largely only to grant him money, and his ability to dominate the Church demonstrate Philip's extensive authority and commitment to Spain.

The Comuneros Revolt, 1520–21

The Comuneros were groups of rebels composed mostly of townspeople, but also including some clergy and nobles. The revolts erupted in the towns of northern Castile sparked by Charles' demands for funds from the Cortes to support his bid for the crown of the Holy Roman Empire.

The Comuneros Revolt overlapped with that of the Germania, albeit in different states of Spain, making it a more dangerous revolt than it might otherwise have been. It was also more serious because a number of revolts broke out in different places at similar times.

Causes

There were a range of factors and events that led to the outbreak of the Comuneros Revolt beginning in May of 1520, only to end with defeat at the Battle of Villalar in 1521.

One of these was that Charles I was basically a foreigner to the Spaniards and remained so for most of his reign. Kilsby quotes a contemporary writer saying, 'amongst Spaniards, no foreigner is accounted of importance'. Charles' 'foreignness' made them anxious about where his loyalties lay and how much he knew about Spain and its people. He spoke no Spanish at first and he had few Spanish advisers in his retinue. In addition, many of the officials appointed were foreigners. He also put his imperial title first, rather than his Spanish one. There was also concern that Charles' responsibilities elsewhere might need to be funded by Spain; this would mean higher taxation. Alternatively, Spain might lose its separate identity and be absorbed into his other territories.

Fig. 2 *Execution of Communards at Segovia*

Another factor was the protests that began in Toledo and other places; the nobility began to divide into factions, some of which were based on long-standing family feuds or were linked to competition for office rather than as a consequence of the national situation. For example, the Riberas family, who had lost some pre-eminence with the death of Ferdinand, were initially sidelined, but soon restored to a position of prominence when the Ayalas family were discredited because they supported Archbishop Cisneros. Loyalties to Castile or Aragon were important. Juan de Padilla, a member of the Riberas faction, made written demands that a meeting of town representatives should be held to discuss the fact that Charles had slighted Castile by spending too long in Aragon. Some of this opposition was also spurred on by Padilla's wife, who felt that her husband had not been justly rewarded for his loyalty to the crown. Castilians were angry that senior government posts were given to Burgundians rather than Castilians.

Religion was also a factor. A group of friars made it clear to their local Cortes in Santiago that they would not support any agreement by the Cortes to grant money to the King. Jews were also scapegoated. In 1521, the Constable of Castile suggested that the *conversos* were the root cause of the revolt despite the lack of evidence. A further grievance was that the much respected Cardinal Cisneros was replaced by a 17-year-old as archbishop of Toledo.

A serious challenge to Charles as the rightful ruler of Castile came from the Cortes of Castile in 1518, led by Juan de Zumel. This challenge failed, but was followed by various demands including that he learn Spanish, use native officials and maintain the laws of Spain. In return for these concessions, Charles asked for money. The Cortes had little choice but to vote the money.

In addition, the towns were already hostile to the nobility, increasingly so after the death of Isabella in 1504. This promoted open opposition between the two groups. There were also concerns

Did you know?

The youth who replaced Cisneros was the nephew of Chievres, one of Charles' advisers from the Netherlands. Earlier, Cisneros, as Regent, had annoyed the nobles by proposing the creation of a militia that would be paid for by the cities rather than the nobles using their own supporters. The nobles felt sidelined. Cisneros abandoned the plan, but the damage had been done.

Did you know?

Demands of the Comuneros

The Comuneros made a wide range of demands that reflect their grievances. Here are some examples:

'After him (Charles) no woman can succeed to the throne of this kingdom; if there are no sons, then sons of daughters and granddaughters born and baptised in Castile shall inherit the throne.

Offices in the royal house must be given to persons born and baptised in Castile and the king, whilst he is in Castile, cannot make use of persons who are not born in Castile.'

J. Cowans (ed.), 2003

Activity

Group activity

In pairs, identify the factors that explain the outbreak of the Comuneros Revolt and produce a diagram that demonstrates the long and short-term causes and the linkages between the causes of the revolt. Make a presentation of your work to the whole class. See how much you all agree.

Activity

Revision exercise

Follow up the group activity above by writing an individual essay: 'Charles' demands for money to support his bid to become Holy Roman Emperor were the main cause of the Comuneros Revolt.' How valid is this assessment?

about the future of the wool trade, which might now be diverted to the empire with consequent loss of earnings for Spain.

The news that the Holy Roman Emperor was dead, and the fact that Maximilian was Charles' grandfather, suggested that Charles would have good prospects of taking over the role of emperor. However, in order to take over the role, Charles had to be chosen by the seven electors; one way to encourage their support was through bribery. Money needed to be raised. Charles, therefore, held a Cortes at Santiago. Santiago was probably chosen because its coastal position made Charles' departure for the empire easier. Charles' demand for money to bribe the electors of the Holy Roman Empire (Germany) was seen as an outrage; it was even more objectionable because Santiago was not even eligible to send representatives to the Cortes being held in their own town in Spain. Matters were made worse by rumours that the demand for finance would lead to taxes on things such as infant baptism and even water. Also, success for Charles would mean an absentee monarch for Spain. Although few representatives had actually been given authority by their towns to grant money, they ultimately agreed to do so after a further change of venue to Corunna. The tax, however, was never actually collected and attempts to do so led to collectors being mobbed.

The combination of all these factors was dangerous; only a spark was needed and that was supplied by the involvement of two rival noble factions, the Ayalas and the Riberas. The Ayalas supported Padilla and his opposition to the crown, and the Riberas became supporters of Charles' chief minister, Chievres. The rebellion finally began in Toledo where Juan de Padilla set up a government in the name of the King, the Queen and the *Comunidad*.

Events

Events followed a pattern of violent outbreaks in several towns, for example in Castilian towns they were aimed at royal officials. Many *corregidores* were driven out; usually a local family of some standing would take over. There were often calls for some kind of representative assembly or commune as set up by Juan de Padilla in Toledo. He was anxious to show that this was not a movement against the crown and declared the new government to be in the King's name. However, fighting in the streets between factions was not uncommon. The town of Medina del Campo, which refused to give up its artillery peacefully to the crown's troops, became the victim of fighting, looting and burning, which literally destroyed large swathes of the city. This only reinforced the rebels in their opposition and actually increased the numbers involved. Towns both south and north joined the movement – for example, Segovia, Salamanca and Valladolid.

Key profile

Juan de Padilla

Padilla (1490–1521) was one of the leaders of the Comuneros. He made a number of demands, for example to see the royal accounts and that posts should be given to loyal Spaniards and not foreigners. He also stated that they, the Comuneros, had freed prisoners, refused to pay tithes, and seized some of the gold from the Indies. He complained bitterly about the absence of Charles I because of his duties as Holy Roman Emperor; he demanded that Charles return immediately to Spain.

A junta was set up by the rebels in Avila, but there was little agreement about how to proceed and what should be the demands made to the crown. The rebels eventually decided to get the support of Joanna, Charles' mother, whom they proposed to present as the real monarch, although she was of unsound mind at this time and would not have been a good advertisement for the cause. Joanna was either well advised or sensible enough to refuse to take action or sign any papers. Adrian of Utrecht, the Regent, was, however, forced to leave Valladolid.

The rebels eventually did present some demands:

■ Economic and social reform, for example reduced taxes.
■ Limitations of the power of the nobles, for example towns refused to pledge loyalty to the local landlords.

They also proposed to continue the uprisings with 'fire, sack and blood … against the estates and properties of grandees, *caballeros* and other enemies of the realm'. This casts the rebellion as a social as well as a political movement, stemming the tide of sympathy from some of the aristocracy for the lower classes. Nobles were not prepared to see their control over land and towns reduced. They worried about the growing demands of the peasants on their estates and the fact that some towns wanted to become independent of all other authority. Some significant figures changed sides and brought a last burst of activity, for example from the Bishop of Zamora who threw his lot in with the rebels.

Cross-reference

Look back to Chapter 7 (page 103) to refresh your memory about Adrian of Utrecht.

Key profile

The Bishop of Zamora

The Bishop of Zamora had been one of Ferdinand and Isabella's representatives in Rome; he had seized his bishopric by force in 1507 (although the Pope had agreed to appoint him). He subsequently became involved in the Comuneros movement and took advantage of the uprisings to go to Toledo and have himself proclaimed archbishop by the people. The previous archbishop, who had resisted his claims, had died. Zamora had a private army of more than 2,000. He was eventually captured and imprisoned for five years. He made a failed attempt to escape and, in the process, killed his jailor. He was condemned to death, tortured and garrotted. His body was put out on show at Simancas as a warning to other would-be rebels.

However, the Constable of Castile gathered an army and met the Comuneros at Villalar, near Toro in April, 1521. The battle was short and decisive; the Comuneros were no match for the royal army. Padilla and another of the leaders were captured and executed. Toledo surrendered and the Bishop of Zamora fled, but was quickly captured and imprisoned, later to be hanged. The casualties were surprisingly few; possibly 200 rebels and 20 on the King's side.

Why did the Comuneros fail? Consider these two different views and decide which is the better explanation:

1 The movement failed because it did not keep to its initial aim of protecting Spain from a foreign ruler. Instead, it became an attack on the aristocracy. It was really a peasant uprising to demand fewer and lighter taxes. There was also uncertainty amongst the participants about what would happen if victory was gained; some factions wanted to create breakaway governments and become independent from the existing Spanish state. Joanna's unwillingness to act as a figurehead for the rebellion was also a factor, although she would have been incapable of taking on such a role.

2 Lack of unity was important, i.e. there were missed opportunities to join with the Germania Revolt, and the rivalry between towns in Castile particularly prevented a coordinated movement.

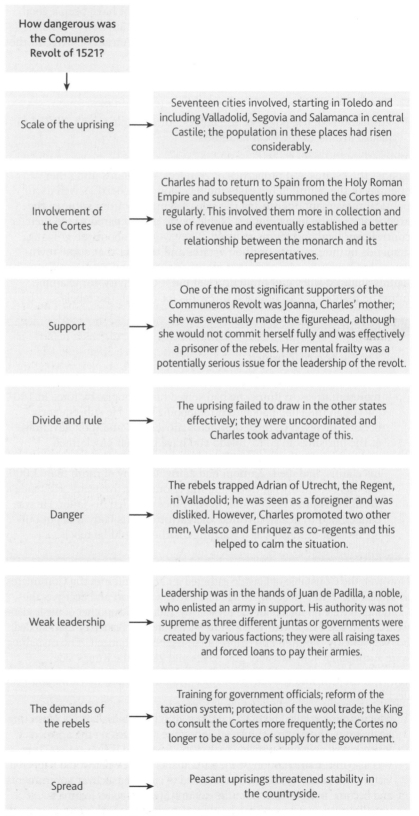

How dangerous was the Comuneros Revolt of 1521?	
Scale of the uprising	Seventeen cities involved, starting in Toledo and including Valladolid, Segovia and Salamanca in central Castile; the population in these places had risen considerably.
Involvement of the Cortes	Charles had to return to Spain from the Holy Roman Empire and subsequently summoned the Cortes more regularly. This involved them more in collection and use of revenue and eventually established a better relationship between the monarch and its representatives.
Support	One of the most significant supporters of the Communeros Revolt was Joanna, Charles' mother; she was eventually made the figurehead, although she would not commit herself fully and was effectively a prisoner of the rebels. Her mental frailty was a potentially serious issue for the leadership of the revolt.
Divide and rule	The uprising failed to draw in the other states effectively; they were uncoordinated and Charles took advantage of this.
Danger	The rebels trapped Adrian of Utrecht, the Regent, in Valladolid; he was seen as a foreigner and was disliked. However, Charles promoted two other men, Velasco and Enriquez as co-regents and this helped to calm the situation.
Weak leadership	Leadership was in the hands of Juan de Padilla, a noble, who enlisted an army in support. His authority was not supreme as three different juntas or governments were created by various factions; they were all raising taxes and forced loans to pay their armies.
The demands of the rebels	Training for government officials; reform of the taxation system; protection of the wool trade; the King to consult the Cortes more frequently; the Cortes no longer to be a source of supply for the government.
Spread	Peasant uprisings threatened stability in the countryside.

Fig. 3 *How dangerous was the Comuneros Revolt?*

As for the aftermath, the Comuneros Revolt has been described as a turning point. There were no more revolts in Castile against the power of the Crown. Nevertheless:

- the failure of the revolt 'left scars' – reminders that revolt could potentially destroy 'Spain' as an individual state; the monarchy could lose support.
- there were still fears that Spain would simply become 'Europeanised' and be treated as only a small part of Charles' overall responsibilities as King of Spain and Holy Roman Emperor. Both of his roles were demanding and Charles could not be in two places at once.
- it was also possible that Charles would try to govern both Spain and the empire in the same way, ignoring their differing needs.
- opposition could have continued; the Zapata family still saw themselves as 'the upholders of the fervent nationalist tradition which had been defeated at Villalar'.

However, as a consequence of their defeat at Villalar, the nobles set out to gain the good favour of the King. Many fought in the war against France in Navarre, in an attempt to redeem themselves. In 1522, Charles I issued a pardon for the majority of those who had taken part in the revolt. The fact that Charles promised he would return to Spain and marry a Spanish princess was also a turning point for both sides.

Some significant changes of a cultural nature diverted the nobles and set them on a gentler course. Peace encouraged interest in the development of humanism; Erasmus and his writings became popular as a result of links with Flanders, and increasingly, high ranking Spaniards were employed in government and some took the opportunities available in the opening up of the New World.

The Comuneros Revolt actually generated substantial, but subtle, positive changes, for example Charles had to work more closely with the nobles as a means of keeping control over their activities. This increased control was not just about providing opportunites for nobles in other parts of his territories, but it was also a process of 'Hispanising' or 'making Spanish' the emperor, Charles, himself. In other words, Charles began to appreciate the strengths of Spain and the need to preserve them. These strengths included:

- The conciliar system of government.
- Castile as the administrative centre just as it had been in the reigns of Ferdinand and Isabella.
- Peripatetic rule.
- Councils acting as givers of advice, rather than having real responsibility for policy.
- Regular use of the Cortes, summoned to agree to grants of money, balanced by a willingness to allow free speech.

This seemed to work and, despite some complaints, there was relative peace after the 1520s.

The revolt had effectively failed, Charles' authority was established and corrupt officials were removed from their posts. Charles then left Spain in 1520 to seek the crown of the Holy Roman Empire. Later, he was willing to concede that this decision was an error, saying in 1520: 'I was not old enough to govern these (i.e. Spanish) kingdoms. And as I left immediately for Flanders, having spent very little time here, and what is more, being unmarried and without an heir, it is not surprising that there was scandal and disturbance.' Although he had learned a lesson, Charles still saw Spain as his second rather than his major responsibility and continued to spend more time in the empire than in Spain.

Exploring the detail

How historians see the impact of the Comuneros Revolt

Elliott supports the view that Spain was now more open to change, for example with regard to domestic change as 'Castilian liberty' was 'crushed and defenceless in the face of restored royal power'. MacDonald, more positively, indicates that nobles were given active roles in Spain and the empire and were exempt from taxation. Kamen says: 'By closer attention to events in Spain, and by actively identifying Spanish officials and soldiers with imperial policy, Charles weaned Castilians away from their isolationism.' Kamen, however, also comments that this development had some negative consequences. The 'Spanish presence actually began to be resented in northern Europe and Spanish culture penetrated the jungles of Central America.'

Did you know?

A contemporary story tells about Charles I meeting a peasant. The peasant did not recognise Charles, but commented that he had lived under five kings in Castile. When asked which was the best and the worst, he identified Ferdinand as the best and Charles as the worst. Charles asked why the peasant thought this. The peasant said the King ruined the peasants with taxes, took all the revenues of Spain and the Indies and abandoned his wife. He also complained about the negative way Spain was viewed in Europe. The story may be untrue, but it suggests considerable dissatisfaction with Charles' performance as King.

Activity

Role play

Work in pairs. Choose to be either Charles I/V or a soldier/rebel fighting for the Comuneros. Explain the causes, events and outcome of the Comuneros Revolt from your chosen perspective. Other members of your class could then question you about the situation and your motives.

Activity

Source analysis

Study Source 1 and answer the following. Compare or discuss your answers with the rest of the class.

1. What do you understand by the term 'absolutism'?

2. To what extent does the writer support the Comuneros? Explain your answer.

3. Why might the *corregidores* be seen in such a negative light?

4. Using Source 1 and your own knowledge, explain why the writer might think that 'Castile lay completely at the mercy of its sovereign.' To what extent do you think this is an appropriate comment?

There were, however, some very positive consequences. Charles had won and his increasing maturity meant he now recognised the need for a strong government and for peace. Spain became more open to the influence of the rest of Europe: religion and culture blossomed. Erasmus was a significant influence; his moral code and piety appealed to many Spanish citizens newly converted to Catholicism. Charles used more Spaniards in his government at home and abroad.

> The defeat at Villalar left Castile even more exposed to absolutism than it had been before. The Comuneros had been concerned not only with objectives but also with means; the revolt was not only a protest against Spain's involvement in the European and and imperial policies of Charles V, it was also an attempt, no matter how vague or rudimentary, to defend the interests of Castile by imposing constitutional checks on royal power. These were now brushed aside and from this moment Castile lay completely at the mercy of its sovereign. Municipal government was already incapable of exercising independent authority. Local elections were far from democratic, but even the elected officers of the towns had little power when face to face with the *corregidores*, those judicial officers who since the reign of the Catholic Monarchs had also been invested with administrative powers and sent to every town in Castile where they acted as royal governors … Owing to a decline in the standards of selection … there were complaints that the nominees of Charles V were not university trained jurists but ignorant favourites.

1   *Adapted from J. Lynch,* **Spain under the Habsburgs, Vol. 1: Empire and Absolutism, 1516–1598,** *1964*

Fig. 4 *The Comuneros uprising in Segovia*

Relations between the crown and the Cortes

Charles had authority to summon a general Cortes that represented all three kingdoms, or he could summon them individually. He did the former six times. However, discussions, even in the general Cortes, were not joint. He had to deal with each of the Cortes of the three kingdoms separately, even if they were gathered in the same place. Achieving any progress was both time consuming and difficult. The Cortes could, as always, be supportive or oppose the monarch, but they could not make laws of their own accord and so, ultimately, the monarch's power was greater. They could, however, petition the monarch to make laws.

Cross-reference

Look back to Chapter 5 (pages 74–5) to compare Charles' attitude to the Cortes with that of Ferdinand and Isabella.

Most importantly, the Cortes could, if they wished, allow Charles to impose new taxes. He usually had to persuade them that this was necessary. However, meetings were irregular and, even when new taxes were agreed, the proceeds were usually unlikely to meet Charles' requirements. He spent at least one-third of what was raised on domestic affairs, whereas his main need was to meet his expenses in other parts of

Fig. 5 *Cortes of Aragon*

his empire, particularly the expenses of war. Nevertheless, this system was a safeguard for Spain ensuring that taxes were not all spent on war and the Holy Roman Empire.

Overall, the Aragonese Cortes was the most powerful, largely because Charles needed its approval for revenue. In Castile, most taxes could be raised without the approval of the Cortes. The most important and useful of the taxes was the *alcabala* or sales tax, payable by all except the Church. Unfortunately for the monarchy, it did not rise with inflation, which was already a significant issue in Spain. Some towns had been allowed by the Cortes, in the previous reign, to pay an agreed total sum in taxation. As this practice became more widespread, it was much harder for Charles to negotiate increases.

A positive aspect of relations with the Castilian Cortes, resulting from the defeat of the Comuneros, was that, by 1523, they had accepted that redress of grievances before deciding money would not be granted. Castile became a useful tax granting body and voted 15 grants during the reign. Unfortunately, even this did not make the crown fully solvent; inflation caused by the circulation of bullion to pay for foreign policies continued to grow. The Cortes petitioned for the banning of exports of bullion from 1515, but this made little impact.

Exploring the detail

Opposition from the Cortes

Opposition from the Castilian Cortes was not just about finances. At the first meeting, held at Valladolid in 1518, Juan de Zumel, the representative for Burgos, declared Charles' claim to the throne as invalid in view of the fact that Charles' mother was still alive. Concerns were also expressed about Charles' inability to speak Spanish and his entourage of advisers, none of whom were Spanish. He was thought disloyal because he wanted to stand for election as Holy Roman Emperor in place of his grandfather Maximilian. Money for bribes was actually granted by the Cortes but the Comuneros Revolt meant that it was never collected.

Activity

Group activity

1. Make a list of the positive and negative factors in the relationship between the crown and the Cortes in this period. Share your ideas with the rest of the class. How far do your fellow students agree with your list? What conclusions can you draw from your final list?

2. How powerful were the Spanish Cortes? Explain your view.

The influence of the nobility

During the last years of Ferdinand's reign and the early years of Charles I's reign, the nobility had something of a resurgence. An increase in their numbers stemmed from the Catholic Monarchs' creation of more nobles as a result of service in the wars. Charles exempted nobles from the heaviest taxes to encourage them to remain loyal. Proof of their loyalty could be seen in their support for the government during the Comuneros Revolt. A cynical observer might comment that this support was simply to preserve their own authority and position in the hierarchy.

However, the older established nobility were being challenged by the advance of some families that Kamen describes as the 'lesser gentry'. This was a consequence of new laws that had allowed property to be passed on between generations and to holders of bureacratic positions, such as

Did you know?

Nobles were ranked in a specific order; at the bottom were the hidalgos, then the *caballeros* or barons; above these were the titled nobility or *titulos*, and finally the grandes or grandees. There were more *caballeros* than any other groups. They had extensive roles especially in Valencia where they dominated the second chamber (or house) of the Cortes. In Aragon, they had their own chamber in the Cortes. There were more nobles in Castile than in any other of the kingdoms. In 1520, Charles singled out a small number of Castilian nobles who could even keep their hats on in the King's presence.

judges. Individuals could also 'purchase' nobility, generating a new-style nobility who sought rank and privilege rather than the responsibilities.

These developments were the beginning of a major change in the role and influence of the nobility and the emergence of different 'types' of nobility. The previous emphasis on family, inherited wealth and estates, posts in government, attendance at court and personal service to the monarch, although still valued, was now being exchanged for success in enterprise, trade and industry. Kamen quotes a contemporary historian who said about the nobility, 'We no longer consider the virtue of a gentleman, but rather how wealthy he is.' Nobles no longer dominated government, although some still retained honorary positions on councils. One example was the Duke of Alva who had an honorary position on the Council of State; most of its other officers were from lower social groups. Lesser nobles took a lead in the government of towns. Their social standing was important in this respect. The experience of the Comuneros had shown that they were able to maintain law and order better than the *letrados* who focused purely on administration.

■ A closer look

Nobles

Specific requirements dictated membership of the nobility; it was not always a matter of birth. A petitioner had to have experience either as a soldier, in government or in the law, finance or trade. They had to be intellectually able and fully committed. Many of the younger members of the nobilty chosen by Cobos to work in government were 'minor gentry who had administrative training and experience, and came from the smaller towns'. They were often very talented and the government benefited from their particular knowledge and skills. As a result, many nobles were now unwilling to be soldiers, as had previously been the norm. By the 1530s, it was claimed that, 'the military estate is decayed and has forgotten its calling'. Although many of these new nobles rose to the rank through service to the crown or because of their sheer ability, they also had to satisfy the *limpieza de sangre* (purity of blood) laws, which ruled that blood and inheritance were the accepted routes to such status. However, the government also considered it important to encourage talent.

A law of 1505 had allowed the 'new nobility' to pass their property on through the generations. They began to establish dynasties in much the same way as the grandees had done before them. Some of the more powerful grandees became involved in trade in addition to their other responsibilites, for example the Duke of Medina-Sidonia had enormous estates and his own port. He benefited from the developing transatlantic trade and contributed to the economy as well as to political life. There was no social bar to trade and commerce for new or old nobles; many of the newly rich families had arisen out of the trade with America.

The trend for seeking status as nobility was noted by a contemporary who said that 'he is noblest who is richest'. The poet Cervantes said, 'money is prized rather than worth'. These changes created some conflict between the 'old' and the 'new' nobles; the 'old' clinging to the idea that only tradition could confer noble status. The new nobility seemed little different to the middle classes.

Fig. 6 *Fortifications were visible symbols of royal and noble power*

A definite shift had occurred in society; the elite was composed of different groups, often with a different outlook and more utility to the state. It did not destroy the 'old nobility', who kept their wealth and their estates, even if their political influence was less pronounced. They often became entrepreneurs, contributing significantly to the economy. The new middle classes conversely grew in influence. The changes were important, but not enough to threaten the stability of the state.

Why did these changes happen? Was the change forced upon the nobles by the monarchs, or was it an evolution, albeit rather rapidly? If it was evolutionary, was it a direct consequence of economic change and a background of rising prices, for example, did nobles have to exchange their courtly pursuits for commerce, which would pay for their lifestyle? Or was it more about the rising influence, greed and ambition of the middle classes threatening the income and status of the nobles? Unfortunately, few detailed records survive of the middle classes. However, we know that petitions for rewards for services given to the crown were made to the various councils. Applications were likely to be accompanied by some kind of bribe or promise; because the bureaucratic system of government was only just developing from the more personal rule of the Catholic Monarchs and the concept of 'grace and favour' was still strong, leading potentially to such corrupt practices. In other words, it was not a specific policy that saw the growth of the rise of the middle classes and changing role of the nobility, it simply happened because the circumstances were right.

Elliott gives us a view of the effects of changes in the influence of the nobility in his study of the provincial aristocracy of Catalonia (Source 2).

> A noble in Catalonia required a substantial income. As a result, the claims of younger sons were bought off with small cash payments. The sons of one such noble were to be maintained until the age of twenty when they would inherit a sum so small that a secular or ecclesiastical appointment, or a good marriage was likely to be essential.
>
> Property and office were essential passports to aristocracy and aspirants to social distinction would either attempt to gain entry into the royal administration – usually by way of the law – or would buy their way into the ranks of the propertied or upper bourgeoisie … like two notoriously rich merchants living in Barcelona, who the day before yesterday were peasants, yesterday merchants and today *cavallers* engaged in commerce – and all in the space of thirty years.
>
> The eventual union of the aristocracy and the dominant municipal families was no doubt facilitated by the constant process of intermarriage. Bourgeois wealth could enable the younger sons of nobles to live as befitted their status and they in turn could bestow their name upon a 'new' family.
>
> If the social gulf seemed forbiddingly wide, it was frequently bridged by an institution peculiar to Barcelona and one or two of the other principal towns, known as 'honoured citizenship'. The title was conferred, either by the king or, more frequently by vote of the existing 'honoured citizens'. Once elected they were entitled to all the privileges of the military aristocracy … and were therefore indistinguishable from the traditional aristocracy.

2   *J. H. Elliott, Spain and its World, 1500–1700, 1989*

Activity

Group activity

To what extent had the nobility become less powerful in the reign of Charles I of Spain? You will need to look back to Chapter 5 to help you with this. Discuss the question in groups and then give a presentation to the class or write an individual essay.

Activity

Source analysis

Read Source 2.

1 How useful is this source in explaining the issues surrounding the growth of the 'new nobility'?

2 To what extent do you think these new nobles would be a threat to government and society?

Activity

Challenge your thinking

To what extent do you think social changes influenced the political development of Spain?

Key chronology

The Inquisition, 1519–29

1519	Muslims attacked.
1521	Lutheran books are banned.
1525	All Muslims are ordered to leave the country.
1525–29	Arrests of Illuminists.
1529	Erasmians persecuted.

Fig. 7 *One of the various torture methods of the Spanish Inquisition*

Key terms

Heresy: used to describe views that are regarded as totally unacceptable. In the 16th century, heresy was associated with scholars who had no confidence In the teachings of the Catholic Church and, through reading some of the original texts of the Bible, found that there were errors in translation which made a significant difference to meanings of particular concepts such as 'penance'. 'Heretic' is derived from 'heresy' and signified a person who no longer accepted the main teachings of the Catholic Church. In non-religious matters, a heretic is someone who is sceptical and wants proof before taking on board new ideas.

There is no doubt that, in this period, the old nobility were pushed towards more peaceful activities, particularly as entrepreneurs, and the new middle classes were growing in influence in government. The contribution made by the old nobility to the economy of Spain was much more significant than in the previous reign. This made them both influential and important, but not too powerful to threaten the stability of Charles I's reign.

The work of the Inquisition

By the reign of Charles I the Inquisition had existed for over 30 years. Fifteen tribunals were operating at this time in Spain, including one in Granada set up in 1526. The Inquisition had originally been set up to deal with the Moors, who were Muslim, and the Jews who had lapsed after conversion. As time went on, this list included Christians who had converted to become Protestants and also Erasmians and *Alumbrados*/Illuminists. Any minor heretics who did not conform were also added to the list. Its work was overseen by the Inquisitor-General; the postholder was nominated by the crown, but had to be approved by the Pope. The monarch had the authority to dismiss the Inquisitor-General. In this period, they were usually bishops.

Over the years, the Inquisition developed systems and spread its powers to deal with witchcraft and other unacceptable practices. Witchcraft was particularly prominent, but its impact was minimised by an Inquisitor-General who was sceptical of the claims made against the accused individuals. However, the Inquisition has often been accused of not being willing to debate issues of **heresy** and of being too quick to condemn.

The Inquisition was a very active body; it was itinerant, arriving in a town or village at regular intervals, as frequently as every four months. The programme would look like this:

- Meeting with the local bishop, priests and ecclesiastical authorities as appropriate.
- Proclamation of a special mass that everyone was compelled to attend.
- Oath to support the Inquisition taken by all; they would raise their right hand, cross themselves and repeat the oath.
- Edict read identifying heresy, including Islam and Judaism.
- All guilty of these heresies to identify themselves.
- A 'period of grace' allowed for confession; this might allow the guilty back into the Church.
- All present expected to denounce others who had not confessed themselves.

This last point in the Inquisition's programme was very important: the campaign against heresy encouraged attempts to get even with members of the community who were disliked, or who were rivals in some way. It was easy to do as the identity of the denouncer was kept secret. Anyone accused of heresy or similar was imprisoned and, in most cases, their property was confiscated. Torture could be administered if considered to be justified. It was a routine method of gaining information or confession; if the subject died as a result, it was because he or she was classed as untruthful.

Lay officials called *familiares*, drawn from all layers of society, were appointed to carry out investigations and take statements from witnesses. These officials are sometimes inaccurately described as denouncers of individuals. However, Edwards states that they were the 'eyes and ears of the inquisitors at times and in places where there was no official visitation'. *Familiares* were usually accompanied by a notary who would write down the confession. Despite the nature of their work and lack of pay, the jobs were highly contested because they gave prestige and privileges. This included protection from arrest by the civil authorities, immunity from prosecution and some exemption from taxation.

A closer look

The torture of Maria Gonzalez

Maria Gonzalez was tortured in July 1513 because 'she has said things which do not seem reasonable'. The inquisitors said this torture 'may be given and continued at our will until she speaks the truth and perseveres in it'. They told her that if she died, was wounded, or lost a limb during the torture, it would be her own fault. They simply wanted to know the truth. Maria insisted that she had spoken the truth. Nevertheless, they told her to undress and tied her to the rack. 'Tighten them and kill me, I will say no more than I have already,' she said, when asked about whether the information she had given about two people was correct. At one point, she said she had made it up. However, under further questioning, she said that she had seen one of the accused making cakes on Friday and eating them on Saturday. More water was then poured into her nose and mouth. The water torture continued. The inquisitors asked about various comments she had made about specific individuals.

'When asked if what she said against Grace de Teva is true; she said it is. They bathed out of ceremony and ate things cooked in earthenware dishes. The order was given to pour another jar of water. She said, I speak the truth … Sirs, I have already told you the truth.' She said that what she had declared was true and she would agree to their throwing her into the fire.

The questioning resumed on 22 August 1513. Maria was clearly seen as guilty, although she continued to claim that she had only spoken the truth. She asked to be reprieved as she had children to care for. However, the inquisitors said that they had no choice but to 'relax her to justice and the secular arm for having falsely confessed'.

'This sentence was read out on Wednesday, September 7th, 1513. Maria Gonzalez was on top of a scaffold … Witnesses were present.'

*Extracts taken from L. A. Homza (ed.), **The Spanish Inquisition, 1478–1614**, 2006*

Exploring the detail

The Inquisition and torture

Torture was usually applied in one of three forms. The first was the *garrucha*, which was a pulley with heavy weights attached to the legs; the accused was then hoisted slowly up and then dropped very quickly. The jerking movement usually dislocated arms and legs. The second method was the *toca*. In this case, the prisoner was placed on the rack and tied down, his or her mouth kept open and water poured in through a linen cloth. The cloth was the *toca*. The third method was the most 'popular'. This involved tying the accused to the rack with ropes that were tightened as the questioning proceeded. Suspects were allowed only limited clothing during these procedures, which was to humiliate them. They were kept imprisoned whilst their misdemeanours were being investigated.

Activity

Source analysis

Why was Maria Gonzalez executed? Was it because the inquisitors had already decided she was guilty? Was it because she confessed to certain crimes? What was her actual offence?

It was not usual for every accused to be found guilty by the Inquisition. However, if there was sufficient evidence, the suspect could be arrested, their goods confiscated and the suspect put in solitary confinement. Conditions in prisons were reasonable; access to doctors was available and the wealthy could usually choose what they ate. They were usually given three separate hearings; the first was about personal details and the reasons for arrest. A formal charge would be made within three weeks if there was no confession. Every conversation was recorded and a

Key terms

Sanbenito: a yellow robe worn by the accused; it had specific markings, usually a red cross, which showed the wearer was guilty of an offence. It was a kind of penance used as a warning to others of the potential consequences of their crimes.

lawyer was allowed to advise the accused. The lawyer's job was usually to get the prisoner to admit guilt. At the trial, witnesses could be called by the accused and those called by the tribunal could be questioned with the purpose of proving that they were not telling the truth. Torture was not always used. It applied to only around five per cent of cases. If torture was used, it did not continue after the confession. Once all the information was available, a jury was summoned and they would vote on the sentence. The latter was not publicly known until the *auto-da-fé* (act of faith). The accused could be acquitted, penanced, reconciled or sentenced to death. The latter punishment could be in person, but an alternative was 'in effigy'. Penances usually meant being imprisoned in a house of correction for a specific period, which could range from a matter of months to life (although this could be in the prisoner's own house), and the wearing of the **sanbenito** for a certain length of time. Sometimes the convicted were sent to serve in the galleys. The shame of the crime and the punishment were attached to the person and, to some extent, their family for lengthy periods of time, even several generations. If they subsequently were found to fall back into their old ways, there would be further punishment. The death sentence was usually burning at the stake following the *auto-da-fé* or formal announcement of the punishment.

There were 21 places of imprisonment available to the Inquisition in Spain; those consigned to them were kept in solitary confinement and often in chains. Surprisingly, there were probably no more than 50 inquisitors for the whole of Spain; that could suggest a limited need and/or that intense or lengthy campaigns against any 'heretics' were unlikely. Although the Inquisition focused on heresy, there were also cases involving withcraft, gypsies, bigamists, homosexuals and priests who had affairs. Witchcraft was less likely to be a matter for the Inquisition after 1526 when witchcraft was pronounced to be a 'delusion'. Lutherans and Judaizers were more regularly brought before it.

The main target of the Inquisition tended to be Jews and *conversos*. The Inquisition continued operating in Spain, and was also exported to the New World, until it was ended by a formal decree in 1834.

The growth of Protestantism

The first effective Protestant challenge to the Catholic Church, Lutheranism, emerged in Germany. It eventually became a limited threat in Spain. Books were banned and the Inquisition did its work; the number of cases brought before the Inquisition was probably less than 100. Most of these cases involved Spaniards. One of the first arrests in Spain was made in 1528; this was Juan Lopez de Celain, burned as a Lutheran in Granada in 1530. Another potential Lutheran was Juan de Vergara; he was a great scholar having helped Cisneros to produce the Polyglot Bible and taught philosophy at Alcalá University.

The founder of Protestantism, Luther, was a German monk and academic working at Wittenburg University. In 1517, he became notorious because of his attack on indulgences in his work 'The Ninety-Five Theses', in which he explored the arguments against

Fig. 8 *Does the Inquisition deserve its sinister reputation?*

indulgences. Luther himself was regarded as a heretic and brought to trial by Charles I of Spain in his capacity as Holy Roman Emperor. His crime was to believe that good works alone would not allow an individual to gain entry into heaven, as the Roman Catholic Church believed. Various attempts were made by the Catholic hierarchy to get Luther to admit that he was wrong, that is, his ideas were against the content of the scriptures and the teaching of the Catholic Church. Luther also believed that people could enter heaven by virtue of their faith alone and not good works or payment. Furthermore, he said that there were only three sacraments and not seven, and that priests were not 'sacred' but simply intermediaries between God and the individual.

Luther would never have been able to get his message across without the help of the Elector of Saxony. He developed his theology and produced books and pamphlets, as well as preaching sermons. The threat of excommunication merely prompted Luther to burn the papal bull (edict) that condemned him.

In 1519, Luther was invited to take part in a public debate with John Eck, a Catholic theologian. Luther would not change his views and he continued to write and preach his ideas. One of his views was that the belief in transubstantiation was misguided. Transubstantiation was a belief that the bread and wine are changed into the flesh and blood of Christ during the Catholic mass. This was strong rejection of the Catholic Church's interpretation. He was eventually brought before Charles V (as Charles I was known in his capacity as Holy Roman Emperor) in 1521 at the Diet of Worms. Luther continued to deny the Catholic view and he was subsequently outlawed. He continued to teach and preach and established a new Church, the Lutheran Church. Some of the princes in the Holy Roman Empire supported Luther's views and subsequently came into conflict wth Charles V. Peace was not made until 1555.

Part of the reason for Protestantism's survival was the nature of the message stressing that it was up to the individual to make up their own mind and that justification came by faith and not by good works. Luther also encouraged his followers to obey their secular leaders as well as the Church. In addition, princes and rulers of the German states were enthusiastic about appointing their own clergy and taking over the monasteries, land and wealth they had gathered over the years. Even more important was the appeal to the ordinary man and woman, particularly in the towns. Artisans and merchants were enthused; Luther's ideas spread along trade routes and from town to town.

In Spain, in the first half of the century, around 105 Protestants were brought before the Spanish Inquisition. Sixty-six of these were not Spanish born; only 39 were native heretics. However, Spain was less open to Protestantism than some other European states, partly owing to the authority of the crown over the Church and the piety of its monarchs who set an example to their subjects. The size of Spain and its lack of large urban centres and a good road system also slowed down its spread. The biggest factor was its relative isolation as a peninsula protected from the rest of Europe by a high mountain range.

Jews, Erasmians and *Alumbrados*

Jews

Jews had been expelled in 1492 at the conquest of Granada, but many remained in Spain as *conversos*, accepting the Catholic faith. It is possible that between 80 to 90 per cent of those who left Spain eventually returned and became Christian at least outwardly. The percentage accused by the Inquisition of lapsing during the period 1516–29 fell from 77 per cent

■ **Key terms**

Mysticism: a form of religion where the individual practises contemplation and, in so doing, hopes to become one with God and to gain an understanding of the meaning and truth of the scriptures.

Reformation: the break from the Catholic Church that was begun by Luther in Germany in 1517.

■ **Cross-reference**

See pages 129–30 for information about *Alumbrados*.

to 2 per cent of all those brought before the tribunal. A good number of these *conversos*, largely from Aragon, were employed in government under Charles I. This was another factor in Castilian anxiety about their new King. However, *conversos* were not always fully welcome in this early part of Charles' reign as he thought they were involved in the Comuneros Revolt, although rigid discrimination did not develop until later in the reign.

Some of the *conversos* were also *Alumbrados;* this means they were Catholic but tended towards **mysticism**, an extreme form of Christianity.

Erasmians

Erasmians were the followers of Desiderius Erasmus (1456–1536), one of the most famous humanists and scholars of the period and a significant figure in the early Renaissance. He was a strong influence on Luther and the development of the **Reformation** in Germany, developing what became known as Christian humanism. This brought faith and learning together, rather than seeing them as distinct and separate. Erasmus emphasised less ritual, greater tolerance and particularly intellectual freedom. He thought there was too much superstition amd immorality in the Church. He encouraged meditation and private prayer and wanted reformers to come together with the traditional Church to generate peace and a universal appeal.

In Spain, Erasmus, whose writings were initially welcomed, especially by university scholars, was eventually perceived as much more of a threat than the Lutherans. He was invited to visit Spain in 1517. His book, *Enchiridion,* was a bestseller, read everywhere and in Spain by people of all classes and in all sorts of places from the royal court to inns. Erasmus also communicated with other scholars by letter and even had an exchange with Martin Luther about Church reform.

■ **Key profile**

Desiderius Erasmus

Erasmus (1467–1536) was born in Rotterdam, became a monk and was ordained a priest in 1492. He was very academic and studied in Paris at Montague College. He continued his studies at Cambridge, eventually becoming a professor of Greek and theology. He published many books, his most famous probably was the satire *In Praise of Folly*. He also published more academic works, for example *The Handbook of a Christian Soldier,* and a Greek version of the New Testament. He was soon well known for his scholarship throughout Europe.

Erasmus:

■ was critical of the monasteries; they needed radical reform

■ wanted more people to be able to read the Bible in the vernacular for themselves, rather than relying on the Church's interpretation

■ translated texts of the early founders of the Church

■ contributed to the Polyglot/Complutensian Bible, which was published in 1522, showing text in Latin, Hebrew and Greek for comparison.

However, as the Reformation developed, Erasmus failed to condemn Luther. He attacked the institution of monks and 'mendicant' or begging friars; as a consequence attitudes generally hardened and the Inquisition struck. One of the first victims was Juan de Valdes who had published a controversial book, *Dialogue of Christian Doctrine*. Another significant victim was the chancellor of the university. Luis Vives, a staunch humanist, also felt it

■ **Cross-reference**

Look back to Chapter 5, page 79 to read the Key profile on Juan Luis Vives.

politic to leave Spain, commenting that: 'We live in difficult times in which we can neither speak nor remain silent without danger.' Charles, who had supported the Erasmians, himself left Spain in 1529 to take up his role as Holy Roman Emperor. He took his humanist courtiers with him and protection for the continuation of the movement disappeared with him.

Persecution of Erasmians continued into the 1530s and many left Spain of their own accord. Although Kamen comments that the impact of humanism has been overplayed, he supports the significance of the movement by reference to the scale of sales of Erasmus' writings; the publishers, having produced thousands of copies, were unable to meet the demand.

In fact, the writings of Erasmus were not heretical as such, but they were critical of aspects of Catholicism, for example the corruption of some religious orders. This would suggest that the attack on Erasmus was not a totally religious issue. It was more a backlash against the support he, Erasmus, a foreigner, had from Charles in his other role as Charles V, Holy Roman Emperor; it was also a likely consequence of the narrow Spanish view of his ideas and possibly more a criticism of the Spanish monarchy than of Erasmus himself. The sheer complexity of the multiracial situation in Spain was also responsible to some extent. In addition, the presence of the Inquisition generated a lack of trust about the religious beliefs of individuals; the simplest way to deal with religious issues, it was perceived, was to ensure orthodoxy, i.e. one faith only.

Alumbrados

This religious group is also known as 'Illuminists' and sometimes *dejados* meaning 'abandoned'. It sprang from the Franciscan Order; a mystical movement, common in Europe at the time. *Alumbrados* believed themselves capable of uniting their soul with God and incapable of committing sins. The movement was shortlived, beginning in 1510, largely dying out by 1525.

One small group, under the patronage of the Duke of Mendoza, was denounced in 1519, followed by the further and specific denunciation of one of its members, Isabel de la Cruz. Investigations went on for several years and links to Lutheranism were identified. Isabel and another member of the group, Pedro Ruiz de Alcaraz, were arrested. Another woman who had influenced the group, Francisca Hernández, was also denounced. The Inquisitor-General, Manrique, drew up 48 propositions demonstrating their heretical beliefs. Isabel and Pedro were sentenced at an *auto-da-fé* in 1529 to perpetual imprisonment. However, they were released after a few years. The individuals involved were all *conversos*.

More denunciations occurred in the following years, for example the preacher Juan de Avila. He was also a *converso*. Despite their condemnation, the general view of historians is that *Alumbrados* ultimately reinvigorated religious and intellectual life with their different views and willingness to reform.

A closer look

Extracts from the Inquisition edict on the *Alumbrados*, 1525

The following is a translation of a list of some of the beliefs of the *Alumbrados* of 1525 with the judgement of the Inquisition shown in italics:

1 'There is no hell, and if they say there is, it is to frighten us, just as they tell children, "Watch out for the bogeyman".'

   This proposition is heretical, erroneous and false, contradictory to the Gospel and the order of divine justice, which arranges for the

The Host: was the bread that was consecrated by the Catholic priest during the mass/Eucharist. It was part of Catholic belief that the miracle of the mass meant that the consecrated bread became the body of Christ. Protestants saw the bread as symbolic only.

Activity

Source analysis

Read the A closer look above and answer the following questions.

1. What do you think was the difference between 'heretical' and 'erroneous'?

2. What were the canonical authorities that gave credence to the replies of the Inquisition? You might need to do some research on this.

3. How effective would this process of denunciation be in ensuring that the *Alumbrados/* Illuminists did 'reform'?

---

eternal punishment of mortal sins through penance when those sins are not removed from us in this life.

2 'That the Father was made flesh like the Son, alleging the authority, "He who sees me".'

This propositon is heretical.

3 'That God could not make a person more perfect or more humble than he already was.'

This proposition is heretical because it denies the omnipotence of God.

4 'That God would enter a man's soul more entirely than He did **the Host** if man did what he should; because the Host was a little piece of dough, whereas man was made in God's image.'

This propositon is erroneous, false and heretical. First because God and man (are both) in the Sacrament of the altar through hypostatic union; next, because the statement seems to contend that after consecration the bread's substance remains.

There were 48 propositions altogether, many with quite lengthy replies. The judgements made were agreed unanimously 'on account of scriptural and canonical authorities'.

The extent of religious unity by 1529

Religious unity in Spain was certainly greater on the surface than in the reign of Ferdinand and Isabella, simply because of the expulsion of the Moors and the attention to other religious groups via the Inquisition. Within the Catholic Church itself, there was greater control and the involvement of the monarchy was significant in generating unity in terms of aims and ideals. This meant that the influence of Protestantism was more likely to be resisted and the Catholic Church was much stronger than it had been. The Pope had also agreed, by 1523, that the monarch could decide which churchmen were appointed to positions as bishops, abbots, etc. throughout Spain. This was a considerable asset to the crown; it gave more authority and, if the power was used wisely, could also ensure greater conformity and uniformity within the Church. The Inquisition was another powerful tool to ensure that individuals did not stray from orthodox religious practices. Also, by 1523, the crown headed the military orders and could make all clerical appointments, leading to greater quality control.

The case of Juan Luis Vives is evidence of this greater religious unity in Spain. He was a humanist but descended from *conversos*; his parents still practised their Jewish faith. He was in line for a post at Alcalá University, but the arrest and burning of his father in 1524 as a Judaizer, meant that he could not take up the post. In 1528, his mother's bones were dug up and burned. Vives had to leave Spain.

In 1527, a debate was held about Erasmus' work; some Spanish clergy were concerned because he had been critical of mendicant friars. These were itinerant religious men who sought food and shelter as they travelled. Although a small number of *Alumbrados* were also arrested, few were actually burned. These incidents, however, suggest that the Church and state were beginning to work together more effectively to deal with differing beliefs.

Despite the above, Lutheranism, had seeped further into Spain. Although a Christian movement, it was not regarded with any enthusiasm by the authorities. By 1521, Lutheran books were found in Spain and were subsequently banned. However, in 1524, it was said that 'there is so much awareness of Luther that nothing else is talked about'.

Although there were several trials in 1528, no further action was taken. A more decisive event was the controversy about a book by Juan Valdes, *Dialogue of Christian Doctrine*. Valdes did leave the country. Several other individuals were denounced as Lutherans, for example Francisca Hernández who was arrested in 1529. Kamen comments that there was widespread interest, but little action taken to deal with it.

Although the size of the country and the difficulties of travel made visitations by prelates and the monarch fairly rare events, the revived Catholic Church of Spain was possibly becoming more 'militant and extremely nationalistic … Purity of blood was underpinned by purity of faith'. In other words, to be Spanish was also to be Christian, particularly an orthodox Catholic Christian. Other faith groups, such as Jews and *Alumbrados*, were becoming less acceptable.

Nevertheless, pockets of 'heresy' remained. Lutheranism was not completely stamped out despite the decree of 1525 imposed by the Inqusition of Toledo; it was seen as being closely linked to Illuminism and the *Alumbrados,* and therefore still a serious challenge.

Activity

Thinking point

Why do you think heresy was never fully stamped out in Spain, in this period? Make a list of your ideas and then compare your list with other students. If there are differences in your views, try to work out why there are differences.

Summary questions

1 Why were the Comuneros a threat?

2 Why do you think the authorities in Spain were so worried about religious developments in this period?

Financial and economic developments

Fig. 1 *Galleon returning with goods from the New World*

In this chapter you will learn about:

- Castile's part as the financial centre of Spain

- the development of Spanish finances and the work of the Council of Finance

- Spain's continuing economic problems and their effects.

With what they pay in other ordinary and extraordinary dues, the common people, who have to pay these servicios, are reduced to such misery that many of them walk naked. And the misery is so universal that it is even greater among the vassals of the nobles than it is amongst Your Majesty's vassals, for they are unable to pay their rents, lacking the wherewithal, and the prisons are full.

1

This was written by Philip, Charles' son, to his father. Charles' wife, Isabella, also wrote often to her husband asking him to leave the Holy Roman Empire and return to Spain to help resolve its problems. Despite these appeals from his family, their obvious concern for the ordinary people of Spain, as well as fear for Charles' reputation, and the stability of the country, his response was largely negative. Charles was more anxious to deal with the religious and political issues, particularly Lutheranism and the ambitious princes, which were rapidly overwhelming Germany at this point.

Cross-reference

Look back to Chapters 3 (pages 43–5) and 6 (pages 84–5) to remind yourself about types of taxation in Spain.

The role of Castile as the financial centre of Spain

Through the various states that made up Spain during the reign of Charles I, the crown had a number of financial resources to draw upon; one of these was the state of Aragon. Unfortunately, its constitution meant the yield was limited and the economy was not strong. Another, more reliable, source was the Church; the Pope was willing to allow a proportion of this income to go the crown. In addition, there was Castile. Castile gained most of the wealth from America, although this only reached its height after 1530. Despite this, however, Charles was faced with the possibility that, in some years, revenue for the following year had already been spent.

The availability of finance and control over spending is a key issue for any government. Without it, a monarch is prey to those social and political groups that do have such resources, and also open to challenges from other states which might take advantage of such a weakness. Castile was the wealthiest state in Spain, but with mounting costs even Castile was not fully able to finance Charles as King of Spain and also as Holy Roman Emperor.

Fig. 2 *Mount Potosi in Bolivia, where rich deposits of silver were discovered*

Sources of income

Charles needed around 1 m ducats per year to break even. He had four main sources of income for Spain: trade, mostly with America; taxation in Castile and Aragon; and the Church.

Trade was a significant source of income by the early 16th century, following the discovery of America. At first, it was the exclusive right of Castile to trade with the New World, but this was gradually relaxed in the 1520s and only reasserted in the next decade.

This relaxation of the rules on trading with America was not particularly successful; the winds and currents between the two continents made the journey difficult and therefore not always profitable. Despite the concessions, Spain did not really want full competition in trade. Castile and the port of Seville therefore continued to hold the monopoly of trade with the Americas until the 17th century. Although usually the right of Spanish landlords and *conquistadores*, collecting tribute from the Indians was always possible.

Bullion, gold and silver, was the main import from the Americas with gold the predominant metal. Some of this precious metal was for the crown, but, over the years, private individuals gained the most. The crown could collect a 20 per cent tax called the 'royal fifth' on all precious metals mined in America. Table 1 shows some figures for this period of study.

Table 1 *Treasure imported from the New World; royal imports for the crown and private imports for other individuals*

Period	Royal imports	Private imports	Total imports
1516–20	312,261	879,575	1,191,836
1521–25	42,183	118,821	161,004
1526–30	326,485	919,640	1,246,125

*Figures taken from J. H. Elliott, **Spain, 1469–1716**, 1963*

Silver was also mined in Europe and its production was higher throughout this period than the imports of gold; silver was also imported from the New World by Spain after 1530 when the mines in Europe were in decline. Contraband and taxes on private bullion also raised around 3.5 m ducats.

Key chronology

The changing view of trade with America, 1524–9

1524   Foreign merchants can trade but are not allowed to settle or create bases.

1525–6 Any subject from Charles I and V's lands can settle.

1529   Concessions are given to 10 ports in Castile to trade with the Indies.

Cross-reference

Look back to Chapter 6 (pages 92–5) for more information about the growth of trade with the New World; compare what was allowed in 1516 with the information given here.

Activity

Group activity

Study Table 1 opposite and look back to Chapter 4, Table 2 (page 55) showing imports of gold from America in the period 1500–16. In groups, analyse both sets of figures.

1   What do they tell you about bullion imports over the whole period represented?

2   Why do you think there are some fluctuations?

3   Are there any links between the dates and information given in the text to explain the figures in the tables?

In 1523, Charles commented that the debts of the government in Castile 'amount to far more than I receive in revenue'. Note that this occurred when imports of bullion were at their lowest. Debt also increased with his role as Holy Roman Emperor and the need to finance the royal household in Castile. Charles therefore insisted that taxes were agreed by the Cortes before other matters were discussed.

Taxes raised in Castile and Aragon were the second and third major source of income; the Cortes rarely rejected a request for finance. In Castile, the *alcabala* was still the most lucrative tax and could be collected without reference to the Cortes. By 1534, however, it was set at a fixed sum and, over time, because of inflation, its value was gradually eroded. Other resources were mainly customs duties and sheep taxes and some extraordinary revenues, for example in 1523 the Cortes of Valladolid had voted a special tax of 400,000 ducats that was to be paid over three years directly by tax payers. *Servicios* yielded 130,000 ducats in 1524. This greatly increased the level of direct taxation on ordinary Castilians, whereas approximately one-tenth of the population were classed as being of noble rank and had only limited obligations to pay tax. By the 1550s, the Cortes were raising 400,000 ducats each year. Nevertheless, Charles also resorted to borrowing through the sale of *juros*, which were a kind of government bond.

Although Aragon was technically also expected to provide revenue, in practice its constitution and limited economy meant that it could not.

A significant source of income was the Church. Athough not usually considered to be taxable, its enormous wealth meant that it was seen as a justifiable source. Not only were the clergy expected to pay the normal taxes, they were also required, at times, to pay additional or extraordinary taxes (see Table 2).

Table 2

Tax paid by the Church	Explanation
Tercias reales	Two-ninths of the income in tithes to the Church.
Subsidio	A proportion of Church income. This tax was first levied in 1519 and was an irregular tax.
Cruzada	Paid by both clergy and laity; served as an indulgence and realised about 121,000 to 150,000 ducats per annum. Only paid regularly by the Church after 1508.
Maestrazgos	From the military orders; by 1525, the Fuggers (bankers in the Holy Roman Empire) were receiving this direct to cover Charles' expenses as Holy Roman Emperor.
Revenues from vacant sees (the term for the area/town presided over by a bishop) and donations.	The latter were 'free gifts'.

The Pope did, however, help Charles I by agreeing that the property and income of the military orders should go to the crown. The only other route to raise money was to borrow and one method was through *juros*.

However, any borrowing Charles made in his role as Holy Roman Emperor had to be paid back by the Spanish treasury. Kamen clarifies that this meant that Spain, and mainly Castile, paid the debts of the Holy Roman Empire. To cancel the debt, the lenders could buy land, mines, offices, etc. in Spain. Kamen considers that this debt was never fully reduced, largely because the nobility could not be counted on not to oppose Charles as long as their tax exemption was untouched.

The urgent need for money and the link between Spanish finances and the rest of Charles' empire can be seen in a letter sent by Adrian of Utrecht (governing the Netherlands) in 1520 (Source 2).

Cross-reference

Look back to Chapter 3 (pages 43–5) for more information on taxation in Castile and Aragon.

> There is no way for us to obtain money for the courier post here; the other day we searched for money to send a despatch to Navarre but were unable to find any. Large sums are owed to the master of the post, but nothing can be found to pay him. My salary is not being paid, and I haven't enough of my own to meet such great expenses. I pray that your majesty will give me permission to leave here honestly and in sufficient time so that I don't disgrace your service.

2   S. Haliczer, *The Comuneros of Castile: The forging of a revolution 1475–1521*, 1981

Cross-reference

Look back to Chapter 5 (page 79) to review *tercias reales* and the *subsidio*.

This lack of cash flow meant that officials often took bribes for favours, offices were sold to people who could afford them rather than those who could do the job. Certificates of nobility were also sold and, over time, reduced the number of tax payers overall. It is possible that, had Charles stopped fighting wars, largely in the empire, he could have been solvent. Most historians believe that his inability to balance the books led to the bankruptcy of Spain in 1557 in the reign of his son, Philip. Kamen summarises this view:

> Charles had set in train two developments of fundamental importance; firstly, it was Castile rather than another realm of the crown that had to bear the cost of empire; secondly, foreign financiers were now in place to dominate sections of the Spanish economy for over a century. In this reign German financiers were permitted to buy land, offices and juros … the Spanish monarchy never shook off the legacy of debt bequeathed to it by the emperor.

3   H. Kamen, *Spain, 1469–1714: A Society of Conflict*, 1991.

The Council of Finance

This was a new body set up in 1522 to 1523 to oversee the accounts and to receive all state income. It was modelled on a council in the Netherlands and Cobos was its first secretary. Although it was first seen as a way of organising the accounts in Castile and the Indies only, it gradually came to deal with finances in general. Daily meetings were held so that a scrutiny could be made of income and expenditure to inform other financial decisions. It kept track of expenditure and credit transactions. Despite this, the financial paperwork was often incomplete as amounts paid were often passed directly to creditors, i.e. the person/ organisation to whom the debt was owed. This was another factor in the rising problem of debt during Charles' reign.

Activity

Group activity

What were the strengths and weaknesses of the financial systems in Spain? Discuss in groups and draw up a chart to itemise your conclusions. Present to the rest of the class and agree a final list for your notes.

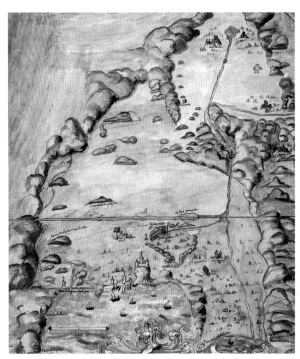

Fig. 3 *Irrigation systems opening more land for cultivation*

Despite the debt and shortfall, Charles was expected to demonstrate his authority through 'show'. Unfortunately, court ceremonial, salaries for new appointments and the trappings of monarchy, for example furnishings and paintings, were at least one-tenth of royal expenses.

Economic problems

Revenue

The lack of government cash flow meant that officials often took bribes for favours, offices were sold to people who could afford them rather than those who could do the job and certificates of nobility were also on offer. The latter excused holders from paying tax. Had Charles stopped fighting wars, it is possible that he would have been solvent.

Cash flow was still a problem in 1523; all of the following year's revenue had already been spent. Unfortunately, it was to remain so throughout Charles' reign. In 1527, he summoned the nobles and clergy to the Cortes of Valladolid to provide funds, but they refused: they feared setting a precedent. Much of the populace lived on fixed incomes and could not afford to pay more in tax. Gold and silver mined in the New World also generated revenue, but led to a significant rise in prices of sometimes more than 100 per cent.

Debt

Borrowing, through the *juro* system, became one of the major sources of cashflow during Charles I's reign. Debt was incurred in many areas, for example war, the upkeep of the royal household, the court ceremonial and its trappings which were intended to display the majesty of the monarchy. Much of the money loaned came indirectly from German bankers, the Fuggers.

This process operated in a complex manner. Initially, a contract for a specific amount was agreed in Spain; this would be cashed by a banker elsewhere, for example in Antwerp on an agreed date. The amount, plus an extra sum, i.e. the interest, was paid back to the agent by the government. From 1520 to 1532, 101 of these transactions took place with a total of 5,379,053 ducats borrowed. Interest charges rose to 17.6 per cent and continued to rise throughout the reign. At the lower level of 17 per cent, the total repayment was 6,327,371 ducats, a difference of more than 1 m ducats. By the end of Charles' reign, the situation had deteriorated so much that he was reduced to drastic measures, for example selling public offices to sustain his finances.

Taxation

Although Charles I had several sources of taxation, they were not consistently reliable. The Cortes tended to choose carefully which projects they were prepared to support; Aragon consistently refused to make grants at all. Although Castile was generally cooperative, Charles had to ask three times for grants during the period 1523–25. After the Battle of Pavia, in 1525, he agreed to a 15-year moratorium, or period in which repayment of the debt to the Castilian Cortes would be postponed, in order to deal with the effects of inflation.

Did you know?

Inflation is a dramatic change in the price of goods and services. This occurred across Europe in the 16th century. Spain suffered more than most. Bread, oil and wine prices rose by a factor of five. Governments, taken by surprise, assumed that an increase in coins in circulation was the cause. Inflation spread across Europe from Spain and the New World as Spain repaid loans from foreign bankers or gave regular pay to their troops. Other factors were, for example, a rise in population and increased demand for goods, or debasement of the coinage, i.e. less precious metal in the coins minted. Merchants then raised prices so that they could maintain the previous level of gold and silver from goods sold.

Inflation – cause and effect

This was not just a Spanish problem; it was a significant issue for Europe as a whole in the 16th century. Its causes were not easy for contemporaries to understand and its effects took time to deal with. Its development was linked to some degree to the voyages of exploration, the discovery of America and the growth of overseas empires. England, France, and Portugal, as well as Spain, became involved. As trade developed, bullion was pumped into Europe. As more precious metal became available, traders demanded more of it for their goods. One Spanish writer in 1513 said that 'Today a pound of mutton costs as much as a whole sheep used to'.

Despite these rising prices and the financial problems it caused, there were still opportunities for entrepreneurs to make money and production of most goods continued. Although fluctuations in an economy are part of a natural cycle, they can affect different states at different times and even different geographical regions of a state at different times. As a developing economy, Spain was particularly prone to these fluctuations which affected some commercial centres rather than others, for example Seville faced heavy competition as an international port, but Burgos and Barcelona were much stronger. The geographical situation of these centres also accounted for some of this difference.

Fig. 4 *In a time of rising prices and low incomes, production of food was an important part of the economy*

A closer look

Spanish influence

Historians have written at length about the financial issues of the reign of Charles I. Bonney notes that for Charles I, his 'total debts to foreign financiers roughly approximated the entire receipts from Spanish America during his reign'. This was largely a result of his role as Holy Roman Emperor, but was also a consequence of the import of bullion that generated an increase in prices. The Spanish historian, Nadal, suggests there was a 2.8 per cent overall price rise in Spain from 1501 to 1562. This seemed astronomic to contemporaries. To make matters worse, prices rose at different rates in different places; wheat prices in Andalucia rose by a staggering 109 per cent between 1511 and 1559. Other factors promoting this rise in prices are suggested by Elliott:

- The use of credit bonds (loans) called *juros*.
- Increased spending by the aristocracy on clothes, jewellery, etc.
- Demand from a growing population for food and goods.

How monarchs and governments responded to the rise in prices was significant for their success in overcoming it. Charles I, for example, was not successful in imposing more taxes on the rich. He also had to raise loans to fund his election as Holy Roman Emperor and other costs such as military expenses. Consequently, debts began to mount.

Activity

Essay question

'Inflation was the most significant factor in weakening the Spanish economy in the reign of Charles I.' How valid is this view?

■ Cross-reference

Look back to Chapter 6 for more information about poverty.

The monarch	→	Had to raise loans, often from foreign financiers, such as the Fuggers of Germany; parliament usually said 'No' to additional taxation; repayment of loans took approximately 36% of income.
Royal officials	→	Took bribes; sold offices; sold certificates of nobility.
Merchants and traders	→	Raised prices to make the same profit as before; bread, wine and oil were the most commonly traded goods.
Ordinary people	→	Rising rents, food prices rose by 100%, the population continued to grow; more mouths to feed.

Fig. 5 *Effects of inflation: who suffered most?*

Poverty, vagrancy and emigration

Poverty was a persistent problem that became greater as a result of the price revolution. An economic historian, E. J. Hamilton, writing in 1934, gave this phenomen that occurred in the early 16th century its name. The Hamilton thesis suggested that after 1530, 20 per cent less goods could be purchased for the same amount of money spent before 1530. As a consequence of inflation, wages rose by only about 30–40 per cent, but prices had risen by 100 per cent.

■ Exploring the detail

Poverty is often a relative term, but the price revolution in Spain created much genuine distress amongst the already poor and generated more people who found themselves in the same situation. Parishes set up registers of vagrants, issued begging licences and tried to offer help. Juan Luis Vives wrote a book in 1526 suggesting that hospitals for the poor be built and provision be made by the government to support the wandering poor.

■ A closer look

The price rise

Rising prices was not a normal event in Spain, or even in Europe, at this time. Contemporaries were puzzled. The most accepted explanation for the price rise is generally known as the 'quantity theory of money'. It was first put forward by a contemporary, Martin de Azpilcueta, of the University of Salamanca. For most people at the time, the idea that the value of money could change was unknown. Azpilcueta deduced, however, that 'money is worth more when and where it is scarce than where it is abundant … in times when money was scarcer, saleable goods and labour were given for very much less than after the discovery of the Indies, which flooded the country with gold and silver.'

This theory was supported effectively by Hamilton who said that 'the close correlation between the increase in volume of treasure (silver) imports and the rise in commodity prices throughout the 16th century demonstrates beyond question that the "abundant mines of America" were the principal cause of the price revolution in Spain.' Although the details of this view have been questioned, the general point is accepted.

Other factors were issues such as the rise in population: more people wanted food and goods and, as those goods were in short supply, the price went up. This can be seen particularly in food prices, which rose dramatically as the demand from the growing population at home and that of the colonists in America grew to create an entirely new market.

Fig. 6 *The Mesta: sheep feeding in protected areas*

Vital commodities such as food and oil were particularly affected. This was not something that just affected the feckless and the sick. Those on fixed incomes suffered badly, including some elements of the noble classes. Worse still were the very poorly paid, many of whom became wandering labourers and often beggars. Peasants who rented land from the Church or the nobility were likely to find their rents rapidly increasing. Day labourers were in an even more difficult situation; along with 70 per cent of the population of Castile. The percentage of poor people in the population rose sharply. The rise in population also contributed, making a significant impact in the latter part of the reign. Gypsies began to be accused of crimes, 'since they steal from the fields and destroy orchards and deceive people.'

Industry slowed despite the resources available; for example, lead, copper and iron were to be found but could not be exploited largely because of the power of the guilds. Small manufacturers found that rising prices and cheap foreign imports were damaging their trade. For many, emigration to the New World became an attractive proposition. Possibly half the emigrants in the New World came from 30 Spanish cities. These people were looking for escape from poverty as a result of rising rents and crippling taxes. They were followed by monks and friars, particularly the Franciscans in 1524. Bartolomé de Las Casas, formerly an owner of land in America but a member of the Dominican Order from 1522, reported meeting individuals who wanted their sons 'to grow up in a free world'.

However, this tide of immigrants had a negative effect on the native population of America, many of whom found themselves slave labourers, unwilling converts to Christianity, and/or the victims of diseases brought by the settlers. The influx created conditions that encouraged a major imposition of Spanish authority in the New World and led to the creation of a Council of the Indies. The effects on the native peoples were catastrophic. In 1516, an expedition went to Hispaniola to study the ability of the Indians to live as free people. It was decided this was not possible. In addition, the sheer distance between Spain and the New World generated administrative delays and misunderstandings; prejudice and slavery grew. Slavery only truly disappeared in the 1560s.

Activity

Group activity

Working in pairs or small groups, answer the following: Why did so many Spaniards emigrate to the New World in this period?

Look at the following suggestions and put them in order of importance. When you have done this, compare your ranking with other groups and discuss why there are differences.

Possible reasons for emigration:

- It would be an adventure.
- To acquire land and become independent rather than working for others.
- To make a fortune from the gold and silver mines.
- To convert the natives to Christianity.
- To escape the control of the Catholic Church.
- To avoid paying taxes that were rising.

Summary question

How secure were the finances of Spain in this period?

Learning outcomes

Throughout this section, you have gained some understanding about the difficult problems that Charles had to deal with in the early part of his reign, despite his youth and inexperience. Understanding of causes and effects of the Germania and Comuneros revolts should have enabled you to appreciate the extent of the threat they posed to a new regime. An awareness of the growing importance of the Cortes, particularly in terms of financial issues, and an understanding of the potential threats posed by the delicate relationship with the nobility, should help you to assess how these issues affected the authority of the crown. An appreciation of the increasing complexity of religious issues, the extent of the work of the Inquisition and its impact on the people and an understanding of the extent to which Protestantism and other non-Catholics were challenging the Church and the state should allow you to make some judgements about the stability of Spain.

Overall, your study of this section should enable you to analyse changes in Spanish society and reach a judgement about the extent to which these changes were beneficial.

 Examination-style question

'A confused affair lacking in cohesion and a sense of purpose.'
To what extent do you agree with this view of the Comuneros Revolt?

(45 marks)

This question asks you to consider two aspects of the Comuneros Revolt – its aims and events. It is probably wise to begin with the idea of 'purpose' before attempting any analysis in terms of 'confusion' and 'cohesion', even though the question does not have the terms in that specific order. As long as you are covering the required aspects, this will not affect the marks you are given. Your initial statement might provide some context, for example, when this event occurred and where.

'A sense of purpose' requires you to think about the reasons why the revolt occurred. There is a wide range of these so perhaps you could organise your points into categories, for example political, social, religious and economic factors. Try to get an example of each type of factor with some supporting information. This means some thinking time before you start writing. It would also be useful, if you have several points within a category, to try to put them in a sequence related to timescale if possible. 'A sense of purpose' could be exemplified by reference to complaints about offices going to Burgundians rather than Castilians, concerns about the future of the wool trade and livelihoods, fears about higher taxation, etc. These are very specific issues that can be explained and linked and perhaps arranged into some order of importance. Links can be made, for example whether the wool trade is going to be viable might depend on the amount of taxes raised through import/export demands. Concerns about Charles' inability to speak Spanish might be very important in the success or failure of the revolt.

'Lack of cohesion' can be identified in the breadth of the demands of the rebels. For example: generation of factions among the nobles and their supporters; the range of people involved in the protest from nobles to clergy; specific individuals like Padilla who wanted a political outcome and rival nobles who wanted to make both personal and political gain; the members of the Cortes who did not want to impose unpopular taxes; and the merchants who wanted to make money and feared that all this wrangling would destroy their business.

Finally, you could draw some conclusions. For example, are both parts of the statement correct or is only part of it correct? Are there other factors involved that don't fit into these two suggested descriptions of the event?

Charles I King of Spain and Charles V Holy Roman Emperor: divided loyalties, 1529–56

Charles V: struggling for survival

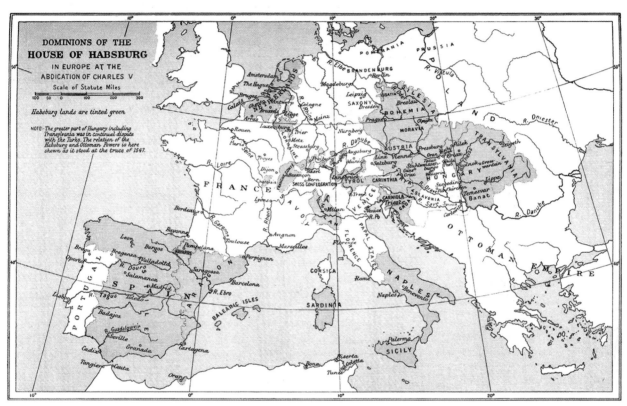

Fig. 1 *Charles' bequest: the Habsburg family lands (shaded)*

In this chapter you will learn about:

- Charles I as King of Spain and Charles V as Holy Roman Emperor

- the regency of Philip from 1543 and the abdication of Charles I/V in 1556

- the challenge and impact of Charles' European responsibilities.

At the tender age of 22, Charles I of Spain had found himself the ruler of two territories; his inheritance of the crown in Spain and the elected role of Holy Roman Emperor. He was the most significant ruler in Europe. By 1529, the responsibilities he held in both territories were an overwhelming burden. In Spain, his young son Philip was acting as Regent, ably supported by the guiding hand of his mother.

Charles' role as both Emperor and King was not easy; he had to spend more time in the Holy Roman Empire than he did in Spain; consequently his ability to speak Spanish was initially very poor, although he had made up for this by 1529. Many Spaniards, throughout Charles' reign, perceived him not as their monarch but more as a visitor. Charles, like Ferdinand before him, was a 'stranger', but he tried to make amends by keeping constantly in touch, usually by courier. Charles was also a moral man and a thinker and got involved in debates about colonial issues as well as purely Spanish matters; one topic he raised was that of the possibility of an 'ethical empire'. This was quite a revolutionary view

Did you know?

Even though Charles was the Holy Roman Emperor, he had no standing army, no consistent means of raising money and his nobles often had members of their families holding important positions, for example in the Church. More positively, Charles was the supreme judge in legal matters and could negotiate with the Reichstag (parliament) about its decisions. He was also usually supported by the Swabian League, which consisted of a group of princes, knights and towns in south-west Germany.

Key terms

The Diet of the Holy Roman Empire: the Diet, or parliament, of the Holy Roman Empire was made up of the electors, princes and free imperial cities. The electors' decisions were binding in theory, but it would probably have been difficult to enforce them across such a multiplicity of states.

in a time when the native inhabitants of Europe saw noble birth and accummulated wealth as the basis of the social and political structures, rather than the concept of contribution and hard work.

Exploring the detail

Holy Roman Empire

This was a collection of more than 300 states ruled by different rulers, owing allegiance to the emperor but having varying authority in their own states. Some were princes, others were electors, some states were run by bishops. Many of these rulers were eager to throw off the authority of the emperor and Charles' predecessor, Maximilian. Maximilian had managed to remain in power, but had been under considerable pressure.

As a devout Catholic, Charles was acutely aware of the growth of alternative faiths; he had already failed to suppress Luther in Germany but was determined that Lutheranism would not take hold and spill across Europe into Spain. He even removed Erasmian scholars from Spanish universities so that the ideas of Protestantism would not spread. Nevertheless, Spain was not to be without heretics.

A significant, although personal, factor in his struggle was Charles' desire to be accepted by his new country; to this end, he learnt to speak both Castilian and Catalan. Unfortunately, he never learned to speak Spanish properly and this did generate some anger in some subjects who felt they had been snubbed.

Charles' elevation to the role of Holy Roman Emperor was more accidental than intentional; it came after a disputed succession, a military campaign and great expense. He was crowned in Bologna in 1530 by Pope Clement VII. This ceremony was a reminder of the secular and spiritual role that Charles had now accepted. In 1529, Charles had stated, 'there are three compelling causes which oblige me to go to Italy. The first is the urge to protect the Christian faith; the second my desire to apply my courage and bravery to this unhappy place; the third my wish to receive the honour and title due to me and achieve a universal peace in Christendom'.

The empire Charles ruled was an issue because of its fractured political condition. The approximately 300 states differed – some were geographically large, Brandenburg for example, and some were much smaller, such as Saxony – and were ruled individually by princes and knights. Charles visited the empire a total of six times. Family members acted as Regents at other times. Maltby suggests that, although the size of the empire created problems, it was in practice difficult for the princes to form a united front about any specific issues. Many ecclesiastical states elected their rulers, so no dynasty could be founded and consistent policies were seldom pursued. Friction between princes, such as the Weltsin family, whose two branches were in almost constant dispute over territory, meant they did not always focus on imperial issues. Furthermore, the princes did not always attend the main governing body, **the Diet of the Holy Roman Empire**, in person. Charles could use this to his advantage.

Historians have suggested that the vast role of Holy Roman Emperor meant that Charles was never really in control. This view also has implications for Charles' role in Spain; he could not give Spain his full attention and had to rely on his son as Regent.

A similar view is promoted by the historian Maland. He says, 'the Diet turned out to be nothing more than a convention of sovereign princes whose power to obstruct any decision they disliked denied the emperor any opportunity to impose his policies on Germany ...' and who also hoped that 'as a busy Spanish king he might leave German affairs to his younger brother Ferdinand'. Charles' earlier agreement to the 'Capitulation' was also a potential stumbling block to the exercise of imperial power as he agreed, for example, that he would support the rights of the princes.

Ruling such a large and varied territory was never going to be an easy task. Charles would not be able to avoid opposition completely. One serious conflict occurred almost immediately with the princes over religious issues. Charles' absence from the empire until 1530, having left his younger brother in control, also meant that there was little change in the way in which the empire was ruled. Some changes that were made only consolidated the power of the princes. One example of this was the disbanding of the Regency Council.

However, Charles was not always willing to delegate his authority. Faced with a range of problems in the 1530s, 1540s and 1550s, he became less democractic. One of his most serious challenges concerned religion and the development of Lutheranism. This created divisions in the empire, provoking not only academic debate, but open conflict between Luther's supporters and those opposing him. Luther was eventually summoned to a Diet at Worms and made an outlaw; this did not end his influence. The issue dragged on throughout Charles' reign. Some princes saw supporting Luther as a way of gaining more political independence for themselves. The Treaty of Augsburg in 1555 eventually brought some compromise. The princes had to make a decision about the religion of their state; it could be entirely Catholic or entirely Protestant. In political terms, Charles also had to strengthen his position by making some changes in the empire, for example replacing some city councils with appointees of his choice.

Charles as an absentee monarch

Charles I spent much of his time after his election as Holy Roman Emperor in the empire rather than Spain. The following dates show when he was actually in Spain:

- April 1533 to April 1535.
- December 1536 to spring 1538.
- July 1538 to November 1539.
- November 1541 to May 1543.
- September 1556 to September 1558.

This amounts to a total of only six years out of a possible 20 years. He needed to spend time in the empire and to establish a relationship with the princes; he had the support of some influential princes, but not all. The Lutheran problem had become a serious issue and, as Holy Roman Emperor,

The Treaty of Augsburg, 1555

- Religious differences were to be resolved by the formula 'cuius regio, eius religio' i.e. whatever the religion of the prince was, so should also be the religion of the territory ruled.

- Any subject who preferred the other choice should sell up and move to the state/territory where his chosen religion was followed; free imperial cities were not bound by this rule.

- Any town or community which had been practising Lutheranism for a length of time in the Holy Roman Empire could continue to be Lutheran.

- Church land taken from Catholic prelates (bishops) who were not directly vassals of the Holy Roman Emperor could be kept if it could be proved that it had been held continuously from 1552. This was called 'Ecclesiastical Reservation'.

- No subjects of any lands should try to persuade the subjects of any other state to abandon their religion.

Fig. 2 *Terms of the Treaty of Augsburg*

Exploring the detail

The Regency Council

The Regency Council was was set up in 1521; it had 22 members. Charles appointed the chairman and four other members; the Diet (parliament) appointed 18 others. Its brief was to maintain law and order and to deal with customs and financial issues. Charles soon realised that the princes were not cooperating and decided that the council could only operate whilst he was in Spain. It was finally disbanded in 1530.

Did you know?

The Imperial Diet or Reichstag was the name given to the parliament of the Holy Roman Empire. Many of the states in Germany also had Diets. The central Diet was made up of three separate bodies; one of these was the meeting of the seven electors, the second was the meeting of the other secular princes and the clergy, and the third represented the free cities.

Activity

Thinking point

How important was the element of prestige for Charles I of Spain in his role as Holy Roman Emperor?

Fig. 3 *Charles I and V in middle age*

Cross-reference

Look back to Chapter 7 (page 109) to remind yourself about Cobos.

Charles was expected to support the Pope in dealing with religious waywardness. Finally, Charles also had to contend with attacks on the Holy Roman Empire from the Ottoman Empire, both on the eastern borders of the empire and along the Mediterranean coast.

Charles was fortunate that his strong system of government in Spain compared favourably to that of the empire, with trustworthy officials who could keep systems going for him. The empire needed a much closer watch. For most of the time, therefore, Charles' son Philip was regent in Spain. There was still no fixed Spanish capital and, although administrators were beginning to work more from Valladolid, councils still followed the progress of the King or his Regent. Cobos, one of Charles' secretaries, as a consequence, set up a useful archive for administrative papers in a fortress at Simancas, making access to records easier.

Records of the Cortes show that Spaniards were not always happy with Charles' absences. The Admiral of Castile is quoted as saying: 'Your Majesty's protracted absences from your Spanish dominions is a thing to which your subjects can hardly reconcile themselves.' However, by choosing mainly Spaniards for court positions, Charles overcame this accusation. The appointed regents were all Spanish:

- 1529–39: Isabella, the Queen and Empress, supported by Cardinal Tavera.
- 1539–43: Prince Philip, with Talavera to advise (his mother had died in 1539).
- 1543–49: Prince Philip, now 15, ruled personally, using the advice of various nobles and two sets of 'Instructions' drawn up by his father.
- 1548–51: The Archduke Maximilian – he later married Maria, sister to Philip.
- 1551–54: Prince Philip again. He then left to go to England to marry Mary Tudor.
- 1555: Joanna, Philip's sister and widow of the King of Portugal.
- 1556: Philip returned as King in his own right.

During this period, there were important developments in the crown's relationship with the Cortes. For example, the Cortes of Castile became more able to bargain with the monarchy. This was the outcome of an agreement made with the Castilian Cortes held in Madrid in 1534 that two of the main taxes, the *alcabala* and the *tercias reales*, would be set at a specific agreed figure. This was called the *encabezamiento*. From 1536 to 1548, the amount collected from this system rose by only 2.5 per cent. By 1550, it accounted for approximately 70 per cent of all taxes collected. A range of other taxes made up the remainder.

However, by 1553, inflation meant that, whilst prices were rising by about 33 per cent, the value of the amount of tax collected had risen overall by only 21 per cent. This was because the Cortes had the right to refuse to impose increases; a significant but dangerous privilege in a period of continuously rising prices. The monarchy consequently had less to spend and did not keep pace with inflation.

A closer look

Conflict with the Cortes

The Cortes had not broken free entirely from crown control in this period. They were still assembled on a fairly regular basis, stimulated by the needs of the crown for finance. But this need gave the Cortes the opportunity to flex their muscles. At the Castilian Cortes held in Toledo in 1538, a tax on food was requested. When the request was not granted, the Cortes was dismissed. The president of the council, Cardinal Tavera, told the Cortes, 'Your lordships are not required any longer: each of you can go home or where you will.' This was not a temporary dismissal, but permanent for the nobles and clergy. They were no longer useful to the crown.

The authority displayed by the monarch suggests that the Cortes, although important, were still not fully in partnership with the crown. They were expected to pay up with the minimum of negotiation, but their demands for 'redress of grievances' were not automatically granted. Elliott suggests that this change turned the Castilian Cortes into a 'rubber stamp'.

Despite this success, Charles only managed to achieve an increase of 50 per cent in taxation over the course of the reign, whereas prices had risen by 100 per cent.

Taxes were increasingly and heavily supplemented by state borrowing via *juros*. This became necessary when estimated income fell drastically short of expenditure, as happened in the 1530s and 1540s. Repayment, however, took up large amounts of incoming revenue – 36 per cent in 1522, 65 per cent by 1543 and 68 per cent by 1556. Loans were also raised for activities in Charles' other territories in Europe, but the backing for these loans came from the Spanish treasury and not the empire. This put Spain in a delicate position of responsibility for the repayment of large loans and also allowed foreign financiers to live and work in Spain, some of them buying offices, land, etc. to the detriment of native businessmen. As early as 1546, Cobos was concerned about the growing financial difficulties (Source 1).

> Remember the importance of finding a remedy for the relief of these kingdoms, because of the extreme need, for otherwise there could not fail to be serious trouble, because the need is so notorious that not only are the natives of the kingdom aware of it and are refusing to take part in any financial transactions, but even foreigners … are doing the same things because they know there is no source from which payments can be made.

1 *Quoted in C. Mulgan,* **The Renaissance Monarchies, 1469–1558,** *1998*

Despite the warnings, debt continued to rise. International bankers, usually the German Fuggers and Italians, charged high rates of interest on money they loaned. Interest rates had reached 48.8 per cent by the 1550s with serious consequences for crown finances.

- Foreign financiers now had an interest in Spanish commercial development and investment.
- Some Spanish producers of goods were unable to organise their business as freely as they would have liked. Many got into debt and often could not pay it off readily.
- The government had difficulty financing its activities. Some bankers were willing to lend money to the government in the expectation of being reimbursed when the next treasure fleet came in; these agreements were set out in contracts called an *asiento*. This meant that banks were handling even more of the government's income.
- Confidence declined rapidly. This was Spain's '**credit crunch**'.

Activity

Thinking point

To what extent did the authority of the Cortes develop during this period?

Key terms

Credit crunch: a term used when borrowing from banks and other financial institutions has reached such a peak that there is a danger that the loans, and the interest on them, cannot be repaid; this, in turn, means there is less money available for banks to lend to clients and other institutions, or to give interest on money invested with them. If this situation continues for an extended period, both lender and borrower will suffer.

Bullion (gold and silver) coming in from the New World was also an important factor in this financial crisis; Mulgan calls it a 'poisoned chalice' because it increased coinage in circulation. This meant that those selling goods raised their prices to acquire more of the coinage. As a result, their income rose in the short term. However, those buying goods were in a more difficult situation, unless their income rose, as they paid more.

Another issue was that bullion was also exported from Spain and spread throughout northern Europe, causing inflation there too. In the longer term, Kamen suggests this was linked to political issues in that the Cortes continued to approve the exportation of bullion to fund Charles' military activities in Europe – war against the Protestants and the German princes who supported them.

Luis Ortiz, a royal official, was clear that 'real wealth came … from labour and higher output', not bullion. However, in many places, land holdings and industry were so small scale, higher output was impossible.

So many issues were feeding into the situation that it became difficult to control and resolve.

■ Philip as Regent from 1543

Philip began work as Regent in 1543, acting as the monarch whilst his father, the King, was dealing with matters in the Holy Roman Empire. Philip was then 16 and so his father wrote out instructions to help him. These took two forms. One was a summary of the ideals he thought he should strive to work towards; the second was his thoughts on his ministers: 'Though they are the heads of rival cliques (Tavera and Cobos) nevertheless I decided to appoint them both, so that you might not be left in the hands of either one of them.' Kamen suggests that this comment about balance may have influenced Philip very much in making his own appointments when he became King.

■ Key profile

Philip II of Spain (King of Spain, 1556–98)

Philip, as King, was known as 'Il Prudente', i.e. cautious and thoughtful. He was very committed to the Catholic faith, hard-working and modest. His strong sense of duty often made him appear cold and detached. However, the Venetian ambassador said, more kindly that 'he displayed great calmness … he held his desires in control … no-one ever saw him in a rage, being always patient, phlegmatic and temperate'. He had four children, but only one survived him.

Fig. 4 *Prince Philip, painted while he was Regent of Spain*

Charles was concerned about leaving his son in charge, particularly regarding the handling of justice and finance. He left copious instructions to Philip; these included:

■ 'Give specal care to finance, which is today the most important department of the state.'

■ 'Trust the Duke of Alva as commander-in-chief.'

Key profile

Duke of Alva

The Duke of Alva (1507–82) was a member of the Alvarez family and was brought up as a soldier; by the age of 14 he was involved in campaigns against the French. He became a general at the age of 25 and commanded an army by the time he was 30. He also fought against the Turks, playing an important role in the siege of Tunis 1535. He also fought with King Charles in the Holy Roman Empire and in Italy and the Netherlands in the reign of Philip II, Charles' son. He preferred to avoid battle whenever possible in preference for sieges. He introduced the use of the musket, and is said to be responsible for the deaths of up to 1,800 Netherlanders in his period as governor of the Netherlands.

Philip was very conscientious and kept his father well informed. He was also critical and concerned about his subjects. In 1545, he wrote to his father commenting on the amount of tax that ordinary people had to pay and the consequences, i.e. 'they are unable to pay their rents since the lack the means, and the prisons are full'. Much of this poverty was to be found in rural areas where most people lived at this time; Hunt suggests that this poverty could have been a consequence of the growth of towns that attracted the most enterprising, leaving the less well motivated, the elderly and the infirm behind. In addition, the opportunity to emigrate to the New World where 'an artisan from Estramadura (might) become a gentleman' was an attractive proposition.

Philip was fortunate in that he had excellent support in Francisco de los Cobos. Cobos had previously worked with Ferdinand. He travelled with Charles as emperor from 1529–33 as an adviser and then spent the rest of his time in office, up to 1547, in Spain.

To assist Cobos, a number of other loyal and hard-working civil servants were appointed, such as Alonso de Idiaquez, Gonzalo de Perez and Francisco de Eraso. Philip was also supported by the members of the *audiencias* or committees set up to deal with different aspects of government.

As in the earlier period of the reign, finance and the economy were potentially the most difficult areas. A quick survey of Spain and its rising population, tripling between 1534 and 1561, might have suggested prosperity. Landowners, traders and merchants were apparently making good livings. Income from the New World was rising, as shown in Table 1.

Table 1 *Total imports from the New World, 1531–55 (in ducats)*

Period	Royal bullion	Private bullion	Total bullion
1531–35	518,833	1,461,445	1,980,278
1536–40	1,621,062	3,104,408	4,725,470
1541–45	909,346	5,035,460	5,944,806
1546–50	1,911,206	4.699,247	6,610,453
1551–55	4,354,208	7,484,429	11,838,637

Cross-reference

Look back to Chapter 7 (page 109) to refresh your memory of the work of Cobos in the reign of Ferdinand and Charles I.

Activity

Research exercise

Find out more about Cobos and his team of civil servants. Try to identify what these men had to offer in terms of skills etc. in supporting the Spanish government.

Activity

Thinking point

1. What information can you extract from Table 1 about imports of bullion from the New World?

2. Compare Table 1 with Table 2 in Chapter 4 (page 55). What comments can you make about similarities and differences?

3. Is what you see here a cause or a consequence of the changes in the Castilian economic and financial situation?

However, the government needed more revenue. The problem began a little earlier, in 1538. The Cortes had been summoned, which, unusually, included the nobles and the clergy, and a proposal for a new tax called the *sisa* was put forward. This would be raised on food and everyone would be liable for this tax. Not surprisingly, the nobles refused. This was the last time the nobles were summoned to the Cortes; nevertheless, the Cortes had to accept the proposed tax. Meanwhile, the situation deteriorated and prices more than doubled at a time when income was increasing by only 50 per cent.

The government mainly relied on:

- taxes raised from ordinary folk, for example *servicios*
- the sale of *juros* or government bonds, although revenue from these was slow to come in
- borrowing.

The consequence was higher interest rates. Charles therefore borrowed, from current revenue, a total of 39 million ducats in order to repay the interest. By 1543, repayments appear to have accounted for more than 43–65 per cent of revenue raised by the Cortes, By 1554, all the money that came into the treasury, plus the anticipated revenue up to 1560, was needed to repay the debt. At least 40 per cent went straight to German bankers who had funded the loans.

The bankers had felt the loans were secure because of the money coming in from America, but soon lenders became concerned about Spain's ability to repay the debt. In 1557, Philip, as regent, had to make a decision. He suspended all payments from the Castilian treasury. It was now obvious that both Charles and Philip had spent far more than their income. Technically, this was bankruptcy.

Was this situation made worse by the actions of Philip's caretaker government? Inflation in the 16th century has commonly been put down, in the first instance, to the arrival of bullion in Europe from the New World in the earlier part of the reign – more coinage in circulation meant that retailers asked for more of it, hence its value fell and prices increased. This did play a part. The rate of inflation overall was about 2 per cent, which seems negligible today, but was exceptional in the 16th century. The rate fluctuated at different times in different places. Although prices were rising overall, wages remained the same or rose only slowly. The effect of this was poverty and a lower standing of living; in some cases, people became totally destitute. This was not just limited to Spain; it was a Europe-wide problem.

The main effect in Spain was felt, as might be expected, by the ordinary people. Philip wrote to his father in 1545 expressing his concern saying, 'The common people who have to pay the *servicios* are reduced to such distress that many of them walk naked.'

■ The abdication of Charles in 1556

Charles' abdication from the Holy Roman Empire was a dramatic response to a complex situation. In part, it was the result of 'apathy and despair' concerning problems such as the spread of Protestantism, which Charles failed to extinguish. Alternatively, the abdication was the product of Charles' failure to appreciate the extent of the determination of its followers to maintain their faith. Neither did Charles support the proposed interim agreement, suggesting that Catholics continued to practise their religion in Protestant areas until the Council of Trent could arrive at some resolution of the issues. This would only have worked in

■ Cross-reference

Look back to Chapter 9 (pages 132–8) to refresh your memory about other views on inflation and financial affairs.

■ Activity

Thinking point

What were Philip's successes and failures as Regent of Spain?

■ Did you know?

The Council of Trent was a General Council of the Catholic Church summoned by the Pope. It had three sessions: 1545–47, 1551–52 and 1562–63. It was a meeting of Catholic bishops who, for example, confirmed Catholic doctrine, agreed the duties and behaviour expected of the clergy of all ranks, set up seminaries to train priests and generally set out to reform the Catholic Church in response to the growth of Protestantism.

areas where Charles' troops were strong enough to keep control.

A further issue was the length of the struggle; Charles had been fighting a battle against the growth of Protestantism and the Schmalkaldic League since the 1520s and he was weary. Lutheran princes such as Philip of Hesse and Maurice of Saxony were his bitter enemies. By 1545, most of north-east and north-west Germany was Protestant. More and more German princes switched their faith, even the Elector of Cologne who was also an archbishop looked as if he might, at one time, become Protestant. Charles found this prospect too hard to bear.

Charles' dual role of Holy Roman Emperor and King of Spain was a heavy burden, even though he had passed some of the responsibility for Spain to his wife and son by the late 1540s. However, he did not want Spain to be sidelined and was anxious that the overall power and authority in Europe of his family would not be diminished. He began to plan for the future.

Fig. 5 *Scene of the abdication of Charles V as Holy Roman Emperor in 1556*

Charles wanted his younger brother Ferdinand to succeed him as Holy Roman Emperor; Ferdinand had achieved the first rung on this ladder through his election as King of the Romans in 1531. Theoretically, he would be the next Holy Roman Emperor. Next, Charles wanted to ensure that his son Philip would have an appropriate inheritance and saw a marriage between Mary Tudor of England and Philip as a possibility. Habsburg territory would neatly surround France and keep the French monarchs in check. For Mary Tudor, this was also a positive move as it supported her plans to return England to Catholicism. Philip tried to make himself popular by distributing pensions, learning some English and being discreet about his influence on government. However, ultimately, the marriage was not a success, there was no heir and Philip had no rights to rule England on Mary's death in 1558.

Key profile

Ferdinand of Spain

King of the Romans, brother of Charles, Ferdinand (1503–64) was brought up in Spain, unlike Charles. In 1521, he married Anna, daughter of the King of Bohemia and Hungary. In 1522, Ferdinand became Regent for Charles in the Holy Roman Empire and controlled the Habsburg lands. In 1556, he became emperor in his own right and ruled until his death in 1564.

Despite lengthy discussions at the Colloquy of Regensburg in 1541, no agreement could be reached about any other European role for Prince Philip. However, during 1548–49, he was accepted as his father's heir to the Netherlands.

Exploring the detail

The Schmalkaldic League

This was a league of Protestant princes set up to defend the faith in the Holy Roman Empire in 1531. It had support from Protestants in France, England and Denmark. By 1545, much of northern Germany was Protestant and the League was less powerful and was finally defeated at the Battle of Muhlberg in 1547. However, its demise did not prevent the Holy Roman Empire being divided between Protestants and Catholics.

More positively, in terms of the empire, a useful development occurred when Francis I of France agreed not to help the Protestants despite his desire to reduce the power of his political enemy, King Charles. Charles also bought-off Maurice of Saxony who was to be allowed to have the title of Elector of Saxony if he would join the Catholic side. The Pope also promised money and troops. The resultant struggle was fierce, and took the Protestants by surprise. In 1547, the Protestants in the Holy Roman Empire were severely defeated at the Battle of Muhlberg. Philip of Hesse surrendered.

Key profile

Philip of Hesse

Philip of Hesse (c.1509–67) was an extreme Lutheran, holding lands in the Holy Roman Empire, and a leading member of the Schmalkaldic League opposing the Edict of Worms, which outlawed Luther, and defended Protestantism. Philip used the revenues of a monastery to fund a university. He also put money into a hospital and the running costs of Lutheran churches. Unfortunately, Philip was subsequently revealed as a bigamist (although Luther is reputed to have condoned it) and had to ask for a pardon from Charles V. In 1552, he was released and continued to support reform of the Church.

Ironically, Charles was, at this point, seen as too powerful by the Catholic forces even though he had 'won the war' for them. His subsequent abdication, therefore, came as a surprise to his contemporaries. The Pope declared it 'the strangest thing to ever happen.' Charles abdicated from his territories in the order in which he had gained them, taking almost a year to go through the process. The only post not handed over to Philip was the Imperial Vicariate in Italy; his uncle, Ferdinand, the new Holy Roman Emperor, refused to sanction this on the grounds that it would mean Philip had to spend time in Italy. His kingdom in Spain needed him more. This was a sound decision in view of the absences of Charles, which had been much resented by his Spanish subjects, despite the prestige of the post. The Habsburgs had now divided their inheritance having potentially learned the lesson of a monarchy overburdened with extensive and scattered territories.

The difficulties created by Charles' responsibilities in Europe

The prestigious role of Charles in the Holy Roman Empire had brought many responsibilities with it. For example, he was expected to:

- champion Christianity
- defend the customs, rights and privileges of his territories
- consult, as appropriate, with his appointed lay and military officers
- protect and defend his territories from attack
- secure the succession.

These issues brought him into conflict with different groups of people and different states such as the French, rather than 'fostering peace'. Six separate conflicts occurred across all of Europe, with fighting in France, the Netherlands, Italy and Scotland. One example was the Habsburg–Valois War, which made the French afraid that Charles wanted 'universal monarchy'.

Despite his success in the Habsburg–Valois War, Charles V later declared that his quarrels with the French King 'would be better resolved person to person with swords, capes and daggers … on land or on sea, in a closed field or in front of our armies, wherever he chooses'. Charles remained wary of the French who suspected that he wanted to rule the world.

During the course of these wars, the Turks besieged Vienna in 1529, gaining a foothold in the Balkans and the Mediterranean. Against the Protestants, Charles fought an internal battle in the Holy Roman Empire. Not only were these conflicts almost continuous, they diverted him from his government in Spain, and consumed resources, creating a heavy financial burden. Alternatively, they also generated respect and sometimes fear of Spain; it was considered to be one of the most powerful European states.

SPAENSCHE TIRANNYE IN NEDERLANDT

Fig. 6 *Growth of opposition to Spanish rule in the Netherlands and its consequences*

The Holy Roman Empire, Protestants and Turks, and the consequences

The Holy Roman Empire that Charles I of Spain came to rule was a complex entity occupying much of the area of modern-day Germany, Austria and Czechoslovakia. There were more than 300 states in total, ranging from those that were basically just a city, for example the Archbishopric of Cologne, and others that were much more substantial such as Brandenburg and Bohemia. In addition, the Holy Roman Emperor's role had certain strengths and weaknesses (Table 2).

Cross-reference

See Chapters 3 (pages 43–5), 6 (pages 84–6) and 8 (pages 133–5) to remind yourself about sources of income and consequent issues.

Table 2 *Strengths and weaknesses of the Holy Roman Emperor*

Strengths	Weaknesses
He, the emperor, had been chosen/elected by the elector princes.	The princes were powerful in their own states, e.g. they administered justice and held their own courts.
He was the secular head of the Christian world and was expected to work in partnership with the Pope as its sprirtual head.	The princes belonged to one of 10 leagues that controlled law and order in specific areas; princes and the cities worked together. The Swabian League operated effectively in the south; but the Schmalkaldic League supported the Protestant cause.
He could raise money and armies.	Diet (or parliament) did not meet regularly.
He set the agenda for meetings of the Diet or parliament.	No permanent royal army or system for raising taxes.
He was the supreme legal authority.	No body existed that had authority over the whole of the empire.
He could give honours, offices and titles to those who supported him/gave good service.	Lesser nobles and knights often teamed up with the more powerful nobles to earn a living as the economy of Germany declined.
Approximately 80 imperial free cities and the imperial knights were traditionally loyal to the emperor; the latter, however, were poor and lacked influence.	The shortlived existence of a Regency Council to govern in the absence of the emperor and to allow princes to negotiate changes, etc. made the princes more resentful of the emperor's power.
	Charles was not always present in Germany.

With such extensive responsibilities, but lacking a standing army, a proper taxation system and having to deal with powerful magnates, Charles' role was always going to be fraught with difficulties. Some of those difficulties were the Protestants and the Turks.

Protestants

Charles was a loyal Catholic and was extremely unhappy to find that differing heretical views in the shape of Protestantism and Martin Luther

Did you know?

Anabaptists were 'extreme' Protestants. They emerged in the Holy Roman Empire in the 1520s. There were many different groups, but they all shared a belief in adult baptism and that the end of the world was imminent. In 1528, Charles V imposed the death penalty, although some princes, for example Philip of Hesse, were prepared to tolerate Anabaptists. Some were burned at the stake. They accounted for no more than 10 per cent of the population, yet stimulated the equivalent of a 'red scare'; the term used in the 20th century for the threat of Communism.

seeped into his territories in Europe, especially in the 'Holy' Roman Empire. Charles, in 1521, said: 'To settle this matter, I am determined to use my kingdoms and dominions, my friends, my body, my life, my soul.' He was not able to attempt to fulfil his promise until the 1530s. By this time, Protestantism was a much stronger movement.

At Charles' coronation as Holy Roman Emperor in 1530, he had tried to get the Pope to agree to a General Council of the Church to deal with some of the religious problems. The Pope was not, however, interested in conciliation, so Charles took matters into his own hands and summoned a Diet at Augsburg, hoping some decisions might be reached. Neither side, however, was prepared to make concessions. Both produced a document; the Protestants had the Augsburg Confession and the Catholics, the Augsburg Recess. The Confession was a statement of Protestant beliefs; the Recess was a condemnation of Protestantism.

The Recess stated that: 'This doctrine (i.e. Protestantism) which has already been condemned, has given rise to much misleading error among the common people. They have lost all true reverence, all Christian honour, discipline, the fear of God and charity to their neighbour – they are utterly forgotten.' Protestants were allowed six months to return to the Catholic Church; the consequence of not doing so would be severe.

However, instead of creating peace, this simply increased the aggravation and led to the formation of the Schmalkaldic League, which was ready to work with other European powers, if possible, to defend Protestantism. For example, the league supported the restoration of the Protestant Duke of Württemberg to his duchy.

Surprisingly, Charles took no effective action, possibly fearing that he would not succeed in suppressing the Protestants. By default, he allowed Protestantism to continue as a force in the empire. In 1539, further concessions were made as a consequence of continued problems with the Turks and the need for troops and money. Charles did, however, pressure a new Pope for a General Council to deal with the Protestant issue, but the Pope, in turn, was pressured by the French not to hold a council. The weaker Charles was in the empire, the more it suited the French who did not want a strong Germany on their borders.

No further progress was made until 1541, when Charles summoned a meeting of the Diet at Regensburg to try and resolve the Catholic/Protestant issue once and for all. He had picked his time carefully; there was scandal in the Protestant camp when Philip of Hesse, the leader of the Schmalkaldic League, was accused of bigamy. The Diet gathered at Regensburg attended by representatives of the Pope, as well as the regular members. Negotiations continued for two months, only to collapse because no common ground could be found.

Over the next few years, both sides attempted to consolidate their position:

- 1544: A meeting of the Imperial Diet at Regensburg asked for reconcilation between the two sides.
- 1545–49: A council met at Trent (as part of the process of the Catholic Reformation); there were no real concessions to Protestant issues.
- 1546: Protestants feared the emperor was planning a military campaign against them and gathered their forces; Charles was allied with England, made peace with France and agreed that the Pope would provide troops to fight the Protestants.

Clearly, both religious and political issues were involved in this situation. Outwardly, Charles emphasised the the need for peace, law and order; privately, the religious issue possibly played the larger part.

Key profile

Maurice of Saxony

A significant supporter of the Reformation, Maurice (1521–53) was educated as a Lutheran and was originally a member of the Schmalkaldic League. He fought for Charles V against the Turks in 1542, the Duke of Cleves in 1543 and the French in 1544. He also supported Charles at the Battle of Muhlberg in 1547, but then switched sides because he felt he had not been adequately rewarded. He died in battle in 1553. He is either described as the saviour of German Protestantism because of his change of allegiance, or as a traitor, depending on the view of the biographer.

As Protestants grew in numbers, another set of 'unbelievers' or 'infidels', the Turks, were waiting to attack; the campaign against Luther was scaled down in order to deal with them.

Charles continued to denounce Lutheranism, but the movement only gained momentum. Attempts to reach a compromise were not successful. Even the Catholic princes did not want Charles to be victorious because they felt it would strengthen his hold on Germany.

The struggle lasted from 1546 to 1555. Charles was able to draw on troops from Italy, the Netherlands and Spain, as well as from the empire. Maurice of Saxony broke ranks with the Protestants and fought with Charles. The Protestants were defeated at Muhlberg in 1547 and Charles produced terms for a compromise set out in the Interim of Augsburg of 1548, but no official agreement was reached between the two religious groups and Lutheranism survived.

Turks

'There are those who say that I wish to rule the world, but both my thoughts and my deeds demonstrate the contrary.' This was a statement made by Charles in 1536 before Pope Paul III and the cardinals. He also said, 'My intention is not to war against Christians, but against the infidel.' Earlier, in 1519, Charles had declared that the fight against the Muslims was, 'the thing most desired by us in this world.'

'Vast, exotic and, above all, non-Christian' is how one historian has defined the Ottoman Empire as it was in the early 16th century. As non-Christians, the Turks were feared; as exotic and different people, they were fascinating and their vast empire, which spread from present-day Hungary to Syria, was envied. Their non-Christian status, their apparent greed for land and their consequent threat to the Mediterranean coast was a diversion that probably prevented Spain from other imperial ventures such as gaining more territory in North Africa and securing the Netherlands.

Did you know?

The Interim of Augsburg, 1548

Stated:

- clergy could marry
- communion bread and wine for everyone
- church property confiscated by Lutherans could be retained if they agreed to return to Catholicism.

Supporters of the Interim were now seen as opponents of the emperor. This, in turn, generated concern about the growth of the emperor's power. Further conflict was a factor in Charles' decision to abdicate in 1555. This led to the Peace of Augsburg; rulers of states could choose which religion they would follow (cuius regio eius religio). Anyone who disagreed with the overall decision could leave for another state.

Fig. 7 *The Ottoman Empire in the mid-16th century*

Fig. 8 *Suleiman I, known as Suleiman the Magnificent*

Key profile

Suleiman the Magnificent

Little is known of Suleiman's (*c.*1494–1566) early life. As Sultan from 1520, he focused on expanding the Ottoman Empire. He used the rivalries of European powers to promote his success; this led to an alliance with France against the Habsburgs which operated on both land and sea. The growth of Protestantism usefully diverted the Holy Roman Emperor; in one campaign, Suleiman reached the gates of Vienna. In his empire, Suleiman was a patron of the arts, had an excellent knowledge of the law and promoted the building of, for example, roads and mosques. He was ambitious; a poet, but also the murderer of his son.

The on land threat from the Turks grew closer in 1520. A new Ottoman ruler, Suleiman the Magnificent had succeeded to the throne, attacked on land and by 1526 he had taken Hungary. He was dangerously close to the Austrian capital Vienna, which he besieged with approximately 100,000 troops. However, it was September and delaying tactics meant that the Turks had to withdraw for winter. When they returned in 1532, Charles took his armies to defend the city. He was cheated of battle, however, as the Turks were held up at the tiny fortress of Guns. The onset of winter and a shortage of supplies drove the Turks back before they could take the city. Fortunately for Charles V, Vienna was saved simply by the distance from the Ottoman bases. Charles' brother, Ferdinand, was keen to pursue the Turks, but failed in 1540 to gain Transylvania. By 1547, Hungary had been divided into three parts; Transylvania became autonomous, Suleiman took central Hungary and Ferdinand gained the western end. More than 20 years of sporadic conflict had resulted in limited gains, but brought relative stability to the area.

The Turks are often seen as cruel and combative, but, despite this, the Turks were more enlightened in their treatment of the peasantry than previous rulers who were Christian. The sultans removed many obligations such as forced labour; for example the requirement to collect wood for fuel, etc. In its place was a **poll tax**. This left the peasants free to cultivate their lands and use its products for themselves, giving them greater security. They also had the right to practise their own religion. This level of tolerance also meant that a good number of Jews settled in the Ottoman Empire after their expulsion from Spain in 1492.

The Turks were probably more threatening to Europe at sea. From 1516 onwards, Barbarossa had attacked Spain and Italy; in 1529 he seized a small island near Algiers on the North African coast and a short sail away from the southern coast of Spain. He also destroyed a Spanish fleet near Ibiza. Despite some retaliation by the Spanish, Barbarossa continued to harass Spanish shipping.

■ **Key profile**

Khairedin Barbarossa

Born in North Africa, Barbarossa (1482–1546), originally a potter, became angry about the Moors expelled from Spain in 1492. He joined an older brother organising raids on the Spanish coast. By 1515, other Muslim rulers were also attacking against Spain. He gained the favour of the Ottoman emperors, Selim I and Suleiman the Magnificent. By 1533, Barbarossa was Grand Admiral of the Ottoman fleet and Governor of Algiers. He promoted Turkish dominance in the eastern Mediterranean, despite failing to take Nice in the 1540s. His death in 1546 called a halt to Turkish activity in the Mediterranean until a suitable successor could be found.

One of Barbarossa's most notorious attacks was in 1534 when he captured Tunis. Charles successfully retaliated in 1535 using a fleet of 74 galleys, 300 transport ships and 30,000 men, one-third of whom were Spanish, the remainder coming from other Habsburg states. Tunis was reconquered for Spain, although Barbarossa escaped. The threat re-emerged when the Turks allied with the French in 1536; but once a truce was declared, Spain allied with the papacy and Venice and launched a naval attack at Prevesa. Spain and its allies were defeated, having limited funds and limited manpower. In1540, Charles failed again. The attack on Algiers failed as a fierce storm arose. Spain had failed to contain the Muslim threat.

Why, therefore, did the Turks not manage to attack and overrun Spain? Historians often stress the power of Spanish religious motivation and 'a great sense of mission'. Spain was inherently hostile towards Muslims having ejected most of them in the reign of Ferdinand and Isabella. The simple answer is probably that it was a matter of logistics; the distance between the two nations was huge. The Ottoman fleet had to overwinter in Toulon in 1540–41; had they not been able to take advantage of the emnity between the French and the Spanish, they would not have been in a position to threaten the western Mediterranean at all. It is also clear that, for the Turks, immediate gain in terms of moveable goods was an acceptable goal; no desire to defeat, convert or gain land and goods beyond the scope of provisioning their forays was sought. They simply wanted to wear down the enemy. The Turks were fully aware of the logistical difficulties of extending their empire, but any advantage they could gain was useful and their control of the Mediterranean was a significant achievement on its own.

Key chronology

The conflict with the Turks

1516 Syria taken.

1520 Suleiman the Magnificent becomes the Ottoman leader; Rhodes is occupied.

1526 Hungary is captured.

1529 Key gains in the Mediterranean.

1532 Siege of Vienna.

1534 Capture of Tunis.

1536 Battle of Prevesa is a resounding defeat for Spain.

1540 Spanish attack on Algiers fails.

Fig. 9 *Clash with the Ottoman Empire, Battle of Prevesa (1538)*

Kamen, however, believes that the conflict did have a distinct effect on the pre-eminence of Spain. From the late 1530s, the Spaniards were losing the struggle at sea and in North Africa. Even after Barbarossa died in 1546, Spain seemed unable to deal with his successors. Although mainland Spain remained inviolate, its North African territories were radically reduced to four fortresses.

The consequences of Charles' responsibilities

Charles' attempts to deal with his diverse kingdoms and meet the challenge of the Protestants and Turks proved an impossible task:

- The Turks were a constant diversion from 1551; in that year the Turks captured Tripoli on the coast of North Africa; in 1552, they defeated a Spanish fleet off the coast of Italy, and, in 1554 and 1555, captured two Spanish outposts on the northern coast of Africa in close proximity to southern Spain. The French support of the Ottomans left Spain isolated, but Malta was retained and, although the Turks remained a constant issue, they never gained complete control.

- German Protestant princes agreed an alliance with the French in the Treaty of Chambord of 1552. This meant Charles was fighting both in Germany with the Protestants and on its borders with the French.

- The Pope was anxious that Charles was becoming too powerful and might threaten the papacy. He was concerned about Charles' victory at Muhlberg in 1546 and became less cooperative about Church reform and the General Council that Charles supported.

- The loyalty of many to the Protestant cause had not diminished, even in those parts of the Holy Roman Empire where Charles' authority was strongest.

- Charles' attempts to impose the Augsburg Interim raised objections among Protestants and Catholics alike, even though it was an attempt to settle the religious conflict.

- Maurice of Saxony changed sides again in 1551 and supported the Protestants, hoping to get more territory; by 1552, he had forced Charles to leave the empire. Ferdinand, his brother, was empowered to settle the peace.

Activity

Thinking point

To what extent were the Turks a threat to Spain in this period?

- Charles was short of money and could not afford to continue the struggle; by 1555, he had borrowed 29 million ducats at high interest (the equivalent of more than £9 million).

Ultimately, Charles abdicated from the Empire and Ferdinand concluded the negotiations for peace that were set out in the Peace of Augsburg in 1555. The Peace established the principle of *cuius regio eius religio*, which can be interpreted as each state deciding the religion it would follow. It had the advantage of providing religious unity within each state, but not in the empire as a whole. There were certain limitations imposed on what could have become a 'free for all', for example all states ruled by a Catholic bishop in 1552 had to remain Catholic, there was to be no attempt to convert people in another state to a different religion; no interference by one state in another to protect a particular religious group.

Some explanations for Charles' failure as Holy Roman Emperor might be as follows:

- Charles had too many responsibilities to focus on this situation and too little power.
- Neither side, Protestant nor Catholic, was willing to make concessions to the other.
- Charles' policy was sometimes confusing; for example he offered concessions to the Protestants and then took them away or changed them.
- Charles did not understand the deep faith of the two sides; he pursued a military solution rather than a peaceful one.
- Charles' resources, for example in terms of troops, were limited; he should not have got into open war.

This chapter started with the view that Charles faced a unique challenge in his two separate roles. Each political entity had its strengths and weaknesses. Each of these responsibilities, in Spain and the Holy Roman Empire, would have been a full-time job for any individual. It is questionable whether Charles could have governed his territories differently. Perhaps he was trapped by his inheritance? However, Charles had tried to ensure that the same dilemma was not passed on to his son. Maybe this was because he thought Philip was not capable, or simply that he did not wish him to have such a heavy load.

Activity
Talking point

Set up a debate in class using this question: 'Spain suffered severely as a consequence of Charles I/V's role as Holy Roman Emperor.' To what extent do you agree or disagree with this view?

You will need to appoint two teams: one to support the proposition; and one to oppose it. Different members of the team can present a case about a specific issue, such as the Ottoman threat, the Lutheran issue, the financial repercussions, etc. You might want to do some extra research to add to your knowledge.

Once you have concluded your debate, you could write a balanced answer to the question, considering arguments for and against the statement and drawing an appropriate conclusion. This would be good practice for exams, especially if you try to write your answer in 45 minutes.

Activity
Challenge your thinking

Read the list of factors creating difficulties for Charles I and V on pages 156–7. Which of these factors was the most important, and which the least important in bringing about the end of the war? Explain the reasons for your choice. Compare your choice with others in the class and agree a common list.

Activity
Thinking point

1 How effective do you think the Peace of Augsburg would be? Give reasons for your answer.

2 Consider how differently Protestants and Catholics might react? What provisions would they find the most acceptable and the least acceptable?

Activity
Talking point

1 In pairs, read the bullet points which provide some explanations for Charles' failure. Take each of the factors listed in turn and identify example(s) that support the view. Compare your examples with others in the class.

2 Try to add some other factors to this list.

Summary questions

1 Why would Charles' role as Holy Roman Emperor cause concern in Spain?

2 What was the biggest problem Philip faced during his regency? Explain your answer.

11 The Spain of Charles I/V

Fig. 1 *A monastery library with frescoes, gold paintings and extensive books collection*

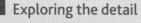

Exploring the detail

The traditional view of Charles is that he was more a failure as a monarch than a success. To some extent this might be influenced by his difficulties in the empire. Nevertheless, significant political changes had been made in Spain and Kamen suggests that, overall, a more collaborative government was created. For example, lawyers were trained in both canon and civil law and so were equipped to work for both church and state.

Letrados worked alongside the nobility on the councils, and Charles was comfortable in leaving Perez and similar officials in charge, confident they would not usurp his authority. The monarchy remained federal, and local interests were often seen to be as or more important than national ones. This, Kamen suggests, did not weaken the crown, but actually reduced bureaucracy and meant the crown could play 'divide and rule'.

Worn down by his role over the years and the impact of change in both the empire and Spain, on his abdication in 1555, Charles said, 'I have done what I could and I am sorry that I could not do better.' Despite his absences from Spain and huge responsibilities elsewhere, he passed on to his son, Philip II, according to Rady, a 'monarchy and empire which both in its territorial and organisational disposition was dominated and led by Spain'.

Charles had been ill since 1553. He set sail for Spain in 1557, where his last years were spent in a monastery at Yuste, regularly attending mass, spending time in prayer and sitting in the sun. He contracted a fever and died on 21 September 1558.

He left behind a range of significant problems. Spain was verging on bankruptcy and price inflation was almost 100 per cent, fed by increasing amounts of gold coming from the New World. The population had grown immensely and the country still relied heavily on sheep farming rather than a mixed agriculture. War against the French and the Turks, as a result of Charles' responsibilities as Holy Roman Emperor, had used up considerable resources, both personally in terms of his health and politically in his ability to oversee events in Spain. His struggle against Protestantism in the empire was also a running sore; followers of Luther and the emergence of even more radical groups in the form of Anabaptists were an affront to his personal faith as well as his imperial role. In addition, the internal wrangling of the princes over religion and their desire for self-rule had worn him down physically as well as mentally.

Despite these difficulties, Charles did not complain. This character trait is shown in a letter to his wife, Isabella in 1536 when he said, 'Madam, there is no need to give way to loneliness and self pity. Take heart and bear whatever God has in store for us.'

The battle against heresy in Spain

Heresy, often compounded by ignorance and superstition, was still an issue in the later years of Charles I's rule in Spain, despite the efforts of the monarchy and the Inquisition. Rural parishes provided bases for probably four-fifths of heretics or non-believers in Spain. Clergy, working in these obscure parishes, had little support. One inquisitor reported in 1539 that he had 'found men aged ninety years who did not know the Hail Mary or how to make the sign of the cross' and in 1547 another report suggested that 'one person in 12 never goes to confession'. In 1543, it was reported by a diocesan visitor that 'parishioners suffer greatly from the ignorance of their curates and rectors', and a later comment in 1568 suggested the situation was not much better: 'The clergy and curates are, in general, idiots, because the benefices are poor.'

Rural areas such as Catalonia and the Basque country suffered even more; there were often no clergy at all because they could not speak the language. As late as 1561, Cardinal Mendoza, when asked to name a Greek scholar who could represent Spain at the Council of Trent, could only produce four individuals. More positively, the extent of ignorance and some explanations for it were becoming clear and some action was taken to assist ordinary people to resist heresy through the work of the Jesuits; some individual clergy, for example, the Bishop of Pamplona, ordered that sermons should be preached every Sunday. However, changes were piecemeal and sometimes blocked by local lords who financially supported churches and monasteries and would not allow interference.

Heresy was basically any challenge to the teachings of the Catholic Church, based in Rome. For example, Jan Hus was branded a heretic because he said that lay people should be given both bread and wine. Another example would be the denial of the miracle of the mass, that is, that the bread became the actual body of Christ. By 1527, the works of Erasmus, a Catholic humanist scholar, began to be seen as potentially heretical, because he reinterpreted some of the scriptures. Charles gave Erasmus his support, but an anti-Erasmus faction grew in Spain, believing that the humanist scholar's views were similar to those of Luther and therefore 'erroneous'. As Charles left for the Holy Roman Empire, more conservative theologians began to dominate; events in Germany; the repercussions of the 'Luther affair', consolidated concern. In Spain, the Inquisition arrested Juan de Vergara in 1533 and accused him of being both a Lutheran and an Erasmian. Despite his strong defence, he had to admit his mistakes at an *auto-da-fé* in 1535. He was then sentenced to a fine and monastic seclusion for a year. Within two years he was free, having had influential friends. However, there were other Erasmian scholars, such as Juan Luis Vives who left Spain, afraid they might meet the same punishment or worse. Within 10 years, Erasmianism had ceased to exist in Spain.

Did you know?

Statistics show that Protestantism/heresy in Spain was not as big an issue as often suggested. From 1540 to 1614, Protestants probably accounted for around 7 per cent of arrests by the Inquisition, Jews for 5.4 per cent and *Moriscos* for approximately 29 per cent. Executions were minimal, running only in single figures every year. Bigamy, sex outside marriage and blasphemy were more likely to merit arrest. There was also concern about witchcraft, considered to be a form of devil worship, but a conference of 1526 concluded that this was untrue. Nevertheless, trials were held in secret and books were banned via the Index.

Did you know?

Rome was the centre of the Catholic faith and the residence of the Pope. Its population was approximately 54,000 in 1527 rising to about 105,000 by 1600. The patronage of the Pope resulted in splendid buildings and encouragement of the arts, for example the painting of the Sistine Chapel by Michelangelo. Cardinals built fine palaces. Montaigne said it was 'all court and nobility; everybody takes his share of ecclesiastical idleness'. There were 'no trading streets ... nothing but palaces and gardens'. However, after the 'Sack' of Rome in 1527 by the army of the empire, the Church returned more to its spiritual role.

Cross-reference

Look back to Chapter 8 (pages 124–31) to review religious developments in the 1520s.

Cross-reference

See Chapter 8 (pages 127–9) regarding the extent of Protestantism in the early years of Charles I.

Did you know?

A total of 56 people suspected of being Protestants were burned in public in the town of Valladolid in 1559. Charles said it was 'necessary to place the greatest stress and weight on a quick remedy and exemplary punishment'. Significantly, Kamen comments that these victims were seen, not just as heretics, but as 'creators of sedition, upheaval, riots and disturbances in the state … they could not expect any mercy'. Heresy now appeared to be a political offence rather than a purely religious one.

Exploring the detail

Charles, in his capacity as Holy Roman Emperor, had struggled with the growth of Lutheranism in Germany. From the early 1520s to 1530, Charles was in Spain but, when he returned to the empire, he found that, despite the Edict of Worms in 1521, Protestantism grew and divisions on religious lines amongst the princes created a civil war. The war ended with a compromise in 1555; the agreement of *cuius regio eius religio* and Charles' resignation as Holy Roman Emperor.

Cross-reference

See pages 165–9 for some further discussion on the growth of censorship and the *auto-da-fé*.

Protestantism in Spain was, however, less of an issue for Charles than in the Holy Roman Empire. In Spain, there were fewer supporters. The strongest growth was in Castile and particularly in Seville, which was a centre of international trade. There were approximately 130 members of the Seville group including some very prominent 'Catholics'. This group had emerged in the latter years of Charles' reign and lasted until the early 1560s. In 1552, the Bishop of Tortosa was revealed as a heretic. Fernando de Valdés, who was Archbishop of Seville and also Inquisitor-General, denounced Constantino de la Fuente, humanist, *converso* and chaplain to Charles V. He was arrested by the Inquisition and eventually died in 1560. The prior of the monastery of San Isidro and nuns from the Santa Paula convent were also victims. An entire family, the Cazallos, were doubly damned as they appeared to have been involved in the heretical Valladolid group of 1559.

The public burning of suspected Protestants indicated a definite change in attitude. It is not clear how much this change owed to Charles V's experiences in the Holy Roman Empire, but it is relevant to the work of Luther which politicised heresy in the empire and brought Charles into conflict with the princes. It may also have influenced the harsh policies of Philip II, Charles' successor, towards heretics.

Another great concern for the Spanish Inquisition was that many ordinary folk knew little about the Catholic faith, for example it was reported by the Bishop of Siguenza in 1533 that 'because priests do not set an example, we observe many men who do not know the Creed, or how to make the sign of the cross, or anything about Christianity'; large proportions of local congregations were not going to confession. It was not until the 1540s and the work of the Jesuits that this situation improved.

Fig. 2 *Men of the Holy Office examining documents for heresy*

Loyola and the Jesuits

The Jesuits were a new religious order founded in 1540 by Ignatius Loyola (1491–1556). His family had always been Christian and Loyola became more interested in the faith after being wounded in the Battle of Pamplona, 1521. He spent some time in hospital where he had a spiritual experience and began to read religious works that led to his conversion and a different kind of Catholicism. In 1522, Loyola lived as a monk in Manresa, begging for food etc. He prayed, fasted, travelled to the Holy Land and conceived a mission to convert Muslims. He wrote in his journal: 'Often and for a long time at prayer, I saw with interior eyes, the humanity of Christ. If there were no Scriptures to teach us these matters of faith, I would be resolved to die for them, only because of what I have seen.'

Loyola studied for the priesthood at the University of Alcalá in 1526. Suspected of being an Illuminist, he was arrested and then released, although banned from preaching. In 1527, he was studying at the Sorbonne in Paris. A group of young men joined him, agreed to take vows of poverty and chastity and to travel to the Holy Land. There he began to write his *Spiritual Exercises* published in 1541. This was a manual of prayer and meditation. Loyola was convinced that the founding of an Order was the next move. By 1540, a papal bull established the Society of Jesus, or the Jesuits. Financial support came from 'alms' or 'voluntary donations'. Jesuits, although a contemplative and missionary order, were seen as Christian soldiers who were to spread their message around the known world. By 1556, there were 1,000 members; by 1565, there were 3,500. Thirty colleges acrosss Europe and the New World provided a good education mainly for those who wished to join the Order. Colleges were established in places such as Bologna (1547) and Rome (1550).

The Jesuits staunchly supported the authority of the Pope and were very influential. However, their close connection with the papacy sometimes was a cause for concern. Their work in Europe and the New World was powerful in restoring Catholicism. For example, Francis Xavier reached India in 1542 and Japan in 1549, founding a church there. In 1552, he was in China. The Jesuits spread their message widely, although were not always welcome, especially in England after the Reformation. They conducted preaching tours in Italy, Spain and France and set up catechism classes. A similar movement developed in Italy for women, known as the Ursulines, with a focus on education, the poor and the sick.

One of Loyola's 'Spiritual Exercises' was a proposition to be used for meditation. 'I will believe that the white object I see is black, if that should be the decision of the hierarchical Church, for I believe that linking Christ our Lord the Bridegroom and his Church, there is one and the same Spirit, ruling and guiding us for God's good.'

The Jesuits were also distinctive for their Fourth Vow of obedience to the Pope. Despite their selfless work, not all Christians welcomed them.

Activity

Essay question

How effective were the Jesuits in preventing heresy taking root in Spain in the period 1540–56?

Fig. 3 *Threat of excommunication for removing or stealing books or parchments from the library*

Activity

Revision exercise

As individuals, in pairs or small groups, look back to the sections in Chapters 2 (pages 30–4) and 8 (pages 124–6) on the Inquisition and consider whether it was more powerful in the reign of Charles I than in the reign of Ferdinand and Isabella. Explain why you have come to your conclusion and give some examples. Compare and discuss your views.

Activity

Thinking point

Why do you think there were still issues of heresy in Spain in the period 1529–56?

Key terms

New Laws: these laws gave the native population the same status as Spaniards. The *encomienda* was abolished. This was a system that virtually enslaved the native population who were expected to work for the Spanish settlers. However, they were replaced by African slaves. Many native Americans died in this period; there were 25 million Mexican Indians in 1520 but only 3 million by the 1550s.

The Inquisition remained active in Spain in this period. Pendrill considers that 'for Spaniards at the time, the Inquisition aroused contradictory sentiments'. Many of them were subject to its ministrations. Different historians and contemporaries have viewed the activities and motives of the Inquisition in different ways.

- John Foxe, an English Protestant in the 16th century: the Inquisition was a 'dreadful engine of tyranny' that might at any time be copied by other regimes.

- John Motley, writing in 1856: the Inquisition prevented rather than encouraged non-Christians to change their beliefs; it made these conquered people, in other parts of the world, more resentful than they might have been about the empire they had to join.

- Elliott, writing in 1963: the Inquisition was 'obnoxious' and 'essentially the product of fear'; the element of secrecy, the slow operation of the system and the inevitable slur on the reputation of the accused were negative elements. However, he considers the 'climate of mistrust' that it created to be the most significant aspect.

- Helen Rawlings comments: the Inquisition was quick to condemn those who did not fully conform, often making a case on fairly flimsy grounds, for example Juan de Avila was arrested for suggesting that it was, 'better to give alms than found chaplaincies'. To Rawlings, this attitude suggests jealousy and the Inquisition's fear of losing its monopoly rather than a genuine criticism of Avila.

- Netanyahu writes: the Inquisition was established to serve Spanish absolutism. He quotes the views of Catholic scholars in 19th century Germany who proposed that 'the Inquisition was actually an instrument of secular authority that served primarily the interests of the state'. However, he then challenges this view by stating that, 'the popes … never gave up their ultimate authority over the Inquisition. Nor did the kings want them to do so. It was in their interests, i.e. the popes' interests, that the Inquisition appear to be the highest ecclesiastical tribunal.'

Heresy was not just an issue for European Spain, but also a problem for Spain's overseas territories, known as New Spain. The Mendicant friars had been sent to convert the native people as early as 1510, closely followed by members of the regular orders such as the Franciscans. Rawlings suggested that Spaniards saw this activity as absolutely essential. However, there was also some realisation that conversion could only occur after social and political control had been achieved. This generated significant debate about human rights and led to the creation of the Laws of Burgos of 1512, devised by Antonio de Montesinos. These were rules about the treatment of the native populations. Some Spanish settlers were also particularly worried about the fact that the Indians were devil worshippers; this led to more proactive ways of converting them, for example, through the destruction of their idols. By the 1540s, the Indians were clearly being exploited and treated much as slaves. Bartolomé de Las Casas, a Dominican friar, protested about such treatment of the Indians, earning the title of 'Protector' of the Indians. In 1542, he produced a Brief *Account of the Destruction of the Indies*, which led to the production of the '**New Laws**'.

However, Las Casas still had concerns. In 1552, in *On the Indians* he wrote: 'The wretched and tyrannical Spanish *encomienderos* (colonists) worked the Indians day and night in the mines and other personal services … I solemnly affirm that so long as these colonists remain, all the authority of the kings, even if they were resident in the Indies, will not be enough to prevent all the Indians from perishing.' Las Casas was then challenged by a Spanish scholar and theologian, Sepulveda, in writing , *The Just Causes of war against the Indians*, in which he stated that the Indians were people 'who require by their own nature and in their own interests to be placed under the authority of civilised and virtuous princes and nations, so that they might learn from their might, wisdom and law of their conquerors to practise better morals, worthier customs and a more civilised way of life'.

In 1550, both men were summoned to the Spanish court at Valladolid to speak to theologians, lawyers and officials about their views. There was no formal outcome to this debate, but Sepulveda was not allowed to publish his treatise. The matter was only resolved by the 1570s when the president of the Council of the Indies declared that the Spanish mission was to bring peace to the Indians and not to conquer them.

From 1518, however, black slaves had been imported into America from both 'Christian lands' and from Africa. Las Casas opposed this just as vehemently as he had opposed Indian labour, but his arguments had little effect. Kamen reports that, by 1560, there were more black Africans than white Europeans in certain areas such as Mexico City and Lima.

Fig. 4 *Bartolomé de Las Casas, Dominican priest, later Bishop of Chiapas, witnessed torture and genocide in the New World*

A closer look

Colonists and the indigenous people of Amerca

(a) Initially, the Indians appeared to be enthusiastic about the Christian faith. There were many missionaries, from monks such as the orthodox Dominicans to the Mendicant Franciscan friars, who began the conversion of the native population. Juan de Zumárraga, a Franciscan, worked with the Aztecs, training native clergy and translating the Bible into different Indian languages. By 1531, the Franciscans were reported to have baptised a million Mexicans and by the 1550s there were more than 800 friars active in New Spain, as it was then called. Approximately 270 churches were built in New Spain by 1576.

(b) Sepulveda, writing in 1547, did not consider the American Indians as equals and was convinced that they needed strong government and direction. This is what he said:

'Divine and natural decree and law … commands that the most perfect and powerful shall rule over the imperfect and the unequal. By this law, wild beasts are tamed and subjected to man's domination. By this law the man rules over the woman, the adult over the child, the father over his children, that is to say, the most powerful … and most perfect over the weakest and most imperfect … And it will be just and in accordance with natural law that such peoples be subjected to the rule of the more cultured and civilised princes and nations, so that, thanks to their virtues and the prudence of their laws, the others may set aside their barbarism and be reduced to a more civilised life and the pursuit of virtue.

And given this, you can easily see … that if you know the customs and nature of one and the other people, then the Spaniards have the perfect right to rule over these barbarians of the New World and its adjacent islands, who are as inferior to the Spaniards in prudence, intelligence, virtue and civilisation, as children are to adults and women are to men … and I would even say between monkeys and men.'

Quoted in J. Cowans (ed.), **Early Modern Spain: A Documentary History***, 2003*

Activity

Group activity

Having read the extract in the A closer look, consider the following questions and discuss your ideas in groups. Report your views to the class as a whole for comparison and debate.

1 What are the differences in attitude of the Spaniards towards the American Indians as expressed in (a) and (b)?

2 Explain Sepulveda's view. Think about the context carefully.

3 What is meant by 'natural decree and law' (line 3 of (b))?

4 Why do you think the writer of (b) is putting forward this view?

5 Carry out your own research to find out more about relations between the Spaniards and their colonies in the New World.

Over time, the settlement of Europeans in America had drastic consequences for the native population. In 1518, there were 25.2 million; in 1568 there were 2.65 million and only 1 million by 1605. Smallpox was one of the biggest factors in this rapid decline in the population; largely because the disease was not known in the Americas. The natives had no immunity and medical support was limited. Very few survived the disease, including the European settlers.

In Europe, the Council of Trent bolstered the drive in Spain against heresy and incompetent Catholic clergy. The Catholic Church realised it was important that some issues of clerical reform be addressed; the laxity and ignorance of the clergy had encouraged the growth of alternative forms of the faith. Although the Inquisition could flush out the heretics, enabling people to understand the Catholic faith was not always achieved effectively, largely because Charles I was not in Spain to make sure it happened. Unfortunately, *counter* reform was seen as more significant than *Catholic* reform.

The three sessions of the Council in the years 1545–63 also helped to confirm Catholic beliefs and explain doctrine more fully. There was a focus on removing corruption and ensuring that clergy, especially bishops, lived in their dioceses and visited their parishes. However, much of this was not fully developed until the reign of Charles' son, Philip II. Some of the changes were:

- An increase in the control by the crown over the Church in Spain which became evident as Charles' reign continued.
- A tax on clerical incomes, already collected by the crown in Castile, was also collected in Aragon from 1534 onwards. The Church virtually became rather like a department of state supporting the religious role of the monarchy.
- The right of the Spanish monarchy to collect income from vacant sees (the term for the area/town presided over by a bishop) was also acknowledged by the papacy.
- The monarchy began to deal with cases of suspected heresy; such interference could turn a religious issue into a quasi-political one.
- Charles nominated bishops and appointed the main officials of the Inquisition. He tended to use scholars rather than the aristocracy, and hence the quality of the higher clergy gradually improved.

The growth in Charles' authority over the Church might also have been influenced by the fact that Pope Adrian VI had been Charles' tutor. But it was also linked to the concept of Charles' power in Europe and his struggle against the Protestants. In the empire this was seen as highly significant, fuelled partly by the religious division amongst the princes and partly by the Lutheran problem itself.

In Spain a process of Christianisation, focused solely on Catholicism, began. This is reflected in the figures in Table 1.

The aim was for ordinary people to know and understand the prayers listed in Table 1. This would help them to understand the basis of their faith. Priests needed to teach their congregations not just to recite the prayers, but to know what they meant.

Activity

Thinking point

What were the most significant issues faced by Spain in the country's New World territories?

Did you know?

The Council of Trent

This was a gathering of clergy (bishops, monastic leaders, etc.) from major European states, although largely dominated by Italians. Their remit was to reform. Decisions were published in the form of decrees, for example 'if anyone says that the sacraments were not all established by Jesus Christ, our Lord; or that they are more or less than seven … let him be anathema (damned).'

Activity

Challenge your thinking

What is the difference between 'counter reform' and 'Catholic reform'? Can you explain why the difference is important in the context of religious developments in Spain in this period?

Table 1 *Percentage of defendants of the Inquisition of Toledo able to recite their prayers successfully, 1550–56*

	Pater	Ave	Credo	Salve	All four prayers
Up to 1550	70	86	45	49	37
1550-4	73	85	49	54	39
By 1556	85	89	69	70	59

*Data source: H. Rawlings, **Church, Religion and Society in Early Modern Spain**, 2002*

It took another century before 82 per cent of the population were able to recite all four prayers. Before 1550, only 40 per cent of the Old Christians in Spain could recite these prayers successfully. Old Christians were those who had always been Christians rather than converts from another faith.

The growth of censorship and the *auto-da-fé*

Censorship

All books coming into Spain had to have the royal licence. Censorship had begun as early as 1502 in the reign of Ferdinand and Isabella and severe penalties were to be imposed on anyone bringing banned literature into Spain. The first list of banned books was publicised in Spain in 1547, followed by a second in 1551 and culminating in the Index of 1559. In this Index, books or parts of books were clearly itemised as being prohibited. The severity of the Index increased over time and by the early years of Philip II's reign, *c.*1558, the following were in place:

- No foreign texts were to be allowed into the country.
- Any such texts, and those condemned by the Inquisition, were to be confiscated.
- The Council of Castile would license all new texts according to the rules imposed by the Inquisition.

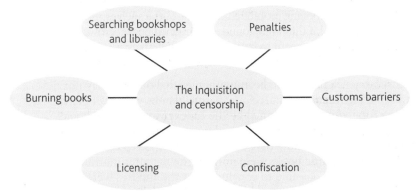

Fig. 5 *The Inquisition and censorship*

- The punishment for being found with one of the prohibited texts was death; it became known as the 'law of blood'.
- Bookshops and libraries were searched on a regular basis.
- All books written by heretics were to be burned publicly.

Activity

Thinking point

Study Table 1.

1. What is the general trend shown in Table 1?

2. Which of the prayers was the easiest to master?

3. How much better was people's knowledge of prayers at the end of the period, than at the beginning?

4. How useful a measure is this change of the 'Christianisation' of the Spanish people?

5. What explanation can you offer for the relatively slow rate of progress from 1550–56?

Exploring the detail

The first Index of Prohibited Books

This was first created in 1543 at the Sorbonne in Paris and was an attempt to identify books that were promoting non-Catholic views. In this first Index, 65 books were itemised. A lengthier list was published in 1559 by Carafa, who had become Pope Paul IV in 1555. It was regularly reviewed and new titles were added.

Exploring the detail

The *Enchiridion Militis Christiani* or *Handbook of the Christian Soldier* was a summary of Christian humanism, published in 1503 and translated into Spanish in 1522. It guided readers through the trials and pitfalls of their lives through an understanding of faith and morality. It suggested, for example, that Christianity was less about ceremony and ritual and more about quiet contemplation and the 'philosophia Christi' or ' wisdom of Christ'.

In addition, all students studying abroad had to return to Spain. This order was published in 1559; a four-month period was allowed for the return. These rules applied specifically to Castile. Heresy was now to be treated as a serious offence against the security of the state rather than a religious matter.

A closer look

The Spanish Index of Prohibited Books

An edict of 1502 had ordered all books to show the royal licence. Ferdinand and Isabella also prohibited reading the Bible in the vernacular, although this was probably directed mostly at *conversos*. A more specific concern was the arrival of Protestant literature in Spain. An inquisitor commented in 1532 that, 'From one hour to the next, books keep arriving from Germany.' Various measures were taken to deal with this; the very first ban had been imposed in 1521, but more detailed instructions were given in 1553 about methods of dealing with this problem.

It is possible that it was booksellers, rather than potential readers, who were most affected by the reaction to this avalanche of literature. Shipments, which could be as large as 3,000 books at a time, were seized; long delays could ensue before the authorities had decided what to do with them. Searches could only be made in accordance with diplomatic arrangements. Consequently, 'unsuitable literature' filtered steadily into Spain. This encompassed the writings of Erasmus including the *Enchiridion*, which was welcomed by Illuminists and other non-Catholics.

Visitations were sometimes made to bookshops by employees of the Inquisition. A certain Thomas de Villanueva was recorded doing this in 1536; another visit in Seville, somewhat akin to a military operation, was recorded in 1566 when, at nine o'clock in the morning, inquisitors simultaneously occupied all the bookshops in Seville. This prevented the owners warning each other and removing prohibited books from the shelves. Bookshop owners were fined if they were found with banned books. However, this kind of operation does not seem to have been repeated; there is no other evidence of such action being taken against bookshops in the town after this episode.

Censorship seems to have been neither carried out properly nor did it have a big impact. In Barcelona, banned books were still on sale a long time after being banned by the Index. Movement of books between Spain, France and Italy had no restrictions. The evidence of the various Indices show that they were slow to keep up with what was being written; some books were only on the list after many years of publication. It is possible to conclude that the Indexes were only a guide to what the Inquisitors would have *liked* to prohibit. These included a fair list of authors such as Erasmus, Valdes, Avila, Loyola and Carranza, whose works were put on the Index. In the latter case, Carranza's *Commentaries on the Christian Catechism* were eventually approved by the Council of Trent in 1563. The inclusion of Loyola and Carranza in a list with authors who would see themselves as unorthodox is explained by the fact that this was 1559 and the reign of the very devout Philip II. However, even then, Spaniards who were studying at foreign universities would bring back new ideas.

Rawlings suggests that the restrictions on printed materials were quite limited; they particularly applied to Castile, and Aragon was never as badly affected. Valencia, Catalonia and Navarre did not impose any controls. Many banned books were subsequently reprinted in the reign of Philip II, despite the fact that he was perceived as far more rigorous in his attitude towards non-Catholic views than his father. It is possible that the original ban was merely a show of force and that the motive was not religious. Spanish students also continued to be allowed to study abroad, albeit in specifically approved places such as Rome and Naples.

However, the Index did shock, adding another barrier to prevent the ideas being circulated without constraints. Libraries, both public and private, were inspected systematically. Rawlings suggests that the newer Spanish Index was not as hard-hitting as the Roman (papal) Index. More frequently, only some passages were deleted rather than a total ban operating. Few books were considered totally unacceptable, or not until much later. By then, they had been read by substantial numbers of people. One such example was a prayer book for *Alumbrados* or Illuminists that escaped the Inquisitorial deletion pen until 1612.

Despite the censorship, books and bookshops flourished in the second half of the century, generating significant developments in Spanish culture. Up to 11 per cent of professors had studied in foreign universities and so brought different ideas into Spain. Although Philip II ordered all Spaniards studying abroad to come home, he could not prevent the movement of people and ideas altogether. Traders were just as likely to come into contact with new ideas as scholars, and were probably less likely to be critical of them. Although not always efficient, these limitations imposed by the government had some positive effect. They helped to maintain Catholicism in Spain whilst other beliefs, such as Protestantism, were actively attacked and never really took hold. Certainly Spain remained largely a devoutly Catholic state. Nevertheless, the growth of censorship was a retrograde step, even though most of the books and articles prohibited would not be known about by the ordinary 'Spaniard in the street'.

A major consequence was the limited and slow circulation of new ideas, as well as the limitations on study abroad. Spain was now more isolated because of feared contamination from other religious groups.

Auto-da-fé

The Inquisitorial *auto-da-fé*, which was still an option, remained a rigorous method of dealing with suspected heresy. Individuals were targeted, brought to trial and questioned closely. However, the scale of such prosecutions varied region by region, and numbers fell substantially in the period after 1530, for example in Valencia. Eighty per cent of the total number of death penalties imposed were issued before 1530.

Alumbrados and Lutherans were the most likely victims of the Inquisitorial *auto-da-fé* in this period. Particular towns and cities were targeted, but individuals were also prosecuted, often after seemingly innocent conversations. An example of this was Diego de Uceda, an Erasmian, who, when travelling, talked too much about religion and particularly about Martin Luther. His travelling companion denounced him and he was arrested, tortured and sentenced although there was no real evidence of his 'crimes'. He was ultimately able to 'abjure' or renounce his 'crimes' at the *auto-da-fé* held in Toledo in 1529. However, this particular case highlights some of the issues in Inquisitorial activity. Uceda wanted to call witnesses but the names were not given to him immediately and it took six months to find them. He was also given so

Did you know?

Despite Spanish piety and concern to know the 'truth', there was no complete Spanish translation of the Bible, or parts of the Bible, available to those who could read. The first such translations were made in 1555, 1556 and 1557. The first complete translation was only finished in 1569.

Did you know?

One famous victim of the Inquisition was Cardinal Carranza. He was a delegate at the Council of Trent set up to reform the Catholic Church and had published *Commentaries on the Catechism*. This sparked substantial criticism from the Inquisition and Carranza was arrested. The case lasted for 10 years as the argument continued about whether the King or the Pope could pass judgement. During this time, the King took the revenue from Carranza's diocese and obtained an agreement from the Pope that the Spanish crown could continue to influence significant appointments in the Spanish Church. Carranza died just after his release in 1576.

Activity

Challenge your thinking

Why were cultural developments censored when the real concern was religion?

Cross-reference

Look back to Chapter 8 (page 125–6) to remind yourself about the *auto-da-fé*.

Cross-reference

Look back to Chapter 8 (pages 128–30) to remind yourself about Illuminists/*Alumbrados* and Lutherans.

little information about the accusation against him that it was difficult to respond; however, he could have a lawyer.

Once questioning was complete, and this might have taken place over several sessions, a *consulta da fe* was formed and the inquisitors, officials with theological qualifications and a representative of the bishop of the locality would vote. There was no cross-examination and no discussion. Victims were never given the identity of those who had accused them.

Sometimes the *auto-da-fé* was held in public; the accused might then be given information about his sentence before the public appearance, particularly if it was the death sentence. Death by burning had become a more rare event; possibly only an average of three people per year, or approximately 2 per cent of those convicted, were condemned to burn at the *auto-da-fé* overall. Sometimes a person found guilty might be burned in effigy. Burning usually took place after and often in a separate place to the declaration of the sentence.

> The accused saw the executioner and asked him, 'Why did you call me a dog before?' The Executioner replied, 'Because you denied the faith of Jesus Christ: but now that you have confessed, we are brothers, and if I have offended you by what I have said, I beg your pardon on my knees.' The accused forgave him gladly, and the two embraced … And desirous that the soul, which had given so many signs of conversion, should not be lost, I went round casually behind the stake to where the executioner was, and gave him the order to strangle him immediately because it was very important not to delay.
>
> When it was certain that he was dead, the executioner was ordered to set fire at the four corners of the pyre … He did this at once and it began to burn on all sides …

1 *Quoted in H. Kamen, **The Spanish Inquisition: An Historical Revision**, 1997*

Iluminism

Illuminists or *Alumbrados* are more difficult to define as 'victims of the Catholic regime'. They were mostly ordinary people with no significant following. They were not really a movement or a coherent group as a religious order might be, but rather a number of different individuals. They are significant, however, as they featured throughout the reign of Charles I; they were irritants and a challenge to the prevailing views of the religious life. One such individual was Juan de Vergara who was arrested in 1533.

Rawlings suggests that the Spanish authorities were afraid of Illuminism. It had no formal structure, and was difficult to root out. Juan de Avila, a reforming Catholic, was suspected of being an Illuminist. Having studied at the University of Alcalá, he became a priest in the south of Spain and was known as the 'Apostle of Anadalusia'. He criticised the quality of priests who followed the family tradition rather than because they had a vocation. In 1531, Juan was arrested following a public statement about the value of giving money to the poor rather than using it to fund more priests. He spent two years in prison. A commentary he wrote on Psalm 44 was confiscated, despite the fact that it pointed out the errors of Illuminism. It was published later and some of his suggestions for reforming the clergy were then put in place by the Archbishop of Granada. He also influenced Ignatius Loyola, the founder of the Jesuits.

Loyola was himself arrested and accused of being an Illuminist as a consequence of his *Spiritual Exercises*, a manual for the good Christian.

Cross-reference

Look back to page 160 in this chapter to remind yourself about Vergara.

Cross-reference

Look back to page 161 to remind yourself about Loyola and the Jesuits.

The work was banned in 1559, but this did not stop the Jesuits and Loyola becoming a major force in the Catholic Reformation. Teresa of Avila (1515–82) was yet another 'victim' because of her mystical experiences, in one of which she said she had been pierced in the heart by an angel with a burning arrow. Some further crimes were the practice of meditation and the fact that her grandfather was Jewish. Her punishment was to be forbidden to publish any of her writings. She was eventually canonised by 1622. The fact that two of the most influential Catholic figures in this period were under suspicion for nonconformity says much about the rigidity of the Catholic Church at this time, and the fear of difference.

Key profile

Saint Teresa of Avila

Teresa (1515–82) was a nun in the Discalced (barefoot) Carmelite Order. She read a lot of devotional literature and often experienced visions; the one best known was of her heart pierced by an angel with a burning arrow. Her aim was to reform her Order, for example she wanted to dispense with various barriers to entry to the Order and encourage the criteria of poverty, humility, faith and obedience as the major characteristics of her nuns. The first convent was eventually founded in 1562; by 1582 there were 17 female communities and 15 for men. Teresa did not consider that wearing a habit made a person good, neither did she believe that ritual would bring forgiveness. She said 'it is dangerous to keep counting the years that we have practised prayer. For even though it may be done in humility, it always seems liable to leave us with the feeling that we have earned some merit by our service … any spiritual person who believes that, by the mere number of years during which he has practised prayer, he has earned the spiritual consolations, will, I am sure, fail to reach the peak of spirituality.' This element of mysticism in her work was to bring her under suspicion of the Inquisition in 1575. Eventually, her mysticism did become more acceptable and her writings became widely available.

Education

Developments in education were partly due to the influence of the Renaissance. The Renaissance (literally rebirth) sprang from a deep curiosity and thirst for knowledge that was influencing most of Europe during the 15th and 16th centuries. The investment of the Renaissance in the arts, sciences and the economy was made possible by the increasing wealth from the New World pouring into Spain and into other parts of Europe through trade. This wealth also gave its recipients an aspiration to move up the social scale or to consolidate their position on it. Social pre-eminence demanded cultured and knowledgeable individuals. The transmisson of culture, new ideas and knowledge was achieved via the printing press. Schools and universities, as well as private individuals, could take advantage of this; the growth in output of fiction and a range of treatises and manuals reflected the thirst for knowledge and also fed it. Books on religion, trade, politics and the economy rolled off the presses. There was even a book of dress patterns published in Seville in the 1520s, making Spanish fashions accessible in the Habsburg empire.

This opening up of horizons caused concerns as well as creating opportunities; the speed of change, the desire to maintain the existing

Activity

Essay question

To what extent was Catholicism under threat in the period 1529–56?

Cross-reference

Refer back to page 161 and the A closer look on the Jesuits; they too were regarded with concern because they were such a different religious group.

Fig. 6 *Saint Teresa of Avila at her prayers*

Activity

Thinking point

Read the Key profile of Saint Teresa of Avila above. Why do you think she was ultimately revered, yet initially faced opposition?

Thinking point

1 What was the most important factor in promoting education in Spain in the reign of Charles I? Explain your answer.

2 Why do you think 'silence has been imposed upon the learned'?

Fig. 7 *The University of Salamanca*

Thinking point

1 Imagine what it must have been like to have little or no education.

   a Individually or in pairs, make a list of all the reasons why the increased availability of education was an important factor in the political and religious development of Spain. You will need to think of what you already know about Spain, not just in this chapter.

   b In pairs or small groups, discuss the relative significance of each factor on your list. Decide which was the most important and which was the least important.

   c Create a diagram to show connections between the factors.

Share your thoughts with the rest of the class. See how far you agree.

social order, the forces of the Catholic Reformation versus the new ideas of the Protestant reformers, the monarchs' need to combine the concept of service with their need for control; all these factors had a disturbing effect. In 1533, the son of the Inquisitor-General said, 'one cannot possess any culture without being suspected of heresy, error and Judaism. Thus silence has been imposed upon the learned … At Alcalá they are trying to uproot the study of Greek completely.'

The problem for Spain, as always, was the tension between the deeply religious nature of Spanish society and its range of cultural and social groups. These groups were loosely brought together, initially by the concept of *convivencia*, but new ideas, such as humanism, alongside the desire to maintain their identity in cultural as well as religious terms were difficult to reconcile. It was feared that these new developments, based on more secular values, could possibly break down *convivencia* and lead to massive changes. One important positive drive, however, was the need of the state for educated men to staff the bureacracy and so education and printing continued to develop.

The growth of schools and universities

Education was still largely confined to the upper classes as a certain cost was attached to it. However, the needs of the state for chroniclers, for example, encouraged its development. A chronicler for Castile had already been established by the Catholic Monarchs and Charles made appointments to Aragon and the Indies. These writers enhanced Spaniards' knowledge of geography, engineering, medicine and navigation.

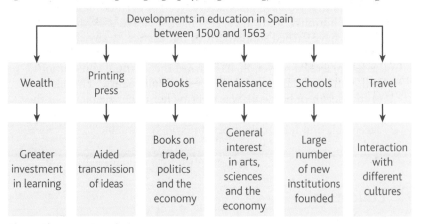

Developments in education in Spain between 1500 and 1563					
Wealth	Printing press	Books	Renaissance	Schools	Travel
Greater investment in learning	Aided transmission of ideas	Books on trade, politics and the economy	General interest in arts, sciences and the economy	Large number of new institutions founded	Interaction with different cultures

Fig. 8 *The expansion of education in Spain*

Schools and universities had been founded in the reign of Ferdinand and Isabella to provide the bureaucrats of the future; from 1500 to 1563, 38 colleges within the universities were established. Some places were available for mature students who came from poor backgrounds. Salamanca and Valladolid, older universities established in the reign of Ferdinand and Isabella, had approximately 7,000 students each. Alcalá was probably the most important newer university with up to 4,000 students. Up to 21 new universities were created after 1516 providing training for government posts. Over time, universities educated more government officials than there were posts available. Influence, however, was also important in acquiring a post. Spaniards were also to be found in France, studying medicine in Montpellier or theology in Paris. Many of these more wealthy students were also to become officials of the state.

The advent of printing was particularly important in producing books for use in schools and universities. There was certainly a printing press in

Valencia by the end of the 15th century. However, by the end of the reign of Charles I, the press was also used to 'express the feelings of ordinary people, rather than being a vehicle for the ideas of the humanist elite'. The use of pictures was important; novels became more popular with topics often drawn from everyday life; poetry was more commonplace.

As a result, education and learning ceased to be just for the wealthy and the privileged. Anyone who could read could expand their knowledge considerably. In addition, it was possible to encourage readers to be more critical and to compare ideas and information. This made readers more aware of debate about significant issues. Eisenstein, who has made a study of the development of printing, comments that it was easier 'to consult and compare different texts … Understanding that there were different approaches to issues encouraged debate. And generated an "intellectual ferment" … Contradictions became more visible, divergent traditions more difficult to reconcile.' So, students in schools and universities had more resources to hand and a greater opportunity to question and debate than many of their predecessors. The impact might well be compared to the advent of computers and the internet in this century.

Population growth and its effects

Assessing population is not straightforward for Spain at this time because of the paucity of figures, different bases for calculations and concern about reliability. At the start of the reign of Ferdinand and Isabella, there were c.9.6 million inhabitants in Aragon and Castile, with Castile having the lion's share of 8.3 million. Between 1529 and the 1590s, the population overall increased dramatically; that of New Castile (in the south east) increased overall by 78 per cent; some individual cities were growing at an even higher rate. This created a demand for food and other supplies, leading to more land under cultivation. However, there were a number of towns scattered across the area that diverged from this pattern and showed a marked decrease. Table 2 shows these figures, quoted to the nearest thousand.

Fig. 9 *Antonio de Nebrija (1441–1522), author of a Castilian grammar book, the first of its kind*

Table 2 *Population figures for 1530 and 1594 showing a decline in some towns*

City/Town	1530	1594
Valladolid	38,000	33,000
Córdoba	33,000	31,000
Medina del Campo	21,000	14,000
Alcázar de San Juan	20,000	10,000
Medina de Rioseco	11,000	10,000
Santiago	5,000	5,000
Orense	5,000	4,000
Vigo	5,000	4,000
Tuy	4,000	3,000
Corunna	3,000	2,000
Betanzos	3,000	3,000

■ Cross-reference

Look back to Chapter 6 (pages 86–91) and the section on the economy and growth in population.

■ Activity

Challenge your thinking

Why is the level of population important for historians in their study of the past?

■ Activity

Thinking point

1. Which of the factors listed opposite do you think is the most important in explaining why Charles' money supply was limited? Discuss your decision with a partner or in a small group and see if you can agree. Are there any connections between the factors?

2. From your research about the reign of Charles I and V, do you agree that his handling of finance and the economy was his greatest failure? Explain the reasons for your view. If you disagree with the proposal, you should be able to argue another factor as Charles' greatest failure.

There are various explanations for this downward trend that seems to have begun in the 1550s:

- Plague in the last decades of the century. In some areas, the death rate was 10 times the normal expectation. From 1565 to 1566, there was an epidemic of plague leading to 16,000 deaths. However, these towns are not all in close proximity to each other; Santiago is on the western coast in Galicia, Medina del Campo was in Old Castile in central Spain.

- Some families moved southwards, away from the spread of piracy on the coast, or the wars in northern Europe. Seville was the centre for trade with America and migrants found employment in, for example, ceramics, leather, silk and the iron industry.

- A fall in the birth rate, possibly a consequence of absent fathers on military activity.

- A general movement into the towns from the countryside; there is some evidence that peasants were getting into debt, some as a consequence of heavy taxes; a poor harvest created financial problems and drove families to seek employment elsewhere.

■ Financial and economic failure

Initially, in the 1540s and 1550s, there appeared to be an economic boom. More land was taken up for agriculture, for example in Valladolid and Segovia. One writer in 1552 declared that, 'Even the wilderness disappeared as everything in Castile was dug up for sowing.' North of Burgos there was a big increase in production of wheat and wine. The woollen industry was a particularly significant example of this growth, with about 600 looms producing 13,000 pieces of cloth in a year.

However, this boom did not last. Methods of agricultural production had not really improved, but more land was ploughed to generate a bigger yield. Another major factor, the birth rate, fell, and some particularly nasty epidemics caused high death rates.

Charles' handling of finance and the economy are sometimes seen as his greatest failure. The accusations are as follows:

- An inordinate emphasis on sheep and too little on agriculture – by 1560, wheat had to be imported.

- Significant levels of taxation, which meant limited cash funds were available to invest in industry; most people wanted to buy *juros* instead hoping to make a quick profit.

- Goods such as textiles were imported from England to send to the colonies; earlier a ban on exports of cloth to the Indies had caused a major depression in the Spanish industry from which it never fully recovered.

- An uneven tax burden; the nobles were exempt and the ordinary people were overburdened. Philip suggested to his father that the situation was so bad that many of the 'common people walk naked' because of the weight of taxation; attempts to remedy this led to stiff resistance from the nobles.

- By 1546, the income from Castile for the next three years had already been earmarked to pay for war in the Holy Roman Empire. In 1552, Charles borrowed money to pay for war in France. Spain was therefore financing the rest of Charles' territories; it would be unlikely that this money could be paid back.

Over the years, there were other economic and financial issues that were difficult to solve.

- Exports of bullion were used to pay for foreign policy as well as goods.
- Raw materials bought from Spain were often reimported as manufactured goods to the detriment of balancing the budget, and generating high prices.
- Up to 1538, Charles was forced to repay his loans by granting permits to trade directly with America.
- The price of grain rose more than any other commodity.
- Trade was in the hands of foreign merchants in places such as Amsterdam and Genoa.
- By the 1560s, gold and silver coming into Spain was often spent outside the country in the purchase of foreign goods.
- The day labourers suffered as wages declined and prices rose.

A further victim of these changes was the concept of 'nobility'. Perez de Guzman declared that 'he is noblest who is richest', although those involved in purely manual work were definitely excluded from this definition. In 1548, the Cortes requested that anyone with 'public shops' should not be allowed to take part in local government; a comment not only on social status, but also on the fact that many shopkeepers were probably more wealthy than some of the nobles. On the other hand, there were demands that such workers be allowed honours and positions. This was not incompatible with the fact that some of the old nobility such as the dukes of Medina Sidonia were now seriously involved in commerce.

Fig. 10 *Financial and economic decline in Spain*

Activity

Research exercise

Choose one of the three activities below. You can work individually or in a small group.

1. Research the life and work of an individual Jesuit, for example Ignatius Loyola, Francis Xavier or Jeronimo Nadal. Use your research to make a presentation to the class. Do not only describe their life; try to explain their motivation, success and failures (if any).

2. Write a newspaper report on *either* the state of the Spanish economy in this period *or* the development of the New World. Make sure you have some earlier background so that you can offer explanations for the changes.

3. You are a member of the nobility and have had to survive through difficult economic times. Write a letter to a relative or a detailed entry in your diary about these changes, saying why you think they happened, what has been the impact on you and your family and what you plan for the future.

Learning outcomes

Throughout this section, you should have some understanding of Charles I and V's later years in Spain and the range of challenges and pressures that he had to face. In addition, you should have some appreciation of the impact of Protestantism and other 'deviant' ideas and the range of ways in which this was combatted. Some understanding of social changes and the importance of education should allow you to analyse the process of creating an elite that could effectively assist in the government of empire. Your knowledge of social change, population growth and economic issues will support a broader view of the extent of the regime's success, both in the New World as well as in Spain.

 Examination-style questions

a) 'Philip's regency was a political success, but a financial failure.' Assess the validity of this view.

(45 marks)

This question has a focus on two different aspects of the regency period, with an expectation that you should assess the validity/accuracy of this statement. You could approach this by initially explaining the situation that Philip is operating within before beginning your analysis of each aspect. Does a regency give Philip the authority to make all his own decisions or does he have to refer to his father/advisers ? How long is the regency period? You will need to pay heed to the dates as there are separate periods in which Philip is acting as King.

There are two aspects to consider: the first is 'political success'. This is where you should be thinking about relations with the Cortes and ministers. You could start by emphasising that Charles considered he was leaving Philip with a sound structure in terms of systems and give some examples, for example the Castilian Cortes' authority had been reduced by Charles and so Philip could expect some cooperation. Then you could consider the support given to Philip by ministers such as Tavera and Cobos, or other members of the royal family. You could also look at the structure of the government that Philip's father had created to assist him, referring back to Chapter 6.

The second area is 'financial failure'. Here, you need to identify what the financial needs were and the effects of the issue of inflation and the income from the New World. Again, you would need to consider the Cortes but also to look at other avenues of supply, for example through financiers. What were the issues regarding borrowing, the impact of bullion from the New World, etc? Why was the condition of the treasury significant?

In your conclusion, you need to finalise your views on success or failure. Your answer could suggest differing levels of succcess or failure for each aspect.

b) 'The expulsion of the Moors from Granada was the most important factor in promoting religious unity in Spain in the years 1492 to 1556.' To what extent do you agree with this view?

(45 marks)

This question has an initial focus on the early part of the period when Ferdinand and Isabella were the monarchs, but requires you to consider the full period to support your answer. This does not mean that you have to work in the same depth throughout the 64-year period, but you do have to identify events and issues that show your understanding of the connections over the period. You should also note that the question uses the word 'promoting' and not 'establishing' in relation to religious unity.

You should start by explaining the nature and extent of the religious mix in Spain in the reign of Ferdinand and Isabella and the extent of disunity. Identifying the attitudes of the Catholic Monarchs to religion, especially Isabella, will also be useful. Some explanation of the relations between Granada and particularly Castile will also help to clarify the reasons for the expulsion of the Moors. You should then move on to a brief reference to the Granadan War and its outcome. Detailed knowledge of the progress of the wars is not required, but an understanding of the outcome is needed. How effective was compulsory conversion to Christianity for the Moors; to what extent did this need policing? Was this a short-term issue or a longer one?

You will also need to look at other religious groups, i.e. Jews and Catholics; to what extent were they prepared to live in *convivencia* with the Moors and each other? How important was the expulsion of the Jews? What was the role of the Inquisition and how did it seek to generate religious unity – force or encouragement? The work of individual Inquisitor-Generals, for example Cisneros, should also be considered.

The role of the monarchy in promoting religious unity is also important. How did they deal with converted Jews and Muslims? What happened when other groups materialised, for example Erasmians, Illuminists (*Alumbrados*). What was the impact of the Catholic Reformation and the work of the Jesuits? How important was censorship?

Finally, you need to draw some conclusions about the most important factor. This should reflect the differing emphasis you have given to the factors discussed throughout your essay. What is important is that your answer is supported by knowledge and links clearly to the question. Remember also that you are offering an explanation and not a description of events.

Conclusion

This study of Spain in the first half of the 16th century began with the very first move towards unity and common policies through the marriage of two young, inexperienced but determined monarchs, Ferdinand and Isabella. It ends with the image of an exhausted Charles I who found his responsibilities demanding but had, nevertheless, built on the foundations laid by his grandparents, even extending his role to that of Holy Roman Emperor; Spain was doubly a European power. What was the extent of change during the two reigns? Had Spain become a Great Power?

Religious issues

Although the whole of Europe was caught up in a debate about the correct route to God, Spain had a greater problem than most other states in the combination of Christians, Jews and Muslims in the population. Many of those who converted to Christianity were not reliable in their new faith. Ferdinand and Isabella had been largely content to achieve *convivencia*, but this was not enough for the devout Charles. A significant change in Spain, therefore, by 1556 was in the religious balance of the country.

Jews, who were relatively small in number, were told that they had to leave within four months following the royal decree of expulsion in 1492 or agree to become Christians. Although this edict was disliked by many Spaniards who were not Jews, nevertheless, a massive exodus occurred. Possibly 40–50,000 left out of a total of approximately 80,000, but many returned and converted, although it is difficult to tell how secure those conversions were. It is apparent, however, that the Jewish faith remained a strong cultural influence in Spanish society.

The 1502 order of expulsion, placed on unconverted Moors, was not fully imposed. Many who remained pretended to be Christians, but retained their Islamic beliefs; some gave themselves away by, for example, dancing the *zamba* or eating couscous. Ultimately, Charles suspended the expulsion order in return for a large payment of 90,000 ducats, which meant the Inquisition was no longer likely to investigate them. Similar compromises were reached by other groups. It was almost as if Spain's *convivencia* had returned, although with a slightly harder edge. However, it was not to last much into the reign of Philip II; his policy was more hardline. The Archbishop of Toledo called the Moors 'diabolical unbelievers'. The ultimate result was expulsion in 1602.

Historians such as Elliott, therefore, see Spain as 'the Spain of the Counter Reformation' and, with particular reference to the influence of Fernando de Valdés as Inquisitor-General. However, this can be challenged; Rawlings refers to Toledo in 1559 where placards were posted stating that the Church was 'an assembly of evil people … not the Church of Jesus Christ …' and to that same diocese in 1595 in which there was 'little or no instruction in the basic foundations of Catholic belief … popular religious practice prevailed'.

■ Political issues

The association of Aragon and Castile in a political alliance was significant; the partnership of Ferdinand and Isabella dominated the peninsula and, by the end of our period, the remaining states were well aware where that power lay; with the monarch of the day and not with the nobility. Nobles became increasingly involved in commerce and the New World. Their role changed, but their contribution to Spain remained important. The new elite in government were the middle-class lawyers, soldiers and lesser gentry, chosen because they had specific talents. However, before long, they too were seeking to climb the social ladder, creating families, acquiring land and becoming wealthy. Cobos, for example, married his daughter to a noble. Spain, therefore, never removed its elite class, but the composition of that class changed rapidly; the old nobility alongside the new. The fact that Charles could leave his young son, Philip, to run Spain, unchallenged, when he was in the Holy Roman Empire, is a significant factor demonstrating this change in noble influence.

Castile, as the major seat of government, was clearly the stronger state. The Cortes was summoned approximately 15 times in the reign of Charles I. By 1544, they asked only to be called every three years. Nevertheless, the Cortes regularly granted the *servicios* tax, which virtually quadrupled and went some way to dealing with the 100 per cent rise in prices. The creation of a conciliar form of government and the work of Gattinara and Cobos suggested a more organised and professional government. However, if the monarch chose to follow a particular policy, there was little his advisers could do.

Law and order were also issues for Spain. Charles had gone through two revolts in the early years of his reign and subsequently wanted to ensure future peace. The effect of the revolts was actually to bring the monarchy, aristocracy and Church into a closer alliance with one another.

Fig. 1 *King Ferdinand and Queen Isabella's partnership represented a significant political alliance*

■ Social and economic issues

In social terms, it is possible to argue that little really changed. The nobility and the clergy still had power and the ordinary people did not. Nevertheless, for some, economic changes were beneficial. The economy under Ferdinand and Isabella had developed slowly and steadily. In the reign of Charles I, however, it burgeoned rapidly with the opening up of America and the opportunities for investment and trade.

Some Spanish towns, and specifically Seville, became boom towns as a result of the trade with the New World. Seville was frequented by foreign merchants and migrants, many of whom travelled from northern Spain to seek their fortune. The areas they travelled through, as well as their destinations, benefited from the additional opportunities to sell goods, promoting materials such as textiles (especially silk) and food such as cereals and olives. Some goods were also sold in northern Europe such as wool, leather and silk. In contrast, however, some basic staples, such as grain, had their prices set at a fixed maximum by 1539. There were also labour shortages – well-trained cloth workers were scarce, for example, just at a time when the home and American market was growing.

Nevertheless, loans were still necessary to fund government. Charles raised 39 million ducats after 1542, based on the security of Castile's credit. A trend to invest in government bonds or *juros* meant more limited investment in trade and industry; there was only a specific amount of money available. The outcome was largely a disaster; many foreign bankers were involved in these investments, rather than native Spaniards, and any profits made simply went elsewhere. When Charles' son succeeded to the throne, Philip could not resolve the debt easily and the influence of foreign financiers grew.

■ The extent of change

Our starting point suggested that Spain might have become, in this period, a 'Great Power' – internally strong and externally respected. Was this really the case?

There is no doubt that Spain, in this period, emerged from a medieval collection of states and forged some limited unity through Ferdinand and Isabella. A government developed that could function effectively without the continuous presence of the monarch; a feature that many other European states could not claim. Spain provided one of the most prestigious rulers of Europe, Charles Habsburg, Charles I of Spain and V of the Holy Roman Empire. Despite Charles' absences, even the challenge of the Germania and Comuneros revolts in Spain was overcome. Philip II was able to build on these developments and, by 1561, had established a permanent court in Madrid.

Mulgan comments that 'the country was better governed, more united and wealthier … with the authority of the crown considerably strengthened and the forces that could threaten it, held in check.' Ordinary Spaniards, however, did not always see themselves as equal partners in their country, they now felt themselves to be under the Castilian yoke. Nevertheless, a growing overseas empire did provide an outlet for the adventurous to acquire lands, status and wealth.

In other ways, too, Spain was changed. Its differing ethnic and religious groups were either dispersed elsewhere or sought a way to live in some kind of *convivencia*. However, in 1533, the son of the Inquisitor-General wrote: 'It is clear that … one cannot possess any culture without being suspected of heresy, error and Judaism. Thus silence has been imposed on the learned.' Yet it seems that even though Philip II was an extremely pious monarch, he could not fully control the seepage of new ideas; despite the ban on Spaniards studying abroad, many were doing just that in Italy, France and the Netherlands. Ideas, as always, are much more difficult to eradicate than the people who promote them, although Spain remained firmly wedded to Catholicism.

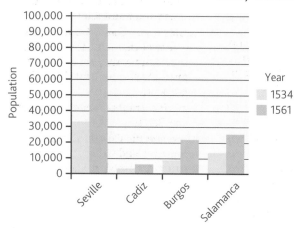

Year
1534
1561

Fig. 2 *Population issues*

In social and economic terms, there had been significant development over the period. The nobles were 'tamed' as the power of the monarchy grew, the economy diversified and the development of the New World brought apparent wealth into the country. However, this period ends with soaring prices, dramatically affecting all classes; the consequences were seen most in the south of Spain where trade with the Americas had its greatest impact. But this was also a time of greater social mobility. Such is reflected in the statements of several contemporaries that, 'We no longer consider the virtue of a gentleman but rather how wealthy he is.' There was also a growing middle class who were merchants, or professionals. Lesser mortals, however, suffered more; beggars and gypsies were on the increase.

Undoubtedly, however, Spain had a major transformation over this relatively brief period, from a disparate set of states into a stronger state with an overseas empire and a foothold in Europe. Spain had found a way of living with the range of different peoples and faiths; the systems of government had been overhauled and greater social mobility and economic diversity had developed. Philip II had strong foundations on which to build.

Glossary

A

alcabala: a 10 per cent sales tax.

alcaldes: magistrates who sat in the courts of the *Hermandad*.

apartamiento: different religious groups or ethnic groups living separately.

audiencias: courts of appeal initially established in Castile, 10 judges resident in Segovia or Valladolid, i.e. Court of Justiciar; also set up later in the New World as administrative as well as judicial bodies.

auto-da-fé: sentencing of a person brought before the Inquisition, following questioning and possible torture. Usually performed publicly.

C

caballeros: a word used to identify a 'gentleman', a 'knight' and a 'good horseman', sometimes included in local government.

canadas: sheep walks.

corregidor: officials created and appointed in the reign of Ferdinand and Isabella to act as town governors in the largest towns. They had wide powers, but were not always able to exercise them effectively.

Cortes: parliament, not elected but chosen by the monarch.

Consejo Real: Royal Council; the main organ of government, staffed by advisers chosen by the monarch.

consulado: trade guild to regulate the wool trade.

consulta-de-fé: jury of inquisitors/ theologians who gave out sentences following trial.

converso: the name given to Jews who converted to Christianity; often also called New Christians.

convivencia: term for all the different religious groups living together peacefully.

E

encabezamiento: tax paid in one lump sum payment rather than previous system of collecting individual taxes.

F

familiares: lay workers for the Inquisition who investigated and collected statements to be presented to the Inquisition; they were often members of the professional classes; there were as many as 12,000 throughout Spain by the end of the century.

fueros: laws and privileges in all provinces of Spain except Castile.

I

Index of Prohibited Books 1559: a list of books banned by the Catholic Church; it was regularly reviewed and new titles were added.

J

junta: a committee set up to deal with a particular issue.

juros: state loan, to be repaid at 10 per cent interest.

L

letrados: lawyers, graduates in law who had spent at least 10 years in practice, experienced and able to make appropriate decisions.

M

Maravedi: a Castilian coin worth approximately 33 pence.

mercedes: royal monetary grants.

Mesta: an organisation that protected the rights of itinerant sheep farmers using the royal sheep walks.

Morisco: a Muslim converted to Christianity, usually thought to be continuing to practise Islam.

Mudéjar: a Muslim living under Castilian rule.

P

pragmaticas: similar to decrees, decisions by the ruler of a country/ state without reference to other bodies or individuals.

R

reconquista: a general term applied to acquiring territory and applied particularly to the defeat of the Moors in Granada in 1492 and gain of New World territory.

regidores: town councillors who were initially chosen by lot or appointed by the crown, ultimately they were always chosen by lot.

S

Sanbenito: a penitential robe of yellow linen with one or more red crosses; it was worn for a fixed period of time as a punishment by the Inquisition; it was often subsequently displayed in the local parish church as a warning to others.

Santa Hermandad: organisations to maintain law and order; they held tribunals and could punish those who flouted the law with death and mutilation.

Sentencia de Guadaloupe: this was a charter that freed the peasants; for example, they could leave their land or sell it without the lord's consent.

servicios: grants of money voted by the Cortes.

Suprema: the Council of the Supreme and General Inquisition; first established in Madrid in 1483.

T

tercias reales: tithes paid to the Church by the Crown.

Bibliography

Introduction to Spain

Edwards, J. (2000) *The Spain of the Catholic Monarchs, 1474–1520*, Blackwell.

Highfield, R. (1972) *Spain in the Fifteenth Century, 1369–1516*, Macmillan.

Hillgarth, J. N. (1978) *The Spanish Kingdoms, 1410–1516*, Oxford University Press.

Liss, P. K. (2004) *Isabel the Queen*, University of Pennsylvania Press.

Section 1 The new monarchy, 1492–c.1500

Students

Kilsby, J. (1987) *Spain: Rise and Decline, 1474–1643*, Hodder & Stoughton.

Netanyahu, B. (1995) *The Origins of the Inquisition in Spain*, Random House.

Woodward, G. (1997) *Spain in the Reigns of Ferdinand and Isabella 1474–1516*, Hodder & Stoughton.

Teachers and extension

Edwards, J. (2005) *Ferdinand and Isabella*, Pearson Longman.

Elliott, J. H. (1963) *Imperial Spain, 1469–1716*, Penguin.

Fernandez-Armesto, F. (1975) *Ferdinand and Isabella*, Dorset Press.

Kamen, H. (1991) *Spain, 1469–1714: A Society of Conflict*, Longman.

Section 2 Strengthening the state, 1500–16

Students

Dor-Ni, Z. (1992) *Columbus and the Age of Discovery*, HarperCollins.

Hunt, J. (2001) *Spain 1474–1598*, Routledge.

Maland, D. (1982) *Europe in the Sixteenth Century*, Macmillan.

Mulgan, C. (1998) *The Renaissance Monarchies, 1469–1558*, Cambridge University Press.

Woodward, G. *Isabella and Ferdinand of Spain: A Reassessment*, History Review no.32, December 1998.

Teachers and extension

Elliott, J. H. (1989) *Spain and its World, 1500–1700*, Yale University.

Elliott, J. H. (1963) *Imperial Spain 1469–1716*, Penguin.

Leach, K. (1980) *Documents and Debates; Sixteenth Century Europe*, Palgrave Macmillan.

Section 3 Charles I: challenge and consolidation, 1516–29

Students

Kamen, H. (1988) *Golden Age Spain*, Macmillan.

MacDonald, S. (1992) *Charles V: Ruler, Dynast and Defender of the Faith 1500–1558*, Hodder & Stoughton.

Pendrill, C. (2002), *Spain 1474–1700*, Heinemann.

Rawlings, H. (2006) *The Spanish Inquisition*, Blackwell.

Rawlings, H. (2002) *Church, Religion and Society in Early Modern Spain*, Palgrave Macmillan.

Teachers and extension

Haliczer, S. (1981) *The Comuneros of Castile. The forging of a revolution 1475–1521*, Wisconsin Press.

Homza, L. A. (ed.) (2006) *The Spanish Inquisition 1478–1614*, Hackett Publishing Company Inc.

Lynch, J. (1964) *Spain under the Habsburgs, Volume 1: Empire and Absolutism, 1516–1598*, Blackwell.

Section 4 Charles I King of Spain and Charles V Holy Roman Emperor: divided loyalties, 1529–56

Students

Baigent, M. and Leigh, R. (2000) *The Inquisition*, Penguin.

Dominguez Ortiz, A. (1971) *The Golden Age of Spain*, Wiedenfeld & Nicolson.

Edwards, J. (1999) *The Spanish Inquisition*, Tempus Publishing.

Goffman, D. (2002) *The Ottoman Empire and Early Modern Europe*, Cambridge University Press.

Maltby, W. (2002) *The Reign of Charles V*, Palgrave.

Stiles, A. (1991) *The Ottoman Empire 1450–1700*, Hodder & Stoughton.

Teachers and extension

Bonney, R. (1991) *The European Dynastic States, 1494–1660*, Oxford University Press.

Cowans, J. (ed.) (2003) *Early Modern Spain: A Documentary History*, University of Pennsylvania Press.

Elliott, J. H. (1963) *Imperial Spain 1469–1716*, Penguin.

Elton, G. R. (1969) *Reformation Europe, 1517–1559*, Blackwell.

Hughes, M. (1992) *Early Modern Germany, 1477–1806*, University of Pennsylvania Press.

Inalcik, H. (1973) *The Ottoman Empire, The Classical Age 1300–1600*, Phoenix Press.

Kamen, H. (1997) *The Spanish Inquisition: An Historical Revision*, Phoenix Press.

Mullett, M. (1999) *The Catholic Reformation*, Routledge.

Po-Chia Hsia, R. (1998) *The World of Catholic Renewal*, Cambridge University Press.

Rady, M. (1988) *The Emperor Charles V*, Longman.

Scott Dixon, C. (2002) *The Reformation in Germany*, Blackwell.

Acknowledgements

The author and publisher are grateful to the following for permission to reproduce copyright material:

Text acknowledgements

Extract from J. Cowans (ed), *Early Modern Spain: A Documentary History*, 2003, University of Pennsylvania Press; Extract from J. Edwards, *Ferdinand and Isabella*, 2005, Pearson Longman (reprinted with permission); Short extracts and two tables from J.H.Elliott, *Imperial Spain 1469–1716*, 1963, Edward Arnold (reprinted with permission of Edward Arnold (Publishers) Ltd); Extracts from J. H. Elliott, *Spain and its World 1500–1700*, 1989, Yale University Press (reprinted with permission of Yale University Press); Extracts from F. Fernandez-Arnesto, *Ferdinand and Isabella*, 1975, Dorset Press (reprinted by arrangement with F. Fernandez-Arnesto with permission of David Higham Associates Ltd); Short extract from G. Griffiths, *Representative Government in Western Europe in the Sixteenth Century*, 1968, OUP (reprinted with permission of Oxford University Press); Extracts from J. Hunt, *Spain 1474–1598*, 2001, Routledge (reprinted with permission of Taylor & Francis Books); Extracts from H. Kamen, *Spain, 1469–1714*, 1991, Longman (reprinted with permission of Pearson Education Ltd); Extracts from H. Kamen, *The Spanish Inquisition*, 1997, Phoenix Press (reproduced with permission of PFD www.pfd.co.uk on behalf of Prof. Henry Kamen); Extracts from J. Kilsby, *Spain: Rise and Decline, 1474–1643*, 1987, Hodder and Stoughton (reprinted with permission of Hodder and Stoughton Ltd); Extracts adapted from J. Lynch, *Spain Under the Habsburgs. Volume 1: Empire and Absolutism 1516–1598*, 2e, 1981, Blackwell (reprinted with permission of Blackwell Publishing); Extracts from S. MacDonald, *Charles V: Ruler, Dynast, Defender of the Faith, 1500–1558*, 1992, Hodder and Stoughton (reprinted with permission of Hodder and Stoughton Ltd); Extract from C. Mulgan, *The Renaissance Monarchies*, 1998, Cambridge University Press (reprinted with permission); Short extracts from M. Rady, *The Emperor Charles V*, 1988, Longman (reprinted with permission of Pearson Education Ltd); Extracts from H. Rawlings, *Church, Religion and Society in Early Modern Spain*, 2002, Palgrave Macmillan (reprinted with permission of Palgrave Macmillan);Table reproduced from H. Rawlings, *The Spanish Inquisition*, 2006, Blackwell (reprinted with permission of Wiley Blackwell); Extracts from *The Comuneros of Castile: The Forging of a Revolution 1475–1521*, by the Board of Regents of the University of Wisconsin System, 1981, Wisconsin University Press (reprinted with permission); Extracts from G Woodward, *Spain in the Reigns of Ferdinand and Isabella*, 1997, Hodder and Stoughton (reprinted with permission of Hodder and Stoughton Ltd).

Photo acknowledgements

Ann Ronan Picture Library 1.2, 4.5, 9.2, 10.6; **Bridgeman Art Library** 5.1; **Edimedia Archive** 2.5, 7.4, 8.1, 10.3, 10.9; **Getty Images** 2.1, 6.3, Conc.1; **Photo12.com** 2.3, 2.10, 3.4, 6.7, 7.2, 8.6, 9.4, 9.6, 11.1, 11.4; **Public Domain** 1.6, 4.3, 4.4, 6.2, 8.5, 11.3, 11.6, 11.7, 11.9; **Siglo d'Oro Collection** 1.1, 1.5, 1.7, 1.9, 2.7, 3.1, 3.3, 3.6, 4.6, 4.7, 5.3, 5.4, 5.5, 5.6, 5.7, 6.5, 6.6, 6.8, 7.1, 7.5, 8.2, 8.4, 8.7, 9.3, 10.1, 10.4, 10.5, 11.2; **The Grainger Collection/Topfoto** 2.8, 3.5, 9.1; **World History Archive** 2.9, 10.8

Photo research by Tara Roberts, Jason Newman and Alexander Goldberg of www.uniquedimension.com.

Every effort has been made to contact the copyright holders, and we apologise if any have been overlooked. Should copyright have been unwittingly infringed in this book, the owners should contact the publishers, who will make corrections at reprint.

Index